ETTA PLACE

Etta Place

Riding into History with
Butch Cassidy and the Sundance Kid

D. J. Herda

TWODOT®

GUILFORD, CONNECTICUT
HELENA, MONTANA

A · TWODOT® · BOOK

An imprint and registered trademark of The Rowman & Littlefield Publishing Group, Inc.
4501 Forbes Blvd., Ste. 200
Lanham, MD 20706
www.rowman.com

Distributed by NATIONAL BOOK NETWORK

British Library Cataloguing in Publication Information available

Library of Congress Control Number: 2021931556

ISBN 978-1-4930-4738-3 (cloth : alk. paper)
ISBN 978-1-4930-4739-0 (electronic)

♾™ The paper used in this publication meets the minimum requirements of American National Standard for Information Sciences—Permanence of Paper for Printed Library Materials, ANSI/NISO Z39.48-1992.

Contents

Introduction

THE MYSTERY BEGAN AT THE VERY BEGINNING. WHO WAS SHE? AS A young woman, she took the name "Place," from the maiden name of lover Harry Longabaugh's mother, Annie. Over the years, she combined the last name with several first-name monikers and slipped on a wedding ring to become widely known as "Mrs. Ethel Place." Eventually, the Pinkertons came to identify her alternately as "Ethel," "Ethal," "Eva," and "Rita" before finally settling on "Etta" for their wanted posters. Harry Longabaugh, the Sundance Kid, knew her simply as his wife.

The two met in late 1899 or early 1900, and from all indications, it was either love or lust at first sight. Understandably so. He was tall for his day with dark hair and chiseled features, deep-set, penetrating eyes, and a full mustache. She was glamour-queen gorgeous, the perfect woman—witty, playful, refined, gregarious. They saw one another for the better part of a year or more before they decided to get married. After Sundance introduced Etta to Robert Parker (Butch Cassidy), the three joined the rest of the Wild Bunch, a gang of outlaws that appeared first in Utah in 1897 and set off on a spree of bank, stagecoach, and train robberies. While Butch was the consummate "good guy," quick to smile and pleasant beyond the norm, Sundance was just as quick with his gun and willing to use it anywhere, anytime. At least, according to legend. He was the quintessential bad boy with whom the archetypical good gal fell in love. While the men went about their calculated business, Etta remained nearby, always aware, keeping a careful watch. But not careful enough.

As the law homed in on the gang, the outlaws rode up to Robbers Roost in southwestern Utah where they laid low until word reached local authorities of their whereabouts. On the run again, Etta accompanied Sundance to New York City, where they purchased a lapel watch and stickpin at Tiffany's before pausing to pose for the famed De Young portrait at a Union Square photo studio on Broadway—one of few photographs in existence of the two together. On February 20, 1901, Etta sailed with Butch and Sundance for Buenos Aires aboard the British ship *Herminius*, as Mr. and Mrs. Harry Place, along with Etta's fictitious brother, "James Ryan."

The three outlaws eventually settled on a ranch they purchased together near Cholila in the Chubut Province of west-central Argentina. The government was anxious to attract outside blood and granted the threesome 15,000 acres of adjacent land to develop, including a 2,500-acre parcel to Place, who became the first woman in Argentina to own property.

On March 3, 1902, Etta and Sundance returned to New York City on the SS *Soldier Prince* to visit her family and friends, lending credence to the theory that she may have been initially born and raised on the Eastern Seaboard, perhaps near Boston. On April 2, the couple registered at a local rooming house before touring Coney Island and visiting Sundance's family in Pennsylvania. They traveled to Dr. Pierce's Invalid Hotel in Buffalo, where Etta underwent an unspecified medical treatment. They sought additional treatment in Denver before returning to South America from New York on July 10, 1902, aboard the steamer *Honorius*, where they posed as stewards. On August 9, Etta registered herself and Sundance at the Hotel Europa in Buenos Aires and sailed with him six days later aboard the steamer SS *Chubut* to return to their Cholila ranch.

Etta made another visit to the States with Sundance two years later in the summer of 1904 when the Pinkerton Detective Agency—by then hot on the outlaws' trail—tracked them to Fort Worth, Texas, and then to the St. Louis World Fair, but the lawmen just missed them as the couple slipped off once more to Argentina.

In early 1905, with the law closing in, the trio sold their Cholila ranch. The Pinkertons had known their whereabouts for several months, but the rainy season had prevented their agents from traveling into the countryside to make an arrest. Governor Julio Lezana issued a warrant, but before it could be executed, Sheriff Edward Humphreys, a Welsh Argentine who was friends with Butch and enamored of Place, tipped the duo off. The trio fled north to San Carlos de Bariloche, where they embarked on the steamer *Condor* across Lake Nahuel Huapi into Chile.

By the end of that year, the three were back in Argentina. On December 19, 1904, Etta, Sundance, Butch, and an unknown male robbed the Banco de la Nacion in Villa Mercedes, four hundred miles west of Buenos Aires. Pursued by armed *federales,* they crossed the Pampas and the Andes and returned once more to the safety of Chile.

But Etta had grown tired of life on the run and lamented the loss of their ranch and the promises it had held for stability. In June 1906, Sundance accompanied her from Valparaiso, Chile, to San Francisco, where she sought medical aid once again and kissed him goodbye for the last time before he returned to South America and infamy.

For Etta Place, the mystery that would last for another century had only begun. Bits and pieces of it would unravel during that time before finally being resolved.

Sort of.

But I digress.

Here is the most complete and accurate biographical history of Ethel Bishop, Ann Bassett, Eunice Gray, Madaline Wilson, and half a dozen other women all rolled into one. Here is the story of the real Etta Place.

CHAPTER 1

The Early Years

*When the Southern end of this band was practically wiped out by the
death, arrest and conviction of the members, a new band was formed,
under the leadership of Harvey Logan, alias "Kid" Curry, which was
composed of O. C. Hanks, alias "Camila" Hanks, alias "Deaf Charlie";
George Parker, alias "Butch" Cassidy; Harry Longbaugh [sic], alias
"Sundance Kid"; "Ben" Kilpatrick, alias "The Tall Texan." A part of
this band on September 19, 1900, at the noon hour, robbed the First
National Bank, of Winnemucca, Nev., a member of the American
Bankers' Association, of $32,640 in gold, holding up the officials with
rifles and revolvers.*
—BALTIMORE SUN, BALTIMORE, MARYLAND, JULY 14, 1907

IT IS CONVENIENT WHEN RECALLING THE LIFE STORY OF SOMEONE AS
famous as Etta Place to begin at the beginning and end . . . well, at the
end. And so it is with Etta.

The fantasy object of all Western fans' intrigues was born in a small
town somewhere around Green Bay, a simple Midwestern gal "from
Door County, Wisconsin," according to Jane Fish, who provided this
information to *True West* magazine editors in 1990. Startled by the news,
the editors enlisted the aid of several outlaw researchers to pursue the
data further, at which time Ms. Fish said that Etta Place was her father's
cousin, a woman who had "got mixed up in a bad crowd," and that her
uncle had been murdered in 1894 in Winnetka, Illinois, possibly by the

Sundance Kid. Fish had harbored the information for most of her life and worried that by sharing it she had opened a "kettle of fish."[1]

Unfortunately, Ms. Fish's kettle proved eminently fishier than even she had hoped, and the account of the earliest days of one of the Wild West's most wily female outlaws was off by a couple thousand miles. Several researchers eschewed Ms. Fish's account in favor of casting their ballots for the Sundance Kid's girlfriend hailing from farther west. According to letters written by Florence Lind in Washington State, who had visited her grandmother in Tacoma as a child, "Grandma went to a home and met with a very refined, quite beautiful woman. Grandma gave her some money and said, 'That's all, there won't be any more.'" The woman I'm sure was Etta.[2] The mystery woman had a male friend who had gone to Portland, but her grandmother didn't want any of the money going to that man, whom Lind was "sure was Sundance."[3]

Understandably, even the most well-intentioned history buffs may have known of ancestors named either Etta or Place and made the leap of faith to the apparent conclusion that the two were one and the same. The only problem was that Etta Place's real name was likely neither Etta nor Place. The name Etta was the result of a Pinkerton Detective Agency mistake: a mistranslation by one of their postal spies reading a New York hotel ledger signed "Ethel Place," which was interpreted as "Etta." Authorities in Argentina didn't help any as Etta, in later years, went around the countryside using the name of Ethel. Unfortunately, Argentinians had difficulty pronouncing that name, which came out sounding like "Etta." The name finally stuck once the Pinkertons began using it on their wanted posters. Little did anyone realize that Etta had adopted Sundance's alias—and his mother's maiden name—while she and her bank-robbing beau traveled the countryside as husband and wife.

As retired Pinkerton detective Frank P. Dimaio, who had investigated Butch and Sundance in Argentina in 1903, recalled decades later, "I know nothing of Etta Place's background, but have the impression that [Sundance] may have met her in a house of ill-fame, and that afterwards she became his common-law wife." He mentioned that "she evidently ha[d] parents in Texas,"[4] but he provided no additional details.

Apparently outcasts made good bedfellows, because the crooks of the day often found their mates in brothels. Sundance was no exception. He reportedly frolicked in bawdy houses in both San Antonio and Fort Worth before he and Butch headed east with Etta in tow prior to their foray to South America. Wyoming rancher John Gooldy wrote in his memoirs that a friend had received a letter from Sundance "with a picture of him and his wife, saying he had married a Texas lady he had known previously."[5]

As convinced as the Pinkertons were that she had been born in Texas, Etta's birthplace is still subject to debate. Other alternatives include the Eastern Seaboard, because she and Sundance may have visited her relatives there later in life, as well as England, from which she was alleged to have emigrated as a child, her "refined," lilting voice betraying her British origins. This theory has regained popularity with the suppositions of Tony Hays writing for the website Criminal Element. Pointing out that, beginning in 1790, the US census has been taken every ten years, Hays deduced: "Since I had a city (San Antonio) and a head of household (Madam Fannie Porter), I thought it would be beneficial to look at the 1900 census of Bexar County, since that's the nexus year, the year they all came together. Lo and behold, there was Fannie Porter, running a 'boarding house.'"[6] Fannie and her family had immigrated to Texas from England in 1874 when she was only an infant. She traveled west to the Lone Star State with her sister at the age of fifteen and began life as a fallen angel in San Antonio, where she soon developed a reputation as a shrewd and formidable businesswoman before she was out of her teens. According to one author, "It was at the tender age of 19, an age at which other young women found themselves teaching school, nursing the sick, or married off, that Fannie utilized everything she had learned and started her own brothel. One day, it would make her a rich woman."[7]

By 1900, Porter, herself not much older than her "girls," had five to eight young women working for her, all born between 1878 and 1880. One girl in particular caught author Hays's attention:

Twenty-two year old Madaline [sic] Wilson appears in the census immediately beneath Madam Fannie. Like Fannie, she is listed as of English birth, immigrating to the United States in 1884 when she was six. Now here's where the conjecture has to come in. It is quite possible that she had changed her name, but does that dictate that she would have changed her date of birth, country of origin, and date of immigration? And a British accent, tempered by 16 years in America, might be described as "refined."[8]

Additionally suspicious, records show that Madaline Wilson disappeared after the 1900 census, when Etta would have relocated to South America. Such circumstantial evidence proves nothing, of course, but it does narrow the possibilities for Etta's place of birth significantly, adding to the likelihood that she may well have grown up on the East Coast, since immigrants arriving in America from Europe landed first at New York's Ellis Island or, before 1892, in New York Harbor.

Also appearing to stoke those fires, a woman going by the name of Eunice Gray (women of the evening often changed their names to shield their activities from friends, family, and the law) appeared in Fort Worth, Texas, in the mid-twentieth century to run a brothel. She was suspected of being Etta for good reason. Eunice had once told a friend that she had been in Fort Worth since 1901 except for a stint in South America. Investigators later produced records proving that Eunice had, indeed, been in the Southern Hemisphere at roughly the same time as Etta Place. After Eunice died in a fire in 1962, researchers recovered some personal photos that, "when compared with known photos of Etta," according to Hays, "prove definitively that Eunice was not Etta Place."[9]

Perhaps, the author continued, attributing the identity of Madaline Wilson to that of Etta Place was a stretch, but the two women did exist around the same time and shared many of the same attributes, making the possibility of their being one and the same at least tantalizing.

Beyond rumors of Etta's place of origin, numerous tales persisted regarding the line of work in which she found herself. Wherever she was born, she was thought at one time or another to be a schoolteacher (her extensive education could have accounted for her refined accent), as well as a nurse's aide, a music teacher, a housekeeper, and a prostitute.

MORE STORIES COME FORTH

Early in 2001, a woman told a *True West* magazine team of contributing editors that her grandmother "knew Etta Place and had visited her several times in Denver" in the 1940s. Naturally, magazine writers Daniel Buck and Anne Meadows took the story with a grain of salt until the woman said that if they didn't believe her, they should call her grandmother, Anne Charter, author of *Cowboys Don't Walk*, a book about the family's life in the West. When the writers contacted the elder Charter at her home in Montana, they asked about her granddaughter's story. Charter sighed and said, "No, that's one of those myths that come around. It was my husband's father who was connected with those people."[10] Her late husband, the woman explained, was Boyd Charter, whose father, Bert, had befriended Butch Cassidy in the 1880s. "It was rumored," she continued, "that Janet Magor was Etta Place. But I never met her, and Magor was not Etta Place." Magor, who was Bert's sister-in-law, was born in 1889 and, therefore, too young to have run off to South America in 1901 with the Sundance Kid. Charter added, "People hear things; they remember things, then improve them." Sometimes, rather than deliberately improving things, they simply misremember them.[11]

This, in fact, turned out to be the case when, a few months later, Utah-based writer Garth Seegmiller mentioned in a telephone call that he had "met Etta Place in the 1950s at her ranch along the Utah–Colorado border." It was, he said, "a big ranch. She hired men to come in and work the cattle and cut the alfalfa. She had an unusual home—clean as could be, but it had a dirt floor." He promised to look up his notes about his visit with Place. Two weeks later, he called the authors back: "I had just started to go through this stuff that I haven't looked at for so many years, and I screwed up. I goofed. It wasn't Etta Place I met; it was Butch Cassidy's girlfriend, Josie Bassett."[12]

If Anne Charter and Garth Seegmiller had not been around to answer questions and set the record straight, their "encounters" with Etta Place might have gone down in history and been accepted as gospel, "percolated through literature for years to come. Such tales murmur on long after their tellers have died,"[13] according to authors Buck and Meadows.

The two writers went on to point out that the most elusive of historical figures often generate the wildest tales. Such appeared to be the case with the "yarns" spun by former Pinkerton detective and deputy New York City police commissioner George Dougherty, who, in 1913, told a reporter that Etta Place had participated in the Wild Bunch's bank holdup in Winnemucca, Nevada. He added that it was she who had encouraged Butch and Sundance to rob a bank in Argentina. Later, she went on a shopping spree in Europe and took a hiatus from outlawry "at the gaming tables in Monte Carlo." At the time of his story, Dougherty confided that Etta Place was "working with the band around Cape Horn."[14]

Of course, it didn't take long for Dougherty's comments to be shredded by several researchers, although not before the rumors were ginned up in a Texas newspaper a few years later. The paper claimed, as did most notable practitioners of yellow journalism of the day, that Etta Place was not merely a member of the gang but its leader. Like the mythical phoenix, she had disappeared in the ashes of anonymity only to rise again as the gang's head, inspiring the wrath of honest citizenry everywhere. And, as a true leader, she was always last in making the getaway and first in placing herself in harm's way. In Argentina, such bravado allegedly led her to become the "virtual ruler" of the Cholila Valley, where she presided over the pampas with Sundance and Butch in the early 1900s. "She lorded over the simple natives and they voluntarily became her abject slaves,"[15] according to one account—the virtual dominatrix of the Wild Bunch reborn.

But, all that taken into consideration, Police Commissioner Dougherty wasn't all that far off regarding the September 19, 1900, robbery of the First National Bank of Winnemucca. As it turns out, it *was* committed by Butch, Sundance, and gang member William "News" Carver, who rode off with $30,000, mostly in gold. All three members of the Wild Bunch had been terrorizing the West for years. Several weeks after the robbery, according to bank manager George Nixon, the mailman delivered a package to the bank of Winnemucca containing a photograph of five men—the three robbers plus two other gang members: Harvey Logan (Kid Curry) and Ben Kilpatrick—along with a note thanking

Nixon for the September 19 "withdrawal."[16] The photograph is still hanging in the bank lobby.

Not everyone believes in the authenticity of the story. The Winnemucca historical society published a slim volume written by amateur historian Lee Berk in which the author disputes the story's authenticity based on several facts:

- For months, bank manager Nixon referred to the gang leader only as "Whiskers" (the man had a light, faded beard, which might have been fake) and didn't name him as Butch Cassidy until January 8, 1901, several months after the robbery, when he learned the Pinkerton Detective Agency claimed that Butch was involved.

- Nixon and other witnesses described "Whiskers" as having "a coyote appearance" (i.e., a thin, hairy face), whereas the picture of Butch Cassidy that the Pinkertons sent to the bank showed, Nixon admitted, "a man with a great deal squarer cut face and massive jaws."

- The strongest evidence to debunk the legend, according to Berk, is the robbery of a Union Pacific train by the Wild Bunch near Tipton, Wyoming, six hundred miles from Winnemucca, on August 29, 1900, just twenty-one days before the Nevada robbery. The robbers had been around Winnemucca for up to ten days before the heist, leaving them—if they were the Tipton bandits— just eleven days to get to Winnemucca, a feat that Berk maintains they couldn't have accomplished in that time.[17]

Supporters of the legend, though, refute Berk's findings. They claim that the "coyote-like" versus "square-cut" facial reference is vague at best, pointing to the ultimate proof: Nixon eventually named Butch Cassidy, regardless of animalistic comparisons. Regarding the Tipton robbery, naysayers are divided into two camps: the Wild Bunch didn't stop the Union Pacific train, *or* the Wild Bunch did stop the train but were still able to make it to Winnemucca in eleven days, most likely traveling in disguise on another train.

And what of Etta Place and her involvement? She likely didn't participate in the holdup simply because she had met Sundance only months earlier in Texas. That said, it's unlikely, considering that she hadn't known the gang member long enough, that she would have been invited along to such an elaborate and intricately woven adventure. Besides, according to an article in the *Chicago Tribune*, she may not yet have decided to follow in her paramour's footsteps because, while "the Boston-educated schoolteacher and mistress" of Sundance eventually participated in a number of the gang's robberies, Etta always remained a lady. The paper added, "She was, after all, almost a noblewoman, being the daughter of George Capel, the bastard son of the 6th Earl of Essex, an English aristocrat. Capel (Etta's surname, Place, is an anagram of her father's name) was a one-time beau of actress Lillie Langtry, "the Jersey Lily," who became the mistress of the Prince of Wales, later Britain's King Edward VII."[18]

Local lore claims that the gang staged the Winnemucca robbery to steal enough money for Butch and Sundance to sail to safety in South America. Butch, writing in August 1902 from Patagonia in the extreme south of Argentina, told a friend in the United States that the country had been "getting too small for me," and added, with typical cheek, "another of my uncles died and left $30,000 to our little family of three so I took my $10,000 and started to see a little more of the world."[19] Sundance's "uncle," no doubt, was the bank of Winnemucca.

While the story about the robbery at Winnemucca may hold more than a shred of truth, it still fails to help identify the mystery woman, Etta Place. Toward that objective, there exists a never-ending trail of claims. One is from a renowned Etta Place exploiter who claimed at times that his name was Robert H. Longabaugh and at other times Harry Longabaugh Jr. (the newspapers dubbed him "Sundance, Jr."), who paraded around the Rocky Mountains in the early 1970s delivering colorful lectures at county libraries on his supposed ties, familial and otherwise, to Old West bandits. At times, he said that Etta Place was his mother, Anna Marie Thayne, whereas on other occasions he claimed that

Etta was his mother's half sister, Hazel Thayne.[20] Neither claim turned out to be verifiable. Some folks can't ever get things straight.

One thing is clear, however. Etta met Sundance at Fannie Porter's in late 1899 or early 1900. After that, all hell broke loose.

Fannie Porter's "boarding house," as it was euphemistically known, served as home in 1900 to five women who ranged in age from nineteen to twenty-four. When the striking Etta Place first saw Sundance, it was likely love—or perhaps lust—at first sight. She must have found Sundance's piercing blue eyes irresistible, and he found her refined ways and elegant features beyond reproach.

It was around this time that Butch told the Wild Bunch he was leaving the country to introduce outlawry "Western-style" to the pampas of South America. The next "raise," or strike, would be in either Bolivia or Argentina. He told the remaining riders they were welcome to come along, saying that he and Sundance first planned on stopping off in New York City to see the sights.

Laura Bullion and Deaf Charley Hanks declined, but Kid Curry said he'd give it some thought. He knew the chances of escaping after a major train robbery were growing slimmer with each passing day, but he told Butch he had planned on making one more strike, this time an express car. He talked long and convincingly, and Butch finally agreed to make his last raid with him in the States. Butch said later that it was only to augment the funds he needed to make a stake in South America. He and Sundance had reached a decision to homestead in the Argentine, build up a ranch with a new herd, and, if necessary, raid a few banks or gold trains to sweeten the kitty.

While Butch and Kid Curry readied their plans, Sundance was busy wooing Fannie's newest girl, the tall and slender beauty to whom the renowned madam had introduced Butch and Sundance, both of whom were stunned by the young woman's beauty.

Author James Horan, writing in *Desperate Men*, fictionalized what may have transpired during their introduction:

"This is Etta Place," Fannie said with the air of introducing a queen. "Etta, this is Butch Cassidy and Harry Longbaugh."

"Pleased to meet you, ma'am," the outlaws said.

"Oh, sit down, boys, Etta knows you're on the dodge," Fannie said. "When's the next raise?"

Cassidy grinned. "Pretty soon, Fannie."

Fannie banged on the table. "Jessie, bring some champagne!"

Jessie, a fat, waddling colored maid who wore a red turban wrapped about her woolly head and a starched white apron to "give the place some airs," brought in the glasses and the bottles of cold champagne.[21]

Not long after, Sundance and Etta became the house's most notorious couple, if not its only one. It was at Ms. Porter's, too, that fellow gang member Harvey "Kid Curry" Logan met his future "wife," Annie Rogers.

But there was still more. Will "News" Carver and Laura Bullion apparently fell in love there as well. Will had been born in Coryell County, Texas, and was briefly married to Laura's aunt. He may also have had a romantic involvement with Etta and a fling with another of Fannie's girls, Lillie Davis, who later claimed to have married him in Fort Worth. Regardless, his heart (more or less) belonged to Laura.

Born in Knickerbocker, Texas, around 1876, Laura was of German and Native American descent. She used the alias of Della Rose when she was a dance-hall girl in Wyoming before working at Fannie's. After Carver died of a posse-fired gunshot wound following a bank robbery, Laura took up with his friend and fellow Wild Bunch member Ben "Tall Texan" Kilpatrick. It was no wonder the Wild Bunch thought so fondly of Ms. Porter's house!

By the time the gang members rode out of San Antonio for good, Etta and Sundance had decided to form an exclusive relationship—either through marriage or some less formal association. Not long after, Fannie and her house faded from the scene, leaving behind a swank business boasting a carpeted parlor, elegant glass fixtures, silk sheets, brass spittoons, and cases of fine champagne, which she allegedly served chilled to her best customers, of whom Butch and Sundance had been two.

Wild Bunch historian Horan provides one of the few personal descriptions of Fannie as being "a hard, shrewd woman . . . well known to the law. More than once she had chased an officer from her place with a broom." William Pinkerton, the founder of the famous detective agency, came down to interview her during the manhunt for the Wild Bunch in 1901. Her "sporting house" had served as a rest stop, hideout, rendezvous, and headquarters for the Wild Bunch and other outlaws for years. Still, she liked Pinkerton because he "treated her like a lady." A photograph of Fannie in the Pinkerton archives shows a formidable-looking, buxom woman dressed to the nines.[22]

The last time the Wild Bunch is known to have visited Fannie's place was in February 1901, between bank jobs at Winnemucca, Nevada, and Wagner, Montana. She apparently threw a raucous going-away party for the members of the gang who had decided to scatter to the four winds to avoid capture. Shortly thereafter, the tide began to turn against active, openly operating brothels. Eventually Fannie sold her building and retired to parts unknown, fading from history. Most researchers agree that she retired semi-wealthy, some saying she married a man of considerable means. Others say she retired into seclusion, while still others insist that she returned to England. None of these stories are confirmed. Later rumors indicated that she lived until 1940 when she was killed in a car accident in El Paso, Texas. However, this also is unsubstantiated.

Regardless of the rumors swirling around Texas like a lone-star dust devil, records show that by late 1900, Etta had traveled with Sundance to New York City, where her real brush with Western history began. It was there that she achieved instant notoriety—or would have, if the truth had been known—when she "married" Harry Alonzo "Sundance" Longabaugh in February 1901. Only the year before, the law had caught up with the gang in Utah, where several of its members had been shot and killed. The gang's leaders, Butch and Sundance, decided the best way to stop the Pinkerton Agency detectives from breathing down their necks was to head east, lie low for a few weeks, and wait for their notoriety to die down.

Needless to say, Etta's insertion into the scene was an unanticipated but presumably welcome occurrence. While the entire law-abiding world was busy searching for two male outlaws on the lam, no one would have thought to look for a threesome that included an incredibly lithe, disarmingly attractive, and refined young lady.

Following the formalization of their relationship, Etta and Sundance had a wedding photo taken, one of only two verified portraits of Etta that has survived the years, and the only one showing her face clearly. Sporting dark brown hair with blue-gray eyes, she was wildly attractive by anyone's account. In the photo, she's wearing what seems to be an engagement ring, which signified that her relationship with Sundance was more than a whirlwind romance and likely had gone on for several months. Several copies of the photo were made and mailed out to friends and relatives. Sundance sent one to a compadre in Wyoming, saying he had "married a Texas lady"[23] whom he had previously known. And while those few words might appear to be the most reliable testimony to Ms. Place's place of origin, they are by no means definitive, since Etta may have been born somewhere else and only happened to be living in Texas when Sundance met her.

The Wild Bunch members appreciated Fannie's establishment because of its owner's solid reputation as both a fair employer and a source of discretion where visiting outlaws were concerned. She made sure her girls kept their mouths shut about their clientele, and in turn, Fannie saw to it that each of her ladies received a generous cut of the bordello's profits.

Over time, several of her girls had become romantically involved with different members of the Wild Bunch and accompanied them when they left. Rampant speculation held that Etta was working under the name of Madaline Wilson, an English immigrant who entered America as a child. Another rumor is that she was using the nom de plume of Ethel Bishop, who had both the right first name and an appealing background as a former music teacher. Ethel was purportedly working in a brothel around the corner from Fannie's place when the Wild Bunch came to town.

Whether or not Ethel was Etta's real first name, her surname of "Place" most likely came into existence from the alias Sundance used on a hotel register in New York, where he signed in as "Mr. Harry Place," and she followed as "Mrs. Ethel Place." The couple had traveled to New York after spending January in Pennsylvania with Sundance's family. There, they enjoyed a brief honeymoon of sorts (no marriage license has ever been found) before the newlyweds and Butch, pretending to be Ethel's brother, "James Ryan," booked passage to Argentina.

Not surprisingly, Butch was often romantically linked to Etta in the press; it was not uncommon at the time for a gang's moll to be passed from one member to another or even to consort with more than one man at a time. Some say that Etta was Butch's girlfriend while they were in Robbers Roost in Utah during the winter of 1896–1897. But that claim didn't surface until decades later and has never been corroborated. In fact, it's unlikely that Etta even knew Butch at the time. No contemporary accounts of the presence of Etta "Ethel" Place existed until she appeared at the side of Sundance in New York in 1901.

The Pinkertons compiled information on the couple's trip east in early 1901, followed by their journey to Argentina and another trip back to the States in early 1902. The detective agency noted that Etta was "said to be [Sundance's] wife and to be from Texas," lamenting that the pair had brazenly commissioned their portrait at the De Young studio right under the agency's nose: "What a great pity we did not get the information regarding the photograph while this party was in New York. It shows how daring these men are, and while you are looking for them in the wilderness and mountains they are in the midst of society." [24]

A Buffalo, New York, clinic that treated Etta and Sundance in May 1902 told the Pinkertons that Etta was "age 23 or 24—5 ft. 5. 110 #, Med Comp., Medium dark hair, Blue or grey eyes, regular features. No marks or blemishes." She was, by any standard, a head-turner—well coiffed and smartly dressed—a classic Gibson girl. [25]

Classic, too, was the perfect description of the woman that phantom Etta Place turned out to be—the perfect enigma, a cross between a sexual siren, a devoted companion, and a wild and wanton outlaw queen. In the end, as Sundance must have realized, he never stood a chance.

CHAPTER 2

Tearing Up the West

There is a belief that Etta in her youth was a Western cowgirl known as Etta Place, and that Longbaugh met her and induced her to run away with him during one of his hold-up raids in this country, some years ago.
—OMAHA DAILY BEE, OMAHA, NEBRASKA, OCTOBER 14, 1906

AS GANGS GO, THE WILD BUNCH OF BUTCH CASSIDY AND THE SUNdance Kid was something of a bust. It's true: They pulled their share of robberies, and they rode on into history. But of the twenty or more different members to join the gang at various times, few rode together more than once or twice, and fewer still were staples of the outlaw bunch under the guiding hands of Butch and Sundance. Nevertheless, this minor caveat did not thwart the gang's dominance over the Western frontier for nearly two decades straddling the turn of the century.

It all began on June 24, 1889, when Butch Cassidy, Matt Warner, and Tom McCarty—and possibly Bill Madden and Butch's brother, Dan Parker—robbed the San Miguel Valley Bank in Telluride, Colorado, netting more than $20,000. The trio formed the core of the Wild Bunch, and their robbery was only the first of dozens more to come.

Under the headline, "Obliged to Give Up $22,000. The Robbers Lose No Time in Their Professional Work—Posses in Pursuit," the facts of the robbery appeared in the *New York Tribune* nearly half a country away:

Ouray, Col., June 25 (Special).—The San Miguel Valley Bank of Tel-luride was robbed of the available cash on hand this morning by four armed men who rode away with their booty. The robbery was com-mitted in broad daylight, and for daring is unsurpassed in the history of this part of the country. About 10 o'clock this morning, while the cashier, C. F. Painter, was out making collections, three men entered the bank and covering the bookkeeper with their revolvers, demanded that he hand over to them the cash of the bank. The bookkeeper was alone and unarmed, and was compelled to comply. Having secured the money the three joined their companion, who was holding their horses in front of the building. All quickly mounted and left town on the run, firing their revolvers in the air as they went. No one interfered with them, and all four escaped without difficulty. The robbers are described as looking like plains men or cowboys and evidently knew the bank and the habits of its officials, as their raid was well-timed. The news of the daring deed and description of the perpetrators has been sent in every direction, and the whole country is on the alert. The last heard of the bank robbers was at Trout Lake, between Rico and Telluride. It is believed by all that they will endeavor to reach Utah. Strong posses are in hot pursuit from Telluride, and the authorities at Durango and Grand River have been asked to organize and head them off if possi-ble. The amount stolen is about $22,000. The depositors will suffer no loss, as the officers and stockholders are wealthy.[1]

As news of the successful heist raced across the wires, other outlaws soon clamored to join the gang, which had suddenly turned into a family affair. Tom McCarty and Matt Warner, along with Tom's brothers Bill and George, his nephew Fred, his brother-in-law Hank Vaughan, and George's wife Nellie, were quick to engage in some ten holdups taking place in Oregon, Washington, and Colorado between 1890 and 1893. The outlaws' tastes were eclectic, hitting trains, banks, stores, and casinos without prejudice. The gang dissolved after Fred and Bill died during a failed September 1893 attempt on the Farmers and Merchants Bank in Delta, Colorado:

The most daring robbery ever committed in this part of Colorado occurred here in broad daylight this morning, the object of attack being the Farmers and Merchants Bank, and while the sum secured was small, the robbery resulted in the death of three people, the cashier of the bank and two of the highwaymen who made the attack.

The robbery was planned on the lines of those in Kansas towns, particularly [at] Coffeeville, where the Daltons secured so much money last year. The belief is the bandits, if not members of that gang, have at least been identified in other robberies of a similar nature. The Bank opened as usual at 10 o'clock this morning. At 10:30, three mounted men rode up to the door and entering quickly rushed up to A. P. Blachley, cashier, presented guns and demanded what money he had. The cashier refused to give it up. The robbers made a grab through the window, secured $500, and opened fire. The cashier fell dead instantly. The robbers then fired at H. H. Wolbert, assistant cashier, but missed him.

The shooting attracted the attention of citizens and Ray Simpson, a leading hardware merchant, and a "dead shot," ran for his Winchester and started for the alley in the rear of the bank, where the robbers had tied their horses.

The robbers had started out of town when Simpson got there, but he succeeded in killing two by shooting them through the head, the third shot killed one of the robbers' horses and together the man and animal fell to the ground. After killing the two robbers Simpson continued after the third one, taking several shots at him but without effect. Simpson then returned to town, and getting together a posse, started at once in pursuit.

The robber is thought to have about a mile head start and is mounted on a fine horse, going in the direction of the mountains. If acquainted with the country there is a chance of his escaping, otherwise the posse will capture him dead or alive. In the latter case he will undoubtedly be lynched on return here.

The two dead robbers were also well mounted and the horse not killed was caught by citizens. Four hundred dollars were recovered from their persons, the escaping robber carrying away the other $100.

The suspicion that the men implicated in the robbery are remnants of the famous Dalton gang seems to be general. They are not known here and their identification can not yet be secured.

The dead bandits are both young men of fair complexion, one strikingly good looking. The coroner has taken the remains in charge.

Mr. Blachley was an old resident of this place and leaves a wife and large family of young children. He and Mr. Baldwin owned the bank.

Delta is the county seat of Delta county and has a population of 900.[2]

Meanwhile, the Rocky Mountain branch of the Wild Bunch wasn't faring much better, marking its inauspicious start on November 29, 1892, near Malta, Montana, with the Sundance Kid, Harry Bass, and Bill Madden robbing the Great Northern No. 32 train. The results netted less than $100. Worse still, Bass and Madden were caught and quickly fingered Sundance, who had managed to escape.

Butch Cassidy, whose fortunes hadn't been much better, resumed his life of crime in 1896, following a two-year stint in prison for horse theft. On August 13, he joined Elzy Lay and Bub Meeks in robbing Idaho's Bank of Montpelier of $7,165, giving the money to an attorney to defend Matt Warner against murder charges. On April 21, 1897, Butch, Lay, and possibly Meeks and Joe Walker stole a $9,860 mine payroll in Castle Gate, Utah. In a strange twist of fate, two of the robbers appeared shortly thereafter in Springville, Utah, a fact that didn't escape the local newspaper or the law:

The latest news concerning the two daring bandits who held up Paymaster Carpenter of the Pleasant Valley Coal Company at Castle Gate a few days ago was received from Provo yesterday. Sheriff Storrs of Utah County received a telegram in the afternoon from Springville informing him that two men answering the published description of the Castle Gate robbers passed through the latter place toward last evening and what aroused the officers' suspicions was that they eagerly asked for copies of the Salt Lake papers containing a story of the holdup. The two men rode off in a southeasterly direction as if going to Spanish Fork canyon although they said they were from Strawberry Valley and were on their way north. Sheriff Storrs and Deputy Sheriff Wilkens a short time after the departure of the suspects took the Rio Grande train to intercept the travelers down the canyon and interview them concerning their movements.[3]

A scant week later, on June 28, 1897, six members of the gang attempted a holdup of the Butte County Bank in Belle Fourche, South Dakota. Tom O'Day was caught hiding in a saloon privy. His compadres included Walt Punteney, George Sutherland "Flat Nose" Currie, Harvey "Kid Curry" Logan (making his debut in the Wild Bunch), and Sundance. Butch may have participated, but his involvement is speculative. Although the robbery was successful, the bandits reaped only ninety-seven dollars. O'Day was tried and acquitted, while Punteney was arrested, although all charges were eventually dropped.

Meanwhile, Butch's reputation, which outpaced his criminal record, continued to grow. In a story headlined "King of the Bandits," a Chicago daily declared in early 1898 that "Butch Cassidy is a bad man." Not just any bad man, but "the worst man" in four states—the leader of a gang of five hundred outlaws "subdivided into five bands." But Butch's brutality went much deeper than that, according to the March 1898 *Inter Ocean* newspaper account:

> *"Butch" Cassidy . . . the worst man in four states. These states are Utah, Colorado, Idaho, and Wyoming, and when the four Governors met in secret conclave last week it was for the purpose of deciding upon a plan of campaign against the most notorious outlaw the West has ever had to cope with. The achievements of Jesse James and his followers pale into tawdry insignificance before those of Butch Cassidy and his 500.*
>
> *For several years in fact, ever since the live stock commission drove the Wyoming rustlers out of business, in 1892 "Butch" has proven a thorn in the flesh of the authorities of the four states in which he carries on his operations. He has laughed the militia to scorn.*

Sheriffs and deputies he regards with pity and contempt. He is a power unto himself.

After the ordinary methods of hunting outlaws had been tried unsuccessfully it was decided that drastic means must be employed. Rewards have been repeatedly offered for "Butch" Cassidy, dead or alive, and after each fresh outbreak these rewards have invariably been increased. If all the offers which have been made from time to time hold good, the slayer of "Butch," should he ever live to claim his reward, would be entitled to upward of $20,000 in blood money. But the rewards have proven as futile as have the efforts of the militia and the deputy sheriffs. And that is why Governor Wells, of Utah, Governor Adams of Colorado, Governor Richards of Wyoming, and Governor Steunenberg of Idaho got their heads together to see what could be done. Just what the result of their conference was has not been divulged.

"Butch" and His Bands.

"Butch" and his bands are the outgrowth of the rustlers of six years ago. Since then they have broadened their field and increased their numbers. It is no idle boast to say that the leader of these notorious bands has 600 men at his beck and call. Their depredations are upon a scale never before reached in the history of frontier crime. All the conditions are favorable to them. They know every foot of the vast territory in which they operate, taking in, as it does, the wildest and most inaccessible portion of four states. Every man of them is thoroughly familiar with frontier life in its rougher phase. The forces are subdivided into five bands, each controlled by its own leader, with Cassidy as the supreme power. The outlaws now practically control the sparsely settled region extending from Central Wyoming southwesterly through Northwestern Colorado and Utah, and almost to the Arizona line. Marauding and murderous bands conduct their raids without restraint. The thefts of live stock run into the millions. Ranchmen are murdered and driven out of business, and the officers of the law are powerless. The outlaws roam the adjacent country and smaller settlements without molestation. Many settlers purchase immunity by extending assistance in various ways, and the robbers even attend

*country dances and other functions, occasionally "shooting up" the town
or indulging in other forms of recreation. It is only when closely pursued by officers of the law that they retire to their mountain retreats.*[4]

With such notoriety ringing in his ears, Butch took a pass on the
gang's next venture. On July 14, 1898, a trio of bandits consisting of Sundance, Logan, and Currie (though they were never positively identified)
held up the Southern Pacific No. 1 near Humboldt, Nevada, escaping
with $450. Two other men were apprehended and tried for the holdup
but were acquitted. The Humboldt Three struck again the following April
3, 1899, robbing a saloon in Elko, Nevada, of several hundred dollars.
Once again, three local cowboys were arrested, tried for the robbery, and
acquitted for lack of evidence.

Shortly before those ventures, other outlaws roaming the Southwest
were equally busy. Three Texas debutants who eventually joined the Wild
Bunch, Tom "Black Jack" Ketchum, Dave Atkins, and Will Carver, held
up a Southern Pacific train near Lozier, Texas, on May 14, 1897, pock-
eting more than $42,000. Reinforced by Ketchum's brother Sam, and
possibly Bruce "Red" Weaver, they robbed the Gulf, Colorado & Santa
Fe No. 1 on September 3, 1897, of several thousand dollars. Weaver was
later tried for the crime and acquitted.

But the outlaws' success bred carelessness. On December 9, 1897, five
bandits, most likely the Ketchum brothers, Carver, Atkins, and Edward
H. Cullen, attempted to rob the Southern Pacific No. 20 near Stein's Pass,
New Mexico. Instead, they met a fusillade from hired guards. Cullen was
killed, and although the others were all wounded, they escaped. Uncowed,
four men—probably the Ketchum brothers and perhaps Carver and Ben
Kilpatrick—robbed the Texas & Pacific No. 3 at Mustang Creek, Texas,
on July 1, 1898, grabbing between $1,000 and $50,000 in cash. (Victims were not always candid about how much was stolen. Employees
occasionally pocketed overlooked money and included it in the amount
said to have been taken; on other occasions, the amounts were intentionally lowballed so as not to encourage copycat capers.) Considering the
amount of fuss made over apprehending the desperadoes, though, the
amount was likely nearer the high end:

The Texas & Pacific west bound passenger train was held up and robbed at 10 o'clock by three masked men five miles west of Stanton, a siding near Midland. The safe was dynamited. No one was hurt. It is not known how much the robbers secured. Blood hounds are on their way from Pecos for the scene. They will reach here late tonight. Three possees [sic] from Midland are in hot pursuit of the robbers.[5]

The use of dynamite, although not unique in train robberies, was a trademark of the Wild Bunch and proved especially useful in opening safes. But despite the gang's successes, times were changing. Elzy Lay joined the bunch just in time for its train-robbing blitz to take a bloody turn. On July 11, 1899, Sam Ketchum, Lay, and Carver overpowered the crew of the Colorado & Southern No. 1 and galloped off with some $30,000. Weaver, probably standing guard nearby, took off on a gallop. Before long, the three perpetrators were surprised by a posse. When the dust cleared, one posse member was dead and two were wounded, one mortally; Sam Ketchum was also fatally shot; Lay was wounded and later captured, and Carver escaped. (Some say the third bandit was Harvey Logan and not Carver.)

Meager details were received here this morning of a pitched battle between a sheriff's posse and the gang of outlaws who held up the passenger train at Folsom, N.M., about a week ago. The affray occurred near Cimarron and Ed Farr, a member of the posse, was killed. Mr. Farr lived at Walsenburg, Colo., and was sheriff of Huerfano County, Colo.

Marion Littrell, live stock inspector, arrived here at 1 o'clock this afternoon, bringing further details of the fight at Cimarron, as he had learned them at Springer.

"It occurred this morning," he said, "in the canon [sic] above Cimarron in a very rough piece of country. The news was telephoned to Springer from Cimarron just before I left there. The posse was led by Sheriff Ed Farr of Walsenburg and United States Marshal Foraker of New Mexico. The posse numbered six members. The force divided, three members advancing upon the outlaws from opposite directions.

One of the outlaws was a dead shot. Sheriff Farr was killed and Henry Love and a man named Smith, members of the posse, were wounded. Love was hit twice, one shot going through his thigh. For- aker returned to Cimarron and telephoned that all of his posse had been wounded.

The identity of the outlaws is not known but little doubt is enter- tained that they are the same individuals who held up the train at Folsom a few days ago and also nearly three years since. While Mr. Littrell did not learn the exact location of their camp it is believed to have been comparatively close to Cimarron, probably two or three miles away.

Cimarron is a place of 200 people, situated close to the mouth of the canon [sic] referred to and 23 miles from Springer. The outlaws had been noticed hanging around in the vicinity for some time past. Although nothing certain is known, it is thought by members of the posse that one or more of the outlaws, who are three in number, have been wounded by the officers.

Sheriff Ed Farr, who was killed, is well known among live stock men. He and his brother have rather extensive cattle interests in Southern Colorado and Northern New Mexico.[6]

Meanwhile, ignoring what had transpired less than a week earlier, Tom Ketchum chose a less than precipitous moment to launch his solo career. On August 16, 1899, he attempted to hold up the Colorado & Southern No. 1 near Folsom but was shot, captured, tried, convicted, and hanged.

These calamities should have been a warning to Carver and Kilpatrick to seek a new line of work. Instead, they served only as a notice of a change of venue as they rode north to join the main branch of the Wild Bunch.

The first crime that fused together the various criminal elements of the Butch-Sundance gang happened around June 2, 1899, with the robbery of the Union Pacific Overland Flyer No. 1 near Wilcox, Wyo- ming. The holdup yielded between $3,400 and $50,000 and brought the Hole-in-the-Wall Gang, as the Wild Bunch was alternately known, nationwide fame.

"They were lawless men who have lived long in the crags and become like eagles," wrote the *New York Herald*, but Butch and Sundance may not have actually participated in the flight that day. Still, numerous witnesses reported six masked men involved in the robbery, and most historians can name only four: George Flat Nose Currie, Harvey Logan, his brother Lonny Logan, and their cousin Bob Lee. The other two? Although they were almost certainly Butch and Sundance, a newspaper account at the time shed light on every aspect of the crime except one: Who did it?

It was learned that the Union Pacific continental west bound mail train had been held up, dynamited, and robbed . . . at 1 o'clock at Wilcox, a lonely station on the Wyoming division.

The train was flagged just east of the little bridge at that point. Two of the men entered the cab of the engineer and presented guns to Engineer W. R. Jones and his fireman, and told him to pull across the bridge and stop. As soon as the train passed over the bridge the gang placed a charge of dynamite on the bridge for the purpose of blowing it out and preventing the second section, which runs ten minutes behind the first section, from coming over. The first section was in a short distance further west, and the express and baggage cars were then looted, the cars being badly damaged by the charges of dynamite used for opening the safe. Engineer Jones, who did not intend to submit to the holdup, was rough-handled by the desperadoes, being struck over the head with a billy and otherwise hurt.

The amount of booty secured by the Union Pacific train robbery is unknown. The shipments of money west are said to have been unusually heavy lately and from this fact estimates as high as $60,000 have been made, but railroads and express officials place the amount low, even to a few hundred dollars. Those who place the amount high do so largely from the fact that a tremendous effort is being made to catch the six men.

One of the men who boarded the engine of the train is described as a man fifty years or more of age and it was he who prevented the other robber from killing Engineer Jones. The air was set on the brakes so that Jones could not start the train when ordered. The robber thought

*Jones was getting foxy and knocked him down with his six-shooter,
when the old man, who seemed to be the leader, interposed and said
"Don't kill him." Woodcock, the express messenger, would not open the
car door when they made the demand and the door was blown open by
dynamite and Woodcock was knocked down and rendered insensible.
One hundred pounds of dynamite was found today near the scene of
the robbery and a piece of a $100 bill was found. This strengthens the
theory that they got a large sum of money.*

*Engineer Jones was not so badly hurt, but that he continued to the
end of his run. The men seem to have been well mounted as the horses
were tied a third of a mile from where the robbery occurred and seem
to have been restless. The two sections of the train were held for two
hours. After the gang left the engineer cut loose from his train and ran
fourteen miles to Medicine Bow, from which point he telegraphed of
the robbery.[7]*

With that heist safely under their belts, the lawless "eagles" swooped
down again, this time on August 29, 1900, robbing the Union Pacific
Overland Flyer No. 3 near Tipton, Wyoming, of between $55.40 as the
railroad claimed and $55,000 as later reported. This time, the five bandits
undoubtedly included Butch and probably Sundance plus Harvey Logan.
Also suspected were Ben Kilpatrick, Tom Welch, and perhaps a sixth
man, Billy Rose. Of the bunch, Logan was a badass. "There was three
Logan brothers [actually four] from Montana," according to local Larry
Roupe. "Harvey used the alias Kid Curry. Killed Ol' Man Pike up there in
Montana, then he robbed this train down on the Wilcox. Butch and Sundance weren't in on that one."[8] One brother, according to researcher and
author Kerry Boren, "died from pneumonia in Steamboat Springs, Colorado. Another was blasted from his horse by a shotgun in the hands of
a Montana rancher, who was in turn killed by Harvey Logan a few years
later. The third brother was shot down at his aunt's home in Missouri."[9]

Tipton is the first crime in which Butch and Sundance are generally
thought to have participated together. They were only six months from
fleeing the country due to the pressure being placed on Butch and his
gang of "five hundred."

With the Wilcox holdup and Sheriff Joe Hazen's killing, Butch, while not named as a participant, suddenly became a national legend. His picture, a likeness based upon his prison photo taken at the Wyoming State Penitentiary at Laramie, appeared in a June 25, 1899, article in the *New York Herald* about the Hole-in-the-Wall bandits. In the article, George Currie and the Roberts brothers were identified as leaders of the gang, but Butch was mentioned as always nearby, ready to grab the helm should anything go wrong.

Several weeks after the Wilcox robbery, law enforcement agencies received a report that two of the robbers had been seen in southwestern Wyoming with thirteen head of saddle horses headed toward Brown's Park. A few days later, the same two were seen passing through Hanksville, Utah, still driving the horses south. One of the two was likely Butch. Pinkerton dispatched two of its most experienced operatives, Charles Siringo and W. O. Sayles, to pick up their trail.

At Hanksville, Siringo and Sayles learned that the men they were after, still driving the horses, had ridden south into Garfield County, Utah, and had crossed the Colorado on Johnny Hite's ferry near the mouth of the Dirty Devil River. When Siringo and Sayles inquired at the ferry, they learned that another man, a single rider with five horses, had crossed the river several days after the first two. Hite said that the second man said he was going to go "where the grass was good and camp until he heard from his friends." This man's description matched that of Harvey Logan, and the detectives assumed that the outlaws had a camp somewhere on the southside of the river where they had arranged to meet.[10]

Siringo and his partner crossed the river and soon picked up the third man's trail, which appeared to lead up White's Canyon. But it was getting late in the day, and the detectives' horses needed to be fed, so they decided that Sayles should return to the ferry to buy some grain. In the meantime, Siringo prepared to track the bandit until dark.

Following the trail up a steep bluff and onto a mesa, the detective lost the tracks in a rocky arroyo. He searched the canyon for another two miles before giving up. About a year later, Siringo learned from a prospector that a man named John Duckett, who was working a claim on a ridge above the canyon, said that the detective had come within half a mile of the outlaw's camp. Duckett told him that he had watched him and the man he was trailing from his vantage point and had seen Siringo give up and leave. He added that the outlaw had camped there for about two weeks before moving on.[11]

Although Siringo failed to spot the lone outlaw's camp on the mesa above White Canyon, he and Sayles eventually found the trail of the two riders who were leading the saddle horses.

From White Canyon, the robbers' trail led southeast to Bluff, Utah, on the San Juan River, about twenty miles north of the Arizona line. At Bluff, the two Pinkerton men learned that two other Pinky operatives had preceded them and were also on the trail of the outlaws, who had headed east out of town after loading up with supplies. By then, Siringo had little doubt that the two men they were following were the Wilcox robbers: A report had arrived that a bill from the express car safe had been traced to Hanksville, and another one had been passed earlier at Thompson's Springs, which also had been on the robbers' path.

From the direction the outlaws had taken out of Bluff, the detectives deduced they were heading either for Colorado or New Mexico. Rather than follow the other two Pinkertons, according to Siringo, "Sayles and I realized we were born leaders of men, hence we didn't like the idea of bringing up the rear," so they rode directly to Mancos, Colorado, and boarded a train for Durango.[12]

Siringo sent a telegram to a friend, J. M. Archuleta, who returned word that the two men he'd been chasing had been spotted near Lumberton, New Mexico, driving thirteen horses. One was a bright cream color and another was a large dapple-iron gray, both easy to spot. Siringo and Sayles took off for Lumberton, but the men they were following were gone by the time they arrived. Believing their quarry had headed south toward Santa Fe, the detectives pressed on, stopping only when they reached the edge of town. There, they split up, Siringo picking up what appeared to be some promising leads that sent him on a wild chase throughout the southern states. Sayles, on the other hand, had better luck. Abandoning the chase to pursue the trail of bills stolen at Wilcox, he headed north, where he eventually found Harvey Logan and his brother, Lonny, in Montana. Between the bills and a positive identification by sheepherder John DeVore at Sullivan Springs, Wyoming, the two Logans were apprehended and charged in the Wilcox robbery.

In the meantime, the men the detectives had been following south, most likely Butch and Elzy Lay, continued toward Alma, New Mexico, where they had been working at the WS Ranch under the names of Jim Lowe and Mac McGinnis.

Once the men had returned, things at the WS began operating smoothly again. But one day in late June 1899, Lowe went to ranch owner William French with the unwelcome news that McGinnis was thinking of leaving. McGinnis's reason, according to Lowe, was that all the broncs had been broken and he just wasn't interested in doing other work around the spread.

By the second week in July, not long after McGinnis had departed, French was in northern New Mexico on business, on his way from Springer to Cimarron in a buggy, when he spotted a man on foot coming across the prairie toward the road. He was in pretty bad shape, and French helped him climb aboard. The man said that he was a special officer for the Colorado and Southern Railroad and that he had been part of a posse that had been chasing several train robbers. French had heard that three or four men had held up an express car on the Colorado and Southern near Folsom, and a posse was looking for them somewhere south of Cimarron.

The stranger, whose name was William H. Reno, had been with the posse that had been formed at Trinidad, Colorado, by Huerfano County sheriff Edward Farr. They had gotten to Raton by rail, where they picked up horses and went looking for the robbers' trail. They found the outlaws' camp in Turkey (or Turkey Creek) Canyon just southwest of the road he and French were on, and a gunfight broke out. Reno was sure that one of the robbers was killed and pretty confident that Sheriff Farr had also been shot. He said that Farr had fallen from his horse, and the frightened beast ran off with the sheriff's Winchester still in its scabbard. Reno, sure they would need the gun, had gone after it before the horse gave him the slip, and he found himself lost in the canyon. French doubted the man's story, figuring that he simply became frightened and ran away. He agreed to take Reno back to Springer so that he could send a telegram to his employers to check in.

The incident had livened up what otherwise would have been a routine business trip for French, but more than that, Reno had said something that bothered the rancher: He said that the robbers, before fleeing the scene of the crime, had mentioned the name of one of the outlaws, and it was McGinnis.

Before French left Cimarron, he learned that one of the train robbers had been captured and identified, a local bad man named Sam Ketchum. French had heard of Ketchum; in fact, Ketchum had stolen two horses from the WS shortly before Jim Lowe and Mac McGinnis hired on at the ranch. The other two train robbers, yet to be found, had not been positively identified. However, if French had any doubts that the man he knew as McGinnis was one of these other two, those doubts disappeared upon his return to the ranch. The ranchers wanted to know if he had learned whether the other two robbers had been taken by the law.

French found that the details of the shootout in Turkey Canyon were not exactly as Special Agent William Reno had described them. According to the story, the robbers had foolishly built a campfire, and the posse had spotted the smoke. As they snuck into position, the robber who called himself Mac McGinnis (Elzy Lay) had grabbed his canteen to fill down at the creek. The other two outlaws were standing near the campfire. Someone may have shouted for the outlaws to surrender, but if they did, the posse didn't wait for an answer. McGinnis was hit immediately, first in the shoulder and then in the back.

As the outlaws returned the lawmen's fire, Sheriff Farr and another member of the posse, F. H. Smith, tried to hide behind the same tree. Smith took a bullet in the calf of his leg. As Farr was trying to wrap his partner's wound, either McGinnis, who may have recovered enough from his injuries to use his rifle, or one of the other outlaws put a bullet into Farr's chest, killing him instantly.

A second outlaw, later identified as Sam Ketchum, took a bullet in the arm just below the shoulder, breaking the bone, and a third member of the posse, Henry Love, was hit in the thigh. The rest of the deputies, seeing their members beginning to fall, promptly retreated, and the outlaws escaped.

The wounds to McGinnis and Ketchum made travel difficult, and the two plus a third robber, later identified as Will Carver, stopped to rest at a cabin near the junction of Cimarron and Ute Creeks. The empty cabin was owned by a man named Ed McBride, whom the outlaws knew well. Once rested, McGinnis was able to go on, but Ketchum was too weak and remained at the shelter. When McBride and his family returned, they bandaged Ketchum's wound, but the following day, they turned him over to authorities.

Several days later, Jim Lowe went to French and told him that their friend, Mac McGinnis, had been arrested as one of the suspects in the Folsom robbery. Lowe was with a former WS hand whom French knew as Tom Capehart. Lowe said that Capehart had just ridden in from Lincoln County with the news about McGinnis. By then, French took everything he heard with a grain of salt. As for Capehart, he was reasonably certain that he, too, was one of the outlaw gang and probably had been involved in the robbery.

Lowe asked French if he would post security for McGinnis's bail until he and the others could scrape together enough money for a bond. French thought about it for a second, probably wondering just how many members of the Wild Bunch he had in his employ and where this entire thing might eventually lead. He liked McGinnis, and despite what the man had done, he felt sorry for him. French told Lowe that he would put up the security for McGinnis if possible but that he doubted he would be given the opportunity since the Territory of New Mexico had made train robbery a capital offense and usually not subject to bail. French did say, though, that if he was given a chance, he would testify to McGinnis's good character during the time that he had worked at the ranch.[13]

French asked Capehart how McGinnis had been captured. Without admitting that he had played a role in the robbery, Capehart replied that he had been helping McGinnis hide out in Lincoln County until his wounds healed, but when McGinnis had been accidentally discovered by a posse looking for horse thieves, he was arrested.

Elzy Lay, still claiming that his name was William McGinnis, was taken to Santa Fe, where he was bound over on a charge of interfering with the US mail. Later, after statements of the posse members were reviewed, he was charged with the murder of Sheriff Farr.

The case against William McGinnis was set for trial at Raton, New Mexico, seat of Colfax County, during the first week of October 1899. His attorneys had tried to get a continuance, claiming their client's fellow cowboys back at the WS Ranch were having difficulty scraping up a defense fund for him because ranch owner William French, who owed them wages, was out of town. This move fell flat when the prosecution introduced affidavits that McGinnis's friends were not paid by French himself but by ranch foreman Perry Tucker.

The trial began on October 2. The evidence proving that McGinnis had fired the shot that killed Sheriff Farr was weak, but the Territory of New Mexico, which was in the process of seeking statehood, was anxious to prove that murder would not be tolerated among its ranks. Although the trial judge's personal feelings are unknown, many of his procedural rulings went against the defense. McGinnis's lawyers put only two witnesses on the stand, one of them the defendant himself. McGinnis appeared convincing when he denied killing Farr, but his credibility was weakened when, on cross-examination, he refused to answer any questions regarding his past or his true identity. The jury found him guilty of murder in the second degree and sentenced him to imprisonment for "any period of time not less than three years." The judge sentenced him to life.

Back at the ranch, Butch, still calling himself Jim Lowe, was likely devastated by Lay's sentence. Lay was his closest friend. But Butch realized that the jury *could* have found Lay guilty of first-degree murder and recommended death.

After the trial, things calmed down at the WS, and operations again became routine, allowing William French time to pursue plans for expansion and other business matters. French, however, was growing increasingly uneasy. He could no longer ignore the fact that he had members of the Wild Bunch in his employ, and he could not help thinking that the law could come knocking at his door at any moment. Sure enough, a month after McGinnis's conviction, a stranger *did* come calling. He identified himself as an operative of Pinkerton's National Detective Agency, and French assumed he was looking for Tom Capehart in connection with the Folsom train robbery. But the detective said that he was investigating a different train robbery, one that had occurred in Wyoming, and a trail of banknotes from that robbery had led him to New Mexico. The bills had shown up at a bank in Silver City and had been traced to the store at Alma. The detective added that these particular bills had been easy to trace because when the robbers dynamited the express car safe, the explosion had blown off the tip of one corner of the packet in which the bills were contained.

The detective claimed that a storekeeper in Alma said that he'd received the bills from an employee of the WS Ranch who called himself Johnny Ward. There were, in fact, two Johnny Wards working at the ranch at the time: "Big" Johnny and "Little" Johnny. French figured Big Johnny was the guilty party since he was the newest hire, so he decided to find Little Johnny for the detective. Much to French's surprise, Little Johnny Ward admitted to spending the bills in Alma and admitted he still had some in his possession. He had gotten them from another WS hand who had since left, a man named McGonigal who had worked for Jim Lowe a week or so on a trail drive. Just before McGonigal had left, Ward sold him a horse, and McGonigal paid him with the tainted bills. This seemed to satisfy the detective, who copied down the numbers from the bills Little Johnny had but allowed him to keep them.

After Ward left, the detective showed French a picture of a group of men and asked him if he recognized any of them. He did: One of them was his trail boss, Jim Lowe. The detective said that the Pinkertons knew the man as Butch Cassidy, that he was believed to be the leader of one of the best-organized outlaw gangs that had ever existed in the West, and that there was hardly a state or territory south of the Canadian line that didn't want him. He added that Cassidy seemed to know precisely when a sizable express shipment was going to be made by rail. He said the Pinkertons had lost track of him, but that he had spotted him that very morning in Alma. French asked if he had come to arrest Cassidy, and the detective laughed, assuring him that he'd be a fool to try such a thing without a regiment of cavalry to back him up. He said he was there merely to follow up on the report of the stolen banknotes and that his job after that was to find the man who called himself McGonigal.[14]

The man whom French knew as Jim Lowe was away from the ranch when the detective had called. On Lowe's return, French told him about the visit, probably adding that the masquerade, at least between the two of them, was over. French said that Cassidy didn't seem the least bit worried. He just grinned that familiar grin of his and said that he knew the detective was in the area snooping around; in fact, he added, after the man had concluded his visit with French, he and Tom Capehart ran into him in Alma and bought him a drink. Butch didn't say what was discussed that evening beyond commenting that he would likely have to leave the WS before long, although he had no plans to pull out yet.

The Pinkerton agent who had called at the ranch was Frank Murray, destined in time to become assistant superintendent of the agency's Denver office. Sometime later, he revealed that the drink he'd had at the saloon that night was nearly his last. He reported that he might well have been shot then and there but for the intervention of a man known only as Jim Lowe.

In exchange for the courtesy, Murray must have convinced Butch that he would keep his mouth shut as to his identity. He also likely pledged that, if the Pinkertons sent any other agents to Alma, Murray would warn Butch in advance. His brush with death that night must have convinced Murray to keep his word or, more likely, if he didn't, he knew the Wild Bunch would make him pay. Murray apparently kept his word: He reported the incident to his superiors but failed to mention that Jim Lowe was Butch Cassidy, saying only that Jim Lowe was the saloonkeeper at Alma.

According to William French, when Butch finally left the ranch, it was of his own accord. Just before they were to drive the last herd of the year to the railroad, Perry Tucker informed French that he was going to be leaving to pursue other interests in Arizona. When French asked him to stay until he found somebody to replace him, Tucker suggested that Butch be put in charge of the outfit. French, however, was hesitant; after the visit by the Pinkerton detective, he knew Butch's days at the WS were numbered. He talked the situation over with Butch, who still didn't appear overly concerned about the Pinkertons knowing his locale. As to Tucker's job, Butch said that he would take it if it were offered, but he added that he understood how French felt about having a famous fugitive running his outfit. French said that he would be glad to keep him on for the last drive, but in the end, Butch decided it was probably time to go.

Before leaving, Butch asked French for a favor: He asked to buy a pair of custom-made kyacks (packsacks) that were sitting around, gathering dust in the stable. French gifted him the pair.

When Butch left, a WS hand named Red Weaver went with him. According to French, they stopped first at the ranch of a neighbor named Ashby with whom Butch and the men at the WS had been having trouble. They suspected Ashby of building his herd at the expense of his neighbors' strays, but when they approached him about the problem, Ashby feigned ignorance. Rather than cause trouble between Ashby and French, who at the time wanted to work out a deal to buy Ashby out, Butch decided upon a more subtle way to resolve the problem. He and Weaver dropped by Ashby's ranch and took every one of his saddle horses with them. The exasperated Ashby was forced to walk several miles to borrow a horse to ride into town to report the loss. French said later that he believed Butch's devilment turned out to be a favor to the WS: He was pretty sure that the theft of all of Ashby's horses had finally persuaded the man to sell out.[15]

But the stunt nearly backfired. On leaving Ashby's ranch, Butch and Weaver, trailing the stolen horses, rode northwest into Arizona. At St. Johns in Apache County, they stopped to buy provisions. Eyeing the horses, the local sheriff became suspicious. When Butch's explanation of where they'd gotten the animals didn't satisfy him, the sheriff marched the two off to jail. Butch told the sheriff that his name was Jim Lowe and that the sheriff should get in touch with William French at the WS because French would vouch for them. The sheriff sent a telegraph to French by way of Magdalena, and French confirmed their identities. The two men appeared in court in Socorro on April 28, 1900, and pled not guilty to the charge of larceny of horses. A trial was scheduled for Weaver on May 4 but was continued to the next term of court, and the two were released on $1,000 bail. The local newspaper offered no further details of the case, implying that the charges had most likely been dropped.

French heard nothing more from Butch until he made a business trip to Cimarron a year later, during which he learned of two men who had been seen in the mountains in Colfax County not far from the scene of the Folsom train robbery. They had come upon the camp of a party in the process of surveying a tract of land being sold by the Maxwell Grant Company. There was nothing special about the pair, and the surveyors would probably never have mentioned the encounter except for a unique set of kyacks one of the men had on his packhorse; they were made of rawhide and wood.

Though Butch may have been indirectly involved in the Wild Bunch's activities while at the ranch, most likely participating in at least one robbery, the months spent there were relatively quiet. He was in hiding—somewhat—right out in the open. His time there, for a change, was as predictable as possible and, most likely, enjoyable.

Among other pastimes, the men of the WS rode into the town of Mogollon on weekends, a ten-mile trip from Alma, for drinking, card playing, and community dances. Butch may also have found romance: A local gal named Agnes Meader Snider apparently had a crush on him.

The days Butch had spent at the WS Ranch were as routine as they could possibly be for an outlaw wanted in four states. That taste of normalcy may have presented him with a different outlook on the course he had taken and helped to explain why he began thinking about reforming. On the other hand, he may also have decided that the Wild Bunch's luck was running out. Elzy Lay, after nearly being killed at Turkey Canyon, was serving a life sentence in Santa Fe, and Henry "Bub" Meeks was doing his third year of thirty-five at the Idaho State Penitentiary.

Butch, for whatever reason, apparently thought seriously about getting out of the outlaw business. At least, that's according to several stories coming from one or both of the attorneys who were involved with Butch at the time: Orlando Powers of Salt Lake City and Douglas Preston.

But before Butch could go straight, he had some accounts to settle. His roots had long been in Utah, where the Parker family were staunch members of the Mormon community. Except for his brother Dan, Butch was the only family member who had crossed the abyss, and even Dan had served his time and had by then returned to a respectable life. Butch was the sole remaining embarrassment to the family, so it was natural that if he were to seek the road back from perdition, he would need to begin in Utah, where Mormons made a big show of family honor.

So, Butch stopped first at the Salt Lake City office of lawyer Orlando Powers, who was both influential and well connected. Just as important, attorney Douglas Preston trusted Powers enough to recommend him for Matt Warner's defense attorney in Ogden.

Butch dropped in unannounced, telling Powers's stenographer that he wanted to see the attorney. The day must have been cold because Butch was wearing both overalls and a blue denim jumper. He carried a battered hat, clutching it in both hands. His face was weathered from months on the range, and he appeared older than his thirty-two years. Powers welcomed him into his office and offered him a seat. The following conversation, according to biographer Richard Patterson, took place:

Cassidy: "Is what I say to you to go as a client consulting his lawyer from now on?"

Powers: "You mean, a privileged communication?"

Cassidy: "That's it."

Powers: "All right then."

Cassidy: "I'm Butch Cassidy."

Powers: "Well, what can I do for you?"

Cassidy: "I'll tell you. There's a heap of charges out against me and considerable money offered for me in rewards. I'm getting sick of hiding out; always on the run and never able to stay long in one place. Now, when it comes to facts, I've kept close track of things, and I know there ain't a man left in the country who can go on the stand and identify me for any crime. All of 'em have either died or gone away. I've been thinking. Why can't I go and just give myself up and stand trial on one of those old charges?"

Powers: "No use. You've robbed too many big corporations in your time. I do not doubt what you say, but if you were ever to go on trial, you can depend on it, some one of those companies would bring some one to the stand who'd swear against you. No, you'll have to keep on the run, I'm afraid."[16]

Disheartened but not defeated, Butch decided to appeal directly to Utah governor Heber Wells. He turned to an old friend, Parley P. Christensen, who at the time was sheriff of Moab County, Utah. Christensen had known the Parker family for years, and Butch had never caused him any problems. To show his good faith, the outlaw turned his guns over to Christensen: the .45 Colt revolver he had bought in Vernal in 1896 and a Winchester 44-40 saddle ring carbine.

Butch's sincerity may have impressed Christensen, who agreed to arrange a meeting for Butch with Wells. But it was a dicey proposition from both a political and a legal standpoint. A sitting governor granting an audience to a wanted outlaw—and one wanted in at least four states, at that—could have ended the governor's career. But the fact that Christensen, a lawman, vouched for Butch's sincerity won the governor over: Wells agreed to a meeting.

From the beginning, Wells seemed receptive. After hearing Butch's plea, he told him that he might be amenable to some form of amnesty provided Butch wasn't wanted anywhere for murder. Butch insisted that he wasn't, and Wells promised to do whatever he could.

But Butch's high hopes were short-lived. At a second meeting several days later, Wells told Butch that he had met with his attorney general, who did some checking and found that Butch was, in fact, wanted for murder in Wyoming. Wells said that he was sorry, but under the circumstances, there was nothing more he could do.

It may not have mattered in the end. Although Wells may have been willing to issue amnesty, he couldn't speak for the governors of the other states where Butch was wanted—Wyoming, Idaho, and Colorado—and they were unlikely to go along.

In the meantime, Orlando Powers had come up with another idea. The railroads had been ravaged by robbers in the previous decade. From 1890 to 1899, some 261 robberies had rocked the railways, mostly in the Western states, during which 88 people had been killed and 86 injured. Powers believed that the railroads, especially the Union Pacific, might be willing to drop all charges against Butch if he'd agree to stop attacking express cars. Even though such an agreement was inherently nonbinding, the railroads held tremendous sway with various Western statehouses. If they asked for it, the states would likely grant it.

Although Union Pacific officials considered Harvey Logan a greater threat to their welfare than Butch, they agreed to discuss the offer, and a plan was worked out with the help of attorney Douglas Preston to arrange a meeting. At the gang leader's suggestion, the site was scheduled for Lost Soldier Pass, about forty miles north of Rawlins and not far from the old stage road to Lander. It was desolate country: If things went south, Butch could make a hasty retreat into the mountains.

On the day of the meeting, Preston set out by buckboard with two railroad representatives; but a violent storm blew up, delaying them, after which they got lost. By the time they reached the prearranged spot, Butch was gone. Tucked under a stone was a note: "Damn you Preston, you have double-crossed me. I waited all day but you didn't show up. Tell the U.P. to go to hell. And you can go with them."[17]

To salvage the plan, Orlando Powers came up with one more idea. Butch's pal, Matt Warner, had recently been released from prison. Powers knew that Butch would trust Warner not to cross him; so, if Warner could be brought in on the deal with the railroad, Butch might reconsider.

Powers went to Governor Wells and suggested that he ask Warner to find Butch, explain the mix-up at Lost Soldier Pass, and beg him to reconsider the deal with the Union Pacific. Warner accepted the assignment and was given $175 for travel expenses. The last week in August 1900, Warner boarded a train at Salt Lake City bound for Rock Springs, Wyoming. He was counting on Butch being either at his Powder Springs hideout or at Brown's Park. But Warner never reached his friend. When the train stopped at Bridger Station just east of Evanston, Wyoming, the conductor handed Warner a telegram from Governor Wells. "All agreements off. Cassidy just held up a train at Tipton."[18]

The town of Tipton, Wyoming, lies on the eastern slope of the Continental Divide, on the Front Range, halfway between Rawlins and Rock Springs. While the holdup Wells referred to in his telegram is referred to as the Tipton robbery, the train—the second section of Union Pacific No.

3 out of Omaha—was stopped by the robbers on the western slope of the divide near Table Rock. The site, also called Pulpit Rock, is a tiny settlement named after a nearby mesa where Brigham Young once delivered a rallying sermon to a group of discouraged Mormon immigrants on their way west to escape persecution.

On the night of the holdup, one of the robbers most likely boarded the train as it was leaving Tipton. As engineer Henry Wallenstine pulled the grade toward Table Rock, the robber, a mask likely covering his face, scrambled down from the tender, shoved a pistol in Wallenstine's ribs, and ordered him to slow the train as they approached a campfire in the distance. A mile farther Wallenstine saw three more masked men waiting just off the right-of-way. Once the train had stopped, the robbers ordered the conductor to uncouple the mail car and express cars from the passenger coaches. As in the Wilcox robbery, the robbers used dynamite to blast their way in. When they entered the Pacific Express car, they saw a familiar face: C. E. Woodcock, the same messenger who had been on duty the night of the Wilcox robbery.

If any doubt remained that the line had been hit by the same gang that struck at Wilcox, it disappeared when Union Pacific detectives took a statement from the postal clerk in charge of the railway mail car. He said he overheard parts of a conversation between the crooks and, from that, deduced that Butch had been involved.

Once again, the actual amount stolen in the heist was never revealed. Two days after the holdup, the general manager of the Union Pacific sent a telegram to the Denver newspapers stating that the outlaws had taken only three money packages containing a total of $50.40 and "two packages of cheap jewelry." However, when the wrecked express car was examined at Green River, three twenty-dollar gold pieces were found on the floor, suggesting that at least one sack of coins had broken open when the robbers blew the safe. A witness at the scene confirmed that as the robbers ransacked the express car, they "stooped over frequently and picked up articles from the floor, which they hurriedly thrust into their pockets."[19] Later, express messenger Woodcock let slip to the press that the actual loss was close to $55,000 and would have been more if he hadn't had the sense to hide several packages of money behind a trunk before the break-in.

Unlike the Wilcox robbery, where little evidence was turned up linking Butch to the crime, Union Pacific officials attributed the Tipton holdup to Cassidy from the start. This was due, in part, to a rancher who ran cattle near the holdup site. The rancher, whose name was not released, told railroad officials he saw Butch, whom he knew on sight, and four well-armed riders on good horses in the area two weeks before the robbery. He said he knew one was Butch because he had watched him through his field glasses. That report, corroborated by statements from several of the train crew that one of the robbers was "sandy complected," smooth-shaven, had gray eyes, and was about five feet ten inches tall, satisfied the authorities that Butch was the man they were after.[20]

Most researchers agree that Butch Cassidy was at Tipton, concluding that he was most likely accompanied by Harvey Logan and Sundance, although they're less sure about the identity of a fourth or even a fifth robber.

The Pinkertons believed they used Jim Ferguson's ranch on the Snake River near Dixon as their staging area. Ferguson, a former butcher from Keystone, South Dakota, had been tied to the Wild Bunch for periodically offering his ranch as a site for the gang's meetings.

One of the robbers at Tipton may have been Tom Welch of Lonetree, Wyoming. According to a fellow who worked for him, Welch and Butch were friends. In escaping from the Tipton robbery, Welch was thought to have caught a bullet in the leg, forcing him to hide out with his parents until the wound healed. Instead of returning to outlawry, Welch apparently took his share of the Tipton loot, formed a partnership with a well-heeled doctor named Hawk, and became a hotel keeper in Green River, Wyoming.

When officials in Omaha were wired about the robbery, Sheriff Pete Swanson organized a posse and rushed by train to the scene, arriving near daylight. Another posse headed by US Marshal Frank Hadsell was dispatched by rail from Rawlins, but a mechanical breakdown near Creston delayed them, and they didn't arrive until 8:30 the following morning.

On leaving the scene of the holdup, the robbers rode southeast toward Delaney Rim, where the Rock Springs posse picked up their trail, but the ground turned grassy and hard just south of the rim, and they lost the robbers' tracks. The landscape slowed Swanson and his riders considerably, and later that morning, Hadsell and the Rawlins posse caught up with them. Both detachments had hurried to secure horses for the chase, with some being young and strong while others were ill-suited for long-distance travel. By that afternoon, attrition had reduced the combined posse to twenty men, less than half the number that had started.

Although at times the posse was strung out as much as two miles from front to back, the lead riders, guided by Deputy US Marshal Joe LeFors out of Rawlins, made good time. By sundown, they had reached the Little Snake River just above the Colorado line, a distance of nearly 120 miles from the holdup scene. As LeFors led his horse down the bank on the north side of the river, he spotted three men and a packhorse climbing the long slope on the facing side.

Hadsell and LeFors quickly counted their remaining deputies: only an even dozen left, enough to handle three outlaws, but it was getting dark fast. They agreed it would be foolhardy to rush the outlaws after dark. Plus, the posse had been without sleep for twenty hours straight, and the horses were spent. Even though they probably were hardly out of shouting distance of the men they were pursuing, they decided to make camp and gamble on picking up their tracks in the morning.

LeFors was up early the next day and set out alone to pick up the outlaws' trail shortly after dawn. Heading due south, he noted that the path showed the group's intent to lose the posse in the wilderness of the eastern edge of Brown's Park. LeFors rode back, awakened his men, and was back on the trail again. The lawmen had ridden around twenty miles when they came upon the robbers' packhorse. The animal had given out and was nearly dead.

Following the tracks of the remaining three horses, the posse rode another fifteen miles until they saw that the trail led to a patch of low ground surrounded by a thick grove of willows. The layout did not look good: It was a perfect spot for an ambush. They drew their weapons and rode instinctively on, slowing their mounts to a walk. When they got closer to the grove, they saw beneath the willow branches what appeared to be the legs of several horses. LeFors dismounted, picked two volunteers, and crawled forward with them on their knees and elbows toward the trees. The remainder of the posse divided into two groups and moved off to the left and right, flanking the grove.

And then LeFors broke in to find the horses—three of them—in the willows, but there was no sign of the outlaws. It was a classic Wild Bunch ploy, one used by Butch during his very first robbery. The outlaws had used the willows to hide a relay of fresh mounts. With their rested animals and a good head start, the posse couldn't possibly catch them before they reached Brown's Park. The posse members rubbed their empty bellies, took a long look at their own exhausted animals, and mounted up for home.

The authorities assumed at the time that the robbers hid out in Brown's Park until things cooled down. Some Wild Bunch historians agree. Others, however, contend that the outlaws rode through the park and kept going west until they eventually reached Nevada, where, on September 19, 1900, they added to their larder by robbing the First National Bank of Winnemucca. And the rest, or so they say, is history.

By February 1901, with the law closing in on Butch Cassidy and his gang, Butch and Sundance decided to split from the others and head for the safety of South America. The two leaders had teamed up on only two or three robberies in the states. As crime sprees go, it was not much of a run. As for the rest of the gang, with their leaders gone, they stumbled on, and within a couple of years, most were either dead or in jail. But that didn't mean the gang was through.

On July 3, 1901, what was left of the Wild Bunch in North America attacked the Great Northern Coast Flyer No. 3 near Wagner, Montana, managing to pluck more than $40,000 in the caper. The gang at the time consisted of four to six bandits, including Harvey Logan, Ben Kilpatrick, and O. C. Hanks. Kilpatrick and Logan were eventually apprehended and sent to prison for passing banknotes from the holdup, and Hanks died the next year in a shootout with the law in Texas.

Still not finished, Logan, who escaped from jail in 1903, enlisted two friends, most likely from Ketchum territory, for his farewell performance, a June 7, 1904, botched holdup of the Denver & Rio Grande near Parachute, Colorado. Wounded and cornered, Logan committed suicide. The list of possible accomplices is long, with George Kilpatrick (Ben's brother) and Dan Sheffield high up among the candidates. George was most likely mortally wounded, his body never found. According to an article in the *Grand Junction News* four days following the incident:

> *Train No. 5 on the Rio Grande was held up Tuesday night a short distance west of Parachute by three men, one of whom boarded the engine at Parachute, held a revolver at the head of Engineer Ed. Allison and compelled him to stop at a point where two other men got aboard. Then the train was uncoupled and the express and mail coaches were taken some distance away and the safe in the express car blown open. There was nothing in it of value, the men having no doubt intended to stop the Midland train and secure a large sum of money. It was an amateur job but the rascals have not yet been caught. The report was received Thursday night that one of the gang had been surrounded and wounded, after which, he had killed himself and the others were close pressed and would be captured, but up to Friday noon nothing farther had been heard.[21]*

This, at last, put an end to the Northern Hemisphere's branch of the Wild Bunch—except for one footnote. Ben Kilpatrick, released from prison in 1911, joined former cellmate Ole Beck to rob the Galveston, Harrisburg & San Antonio No. 9 near Sanderson, Texas, on March 13, 1912. Quick-witted Wells Fargo messenger David Trousdale fatally bludgeoned Kilpatrick with an ice mallet before grabbing the man's rifle and shooting Beck dead.

So, between the late 1880s and early 1900s, a gang called the Wild Bunch, which was comprised of several smaller outlaw groups and several dozen bandits, added to the legend and the lore of the Old West. The fact that the McCarty-Warner and Ketchum Gangs proved more durable over the years than the Rocky Mountain Wild Bunch, possibly because they were made up mostly of family, was irrelevant. All told, the Wild Bunch committed more than two dozen holdups. They probably weren't responsible for some they'd been blamed for, and they most likely pulled off a few others for which they'd never been accused. Such is the stuff of outlaw legends.

Of the approximately twenty bandits who can be counted among the Rocky Mountain Wild Bunch during its heyday, few participated in more than a couple of the gang's crimes, and the combined holdups in that eight-year period numbered a scant five to seven. Butch and Sundance, that inseparable gun-toting duo destined to go down in Western film history, pulled off no more than two or three crimes together. If they hadn't gone to South America, where they were reported shot and killed following the departure of Sundance's paramour, Etta Place—waiting patiently in the wings for her real-life, on-stage performance—for the States, the 1969 movie would never have been made, and the twosome's legend would never have spanned the decades.

But such is the nature of fame and infamy. While more successful and longer-enduring gangs plied their trades around the Old West, none quite stirred the imagination or the admiration as much as one of the nation's most remembered, feared, and revered. None could ever quite compete with Butch, Sundance, and the Wild Bunch.

CHAPTER 3

The Pinkertons Meet Ethel Place

A certain romantic interest is thrown about this little coterie of des-
peradoes by reason of the presence among them of Etta Longbaugh, the
intrepid wife of the leader. She is but twenty-six years of age, with
graceful, girlish figure, dark, flashing eyes, regular features, brilliant
white teeth and a mass of wavy dark hair. She can shoot with the
rapidity and precision of a professional marksman, handling rifle
and revolver with equal deftness. She wears masculine attire almost
invariably and rides astride of her horse quite as well and with fully
as much fortitude as her male associates. Where she originally found
Longbaugh, or where he found her, is not an item of police history, but
the Pinkertons would probably pay any one who could identify and
furnish her pedigree.
—OMAHA DAILY BEE, OMAHA, NEBRASKA, OCTOBER 14, 1906

THE WILD BUNCH RIDERS FREQUENTLY CHANGED IN PERSONALITY AND
number during the course of their run, but the core members most often
included Robert Parker (Butch Cassidy); Elzy Lay; Harvey and Lonny
Logan; Tom O'Day; Harry Longabaugh (the Sundance Kid); Ben Kilpatrick (the Tall Texan), and Will Carver. Two women—Laura Bullion
and Etta Place—were also bona fide gang members, along with several
prostitutes and hangers-on who swept in and out like so much wind off
the valley floor.

The gang's principal hideout was a ranch in Alma, New Mexico, where Butch Cassidy was known as Jim Lowe. Some historians of the outlaws have insisted that Butch never robbed a train, but they're incorrect: His original photograph in the Pinkerton Criminal Gallery lists him as "Bank Robber, Train Robber and Outlaw." Agency reports also connect him with at least one train holdup in Wyoming.

The Wild Bunch members were tough ex-cowboys and mostly illiterate, like Ben Kilpatrick, who never ordered anything but ham and beans because he couldn't read the whitewashed menu on the bar mirrors in the frontier saloons. Elzy Lay, from men who knew him, had some education and was an intelligent man, but although he's listed as the discoverer of one of Utah's most promising oil fields, he gave up his claim before it could be worked.

Such a nefarious group of men needed a special place to unwind, relax, and let their hair down, and for Butch Cassidy and his men, that place was Fannie Porter's Sporting House in San Antonio's "Hell's Half Acre." Lillie Davis and Maud Walker, two of Fannie's most in-demand girls, were the favorite companions of gang regulars Kid Curry and Will Carver—and, as it turns out, of a man by the name of Will Pinkerton, to whom Lillie Davis agreed to talk during the long, depressing, dreary winter of 1901.

Throughout history, America's idea of the Western outlaw as a lying, cheating, drinking, stealing, train-robbing, card-sharking, goodness-shirking, gun-wielding, whoring example of all that is wrong with America has been pretty accurate. And it is accurate to this day if you swap "drug dealing" for "train robbing," and "ganging" for "card sharking." While all these traits are unquestionably antisocial, they are simply symptoms of the times when dropped in the lap of someone who lived a century or so ago.

Yet, just as with modern criminality, Western Americana's outlaws were, in reality, few and far between. If you watch a contemporary Western film such as *The Unforgiven* or *Tombstone* today, you have the feeling that death lay around every turn of the cue stick. In reality, life back before the turn of the century was every bit as precious and relatively free from disaster dealt from the hand of really bad dudes as it is today. In fact, you had a much greater chance back then of dying of syphilis or even dysentery than you did of gunfire down at the O.K. Corral.

Part of the reason was that good, law-abiding citizens didn't often hang out in places that outlaws called home. Another reason was that lawmen were very good at what they did, which was keeping the peace. And for that expertise, they could thank a former military spy by the name of Allan Pinkerton.

Pinkerton entered the burgeoning field of detective work well before the outbreak of the Civil War in 1860. Nearly twenty years earlier, he emigrated from his native Scotland to settle on the Fox River in Dundee Township, Illinois, fifty miles northwest of Chicago. He built a cabin and started a cooperage, making barrels of such superior quality that he soon cornered the market. When at last he'd finished building his personal cabin, he sent word to Chicago for his wife to join him.

As early as 1844, Pinkerton worked with Chicago's abolitionist leaders, turning his Dundee home into a stop on the route of the Underground Railroad. His antislavery views would remain with him his entire life.

To indulge his beliefs, "Pinky" required money. When he realized he could save a great deal in production costs by not paying someone else for poles to make barrel staves, he decided to go out and harvest the timber himself. He began his search on a small deserted island in the middle of the Fox River and rowed out to cut down his own supply of wood. But when he got to the island, he noticed signs that others had been there before him. Knowing that counterfeiters had been working the area, he wondered if the island might be their hideout.

After keeping his eyes open for several days, Pinkerton noticed several men coming and going. On a hunch, he watched the group's activities for several hours at a time. When he returned to shore, he recorded his findings before notifying the local sheriff of his suspicions. The two men teamed up the next day to stake out the island, eventually leading to the arrest of the counterfeiting band, known locally as the Banditti of the Prairie. Unfortunately, the ringleader managed to escape, and Pinkerton found himself hot on his trail, tracking him down and turning him over for prosecution.

This undercover escapade led to Pinkerton being appointed sheriff of Kane County in 1849, after which he was named the first police detective in Chicago, Cook County, Illinois. The following year, in 1850, he partnered with Chicago attorney Edward Rucker to form the North-Western Police Agency, which later became Pinkerton & Co, and finally Pinkerton National Detective Agency, still in existence today as Pinkerton Consulting and Investigations.

While Allan Pinkerton was building up his new business, his brother, Robert, who had formed a business of his own called Pinkerton & Co in 1843, set up his employees as railroad contractors and, finally, as detectives. Through his railroading contacts, he managed to secure several contracts with Wells Fargo to provide guards on stagecoaches. Robert's business expanded so quickly that he was continually hiring new men to serve as railroad and stagecoach detectives and guards.

Meanwhile, as Robert's business grew, Allan and Rucker's company fell on hard times, dissolving a scant year after it was formed. Allan joined his brother Robert in his new company, and the two changed the name to Pinkerton National Detective Agency. The "new" and greatly expanded company provided a variety of detective services, from private military contractors to security guards, but it specialized in the capture of counterfeiters and train robbers. Although several other detective agencies existed at the time, most had unsavory reputations. But the Pinkertons, who were the first to set uniform fees and establish standard practices, quickly earned the respect of the community.

As the United States expanded in territory and grew in size, rail transport increased. More goods and money traveling by rail meant more opportunities for robbers. Pinkerton's agency was called in to solve a series of holdups in the 1850s, which brought Pinkerton to the attention of George McClellan, then chief engineer and vice president of the Illinois Central Railroad. He also caught the eye of the railroad's corporate attorney, a man by the name of Abraham Lincoln.

In 1859, Pinkerton learned of several secret meetings held by John Brown and Frederick Douglass in Chicago, along with abolitionists John Jones and Henry O. Wagoner, and he quickly volunteered to join. At those meetings, Jones, Wagoner, and Pinkerton helped purchase clothes and supplies for John Brown and his sons and followers. John Jones's wife, Mary, guessed that the supplies Pinkerton helped to provide included the suit John Brown was hanged in after the failure of Brown's insurrection at Harpers Ferry, Virginia, in November 1859, which is sometimes referred to as a dress rehearsal for the Civil War.

Early in 1861, while investigating a railway robbery case, the agency uncovered an assassination plot against Abraham Lincoln in which several conspirators planned to kill Lincoln in Baltimore during the president-elect's stopover on his way to his Washington inauguration. Thanks to Pinkerton's quick action, Lincoln's itinerary was changed. When the Civil War broke out later that year, President Lincoln showed his gratitude by hiring the Pinkerton Detective Agency to organize a "secret service" to obtain military information on the Confederates and serve when needed as Lincoln's bodyguard.

Working diligently for the Union Army, Pinkerton traveled under the pseudonym of "Major E. J. Allen." He and his agents often worked undercover as Confederate soldiers and sympathizers to gather military intelligence. One of them, John Scobell, was the first African American ever to hold such a position. Pinkerton himself served on several under-cover missions as a Confederate soldier under a pseudonym. He traversed the Deep South in the summer of 1861, focusing on fortifications and Confederate plans, but he was unmasked in Memphis, barely escaping with his life.

Pinkerton eventually surrendered his duties as Intelligence Service chief to Lafayette Baker, and the Intelligence Service became the prede-cessor of the US Secret Service. In fact, a study of all the detective, secu-rity, and bodyguard work done in America during the last century shows they are all traceable to Pinkerton. He was Arthur Conan Doyle's real-life Sherlock Holmes, a person after whom Doyle might very well have structured his fictional private eye and, in fact, upon whose union-busting successes Doyle based his 1914 Holmes whodunit, *The Valley of Fear.*

Following Pinkerton's service with the army, he returned to his pursuit of train robbers, which included the notorious Reno Gang. He was also hired by the railroad express companies to track the outlaw Jesse James, but after Pinkerton failed to capture the bandit, the railroad withdrew its financial support. Pinkerton was so focused on his task, though, that he continued to track James at his own expense. After James allegedly captured and killed one of Pinkerton's agents (who was working undercover at the farm neighboring the James family homestead), Pinkerton staged a raid on the bandit's hideaway. Failing to apprehend the gang's leader, Pinkerton abandoned the chase shortly thereafter. Some consider this failure his most significant defeat, although the raid left the James Gang so financially stressed that they all but disbanded after they tried recouping their losses with the failed bank robbery at Northfield, Minnesota. James's life as an outlaw had effectively ended with Pinkerton's raid. From then on, James lived in hiding, sneaking out for the occasional robbery, until his eventual death at the hands of Robert Ford in 1882.

The Pinkerton Detective Agency had proved groundbreaking in several areas. In 1856, it was the first agency to hire women and minorities, a practice uncommon at the time, when twenty-three-year-old widow Kate Warne walked into Pinkerton's Chicago office and requested a job. Pinkerton was hesitant to hire a female investigator, but he gave in after Warne convinced him that she could "worm out secrets in many places to which it was impossible for male detectives to gain access." True to her word, she proved invaluable at working undercover, once busting a thief by cozying up to his wife and convincing her to reveal the location of their loot. During another case, she got a suspect to feed her critical information by disguising herself as a fortune-teller. Pinkerton later listed Warne as one of the best investigators he had ever hired. Following her death in 1868, he had her buried in the Pinkerton family plot.

Following the end of the Civil War, the Pinkerton Agency continued its work for the railroads and overland stage companies, playing an active role in chasing down several outlaws, including various members of the Wild Bunch. On their three-story headquarters in Chicago was their logo, which included the phrase "We Never Sleep" below the image of a black-and-white eye, which quickly became the origin of the term "private eye."

When Robert Pinkerton died in 1868, Allan assumed full control of the agency. However, just a year later, in the autumn of 1869, he suffered a paralyzing stroke that nearly killed him. Robert's and Allan's sons took over most of the responsibilities of running the business. Not surprisingly, a rivalry grew between them, and the agency struggled for lack of leadership. At the same time, it suffered financially.

Despite the business's economic hardships, the Pinkertons helped revolutionize law enforcement by constructing a so-called Rogues' Gallery, which consisted of a collection of mug shots and case histories that the agency used to research and keep track of wanted men. Along with noting suspects' distinguishing marks and scars, agents also collected newspaper clippings and generated rap sheets detailing the criminals' previous arrests, known associates, and areas of expertise. A more sophisticated criminal library wouldn't be assembled until the early twentieth century with the birth of J. Edgar Hoover's Federal Bureau of Investigation.

By the early 1870s, the Pinkerton Agency's collection of mug shots and "criminal database" had expanded to become the world's largest. During the height of its existence, the agency had more agents than the standing army of the United States, causing the state of Ohio to outlaw the organization because of the possibility that it could be hired out as a "private army" or militia to overthrow local governments.

Despite the agency's phenomenal success, its fortunes once again plummeted when, in 1871, Chicago suffered the Great Fire that began on the evening of October 7. Before the fire burned itself out three days later, the city's entire business district had been destroyed, including the Pinkerton buildings and many of the agency's records. When the fire had finally ended, martial law was declared in Chicago, and guards from the Pinkerton Detective Agency stepped in to prevent looting. Robert Pinkerton's widow, Alice Isabella Pinkerton, and his dependents were among the thousands of survivors left homeless. When Isabella approached Allan for assistance, he encouraged her to return to Great Britain, offering to pay the way. Alice and her sons accepted his offer and sailed for Liverpool, leaving the agency entirely in the hands of Allan and his sons.

Pinkerton, not surprisingly, had long opposed labor unions, which he viewed as little more than organized conscription or slavery; his men often served undercover, posing as union members, in reality working to break the unions' strength through divisiveness and, occasionally, brute force. One of the earliest examples involved a secret Irish society known as the Molly Maguires.

The Molly Maguires was a nineteenth-century society active in Ireland, Liverpool, and parts of the eastern United States, where its members were best known for their activism among Irish American immigrant Pennsylvania coal miners. After a series of often violent conflicts, twenty suspected members of the Molly Maguires were convicted of murder and other crimes and were executed by hanging in 1877 and 1878. The history remains an integral part of local Pennsylvania lore.

The Mollies were believed to have been present in the anthracite coal fields of Pennsylvania since at least the Panic of 1873, until becoming largely inactive following a series of arrests, trials, convictions, and executions. Members of the organization were accused of murder, arson, kidnapping, and other crimes, based partly on allegations by Franklin B. Gowen, head of the Philadelphia and Reading Railway Company, along with the testimony of a Pinkerton detective, James McParland (also known as James McKenna), a native of County Armagh, Ireland. Fellow prisoners testified against the defendants, who were arrested by the Coal and Iron Police. Gowen acted as a prosecutor in some of the trials.

Some historians, such as Philip Rosen, former curator of the Holocaust Awareness Museum of the Delaware Valley, believe that Irish immigrants brought a form of the Molly Maguires organization into America with their mass immigration in the nineteenth century, carrying on the group's activities as a clandestine society. They were located in a section of the anthracite coal fields called the Coal Region. Irish miners in the organization employed the tactics of intimidation and violence used against Irish landlords during the "Land Wars" in violent confrontations against the anthracite, hard-coal mining companies in the nineteenth century.

In the end, the Molly Maguires were an outgrowth of the long-simmering and often violent feud between mine owners, corporate America, and organized labor.

A Pinkerton agent, Robert J. Linden, was brought in to support McParland while serving with the Coal and Iron Police. On August 29, 1875, Allan Pinkerton wrote a letter to George Bangs, Pinkerton's general superintendent, recommending vigilante actions against the Molly Maguires: "The M.M.'s are a species of Thugs. . . . Let Linden get up a vigilance committee. It will not do to get many men, but let him get those who are prepared to take fearful revenge on the M.M.'s. I think it would open the eyes of all the people and then the M.M.'s would meet with their just deserts." On December 10, 1875, three men and two women were attacked in their home by masked men. Author Anthony Lukas wrote that the attack seemed "to reflect the strategy outlined in Pinkerton's memo."[1]

The victims had been targeted by McParland as Mollies. One of the men was killed in the house, and the other two Mollies were wounded but able to escape. A woman, the wife of one of the reputed Mollies, was shot dead. McParland was outraged that the information he had been providing had found its way into the hands of indiscriminate killers. When he learned the details of the attack at the house, he protested in a letter to his Pinkerton supervisor, who couldn't see why McParland was so upset, since the protestors only "got their just deserving." McParland resigned when it became apparent the vigilantes were willing to commit the "murder of women and children," whom he thought to be innocent victims.[2] His letter stated:

Friday: This morning at 8 A.M. I heard that a crowd of masked men had entered Mrs. O'Donnell's house . . . and had killed James O'Donnell alias Friday, Charles O'Donnell and James McAllister, also Mrs. McAllister whom they took out of the house and shot. . . . Now as for the O'Donnells I am satisfied they got their just deserving. I reported what those men were. I give all information about them so clear that the courts could have taken hold of their case at any time but the witnesses were too cowardly to do it. I have also in the interests of God and humanity notified you months before some of those outrages were committed still the authorities took no hold of the matter. Now I wake up this morning to find that I am the murderer of Mrs. McAllister. What had a woman to do with the case—did the [Molly Maguires] in their worst time shoot down women. If I was not here the Vigilante Committee would not know who was guilty and when I find them

shooting women in their thirst for blood I hereby tender my resigna-
tion to take effect as soon as this message is received. It is not cowardice
that makes me resign but just let them have it now I will no longer
interfere as I see that one is the same as the other and I am not going
to be an accessory to the murder of women and children. I am sure the
[Molly Maguires] will not spare the women so long as the Vigilante
has shown an example.[3]

There appears to be an error in the detective's report (which also constituted his resignation letter) of the vigilante incident: He failed to convey the correct number of deaths. Two of the three men "were wounded but able to escape."[4] In the note, McParland reported that the two had been killed by vigilantes. Such records, possibly containing erroneous or still unverified information, were often forwarded daily by Pinkerton operatives. The content was routinely made available to Pinkerton clients in written reports. Pinkerton detective reports now in the manuscripts collection at the Lackawanna County Historical Society reveal that Pinkerton had been spying on miners for the Scranton mine owners for months. Pinkerton operatives were required to send a report each day. The daily reports were typed by staff and conveyed to the client for a ten-dollar fee. Such a process was relied upon to "warrant the continuance of the operative's services."[5]

McParland believed his daily reports had been made available to the anti-Molly vigilantes. Benjamin Franklin, McParland's Pinkerton supervisor, declared himself "anxious to satisfy [McParland] that [the Pinkerton Agency has] nothing to do with [the vigilante murders]." He urged McParland not to resign. Meanwhile, the Pinkerton Agency was having a difficult time at home just as their reputation was growing overseas. In 1872, the agency—which by then had achieved universal acclaim—was allegedly hired by the Spanish government to help suppress a revolution in Cuba whose goal was to end slavery and give citizens the right to vote. The Spanish government abolished slavery in 1880, and a royal decree abolished the last vestiges of it in 1886, two years after Pinkerton's death in Chicago on July 1, 1884. Following his demise, the agency was taken over by his sons, Robert and William. Like their father, they became involved in the labor unrest of the late nineteenth century when they were hired by several businesses to keep strikers and suspected unionists out of their factories.

But the rapidly expanding agency began to develop an unsavory reputation for less admirable activities as they often became the "law" in and of themselves. Accused of using heavy-handed tactics, such as firebombing Jesse James's mother's home and using intimidation against union sympathizers, public support began to turn away from the agency, and a disagreeable feeling was elicited at the very word "Pinkerton."

Labor sympathizers did little to help, accusing the Pinkertons of inciting riots as the agency's reputation continued to suffer. One of the most notorious examples of its anti-union activities involved the Homestead Strike of 1892, when Pinkerton agents killed nine striking workers while losing seven of their own employees in their attempts at strikebreaking. It began on July 6, 1892, when three hundred Pinkerton detectives from New York and Chicago were called in by Carnegie Steel's Henry Clay Frick to protect the Pittsburgh-area mill and strikebreakers from union protesters.

Homestead Steel Mill plant superintendent Frick intended to open the works with nonunion men on July 6. Carnegie Corporation attorney Philander Knox devised a plan to get the Pinkertons onto the mill property to help forestall any union interference. With the mill ringed by striking workers, the agents needed to access the plant grounds from the river. Three hundred Pinkerton agents assembled on the Davis Island Dam on the Ohio River about five miles below Pittsburgh at 10:30 p.m. on the night of July 5, 1892. The armada was provided Winchester rifles, placed on two specially equipped barges, and towed upriver. They were also given badges reading, "Watchman, Carnegie Company, Limited."[6] Many had been hired out of lodging houses for $2.50 a day and were unaware of what their assignment was to be in Homestead.

The strikers were prepared for the Pinkerton agents; the Amalgamated Association of Iron and Steelworkers (AA) had learned of the Pinkertons' plan as soon as the agents had left Boston on two barges bound for the embarkation point. A small flotilla of union boats went downriver to meet them. Strikers on the steam launch fired a few random shots at the barges before withdrawing, blowing the launch whistle to alert the plant. The whistle sounded at 2:30 a.m., drawing thousands of men, women, and children to the plant. The resulting battle was a firefight and siege in which sixteen men were killed and twenty-three others were wounded. To restore order, two brigades of the Pennsylvania militia had to be called in by the governor.

As a legacy of the Pinkertons' involvement, a bridge connecting the nearby Pittsburgh suburbs of Munhall and Rankin was named Pinkerton's Landing Bridge.

Another high-profile case involving the Pinkertons was the Steunenberg murder and trial. In it, Harry Orchard was arrested by the Idaho police and confessed to Pinkerton agent James McParland that he had assassinated former governor Frank Steunenberg of Idaho in 1905. Under threat of hanging, Orchard testified against Western Federation of Miners (WFM) president "Big Bill" Haywood, naming him as having hired the hit. With a stirring defense by none other than Clarence Darrow, the most famous defense attorney of his day, Haywood and the other defendants of the WFM were acquitted, despite the Pinkerton man's testimony in a nationally publicized trial. Orchard received a death sentence, but it was later commuted.[7]

In light of this string of less-than-sterling public displays, Pinkerton's two sons, Robert and William, decided they desperately needed some positive public relations to overcome the bad reputation the agency had developed with the public. The two Pinkertons decided to turn their attentions westward in pursuit of a gang of desperadoes and train robbers that had been plying the Southwest. The name of the gang: the Wild Bunch.

As resourceful as they were daring, the Pinkertons used every trick in the book to gain a foothold in the ever-devious minds of the master criminals challenging them. So, in winter 1901, Will Pinkerton befriended and persuaded a disgruntled Lillie Davis to talk with him about her short-lived marriage to Wild Bunch gang member William Carver and other, more thoughtful matters. Pinkerton's interview with the frontier whore presents a less romantic but more realistic version of life among the West's wildest outlaws. As Lillie revealed, the Wild Bunch had taken to riding bicycles, using the telephone to stay one jump ahead of the authorities, and filing charges against rival gangs for stealing their guns. In spilling her life's story, Lillie explained that she had run away from home when she was only eight, "and I have been wild ever since."

An only child raised by her father, W. F. Hunt, and her older brother Joe in a relatively well-to-do section of Palestine, Texas, she was a product of the cow towns along the Texas border and soon "slipped down the two-rung ladder from dance hall girl to prostitute." Fannie found her in a saloon in San Antonio and brought her back with her to Fort Worth. She still had her looks and could carry a tune in a deep, husky voice. She would like nothing better, she told Fannie, "than to go home with a husband and a new hat with a long, drooping ostrich plume to show how well I had made out."[8]

Her best friend, Maud Walker, around twenty-two, was a stunning, buxom girl with long, copper-colored hair and wide, greenish eyes. Kid Curry met her and was smitten. He, Maud, Will Carver, and Lillie formed a foursome one night and did the town.

They ended in Maddox Flats, Texas. After partying the whole night through, Carver swept Lillie up in his arms, threw her onto his horse, and rode to the nearest preacher, where they were married. Kid Curry and Maud stood up for them. Kid Curry wanted to marry Maud as well, but she said she had to wait and see "what kind of man he was."[9]

They stayed in the Flats for five days, went on to Houston for two more, and then traveled to Fort Worth,[10] where Fannie threw Carver and Lillie a rousing party at which all the prostitutes were present. Butch Cassidy, the most wanted outlaw in America, "rode a bicycle up and down outside the cribs while the girls leaned from the windows, shouting their encouragement. Jim Lowe [Butch Cassidy's alias] was real athletic," Maud recalled.[11]

But the bridal party hadn't finished celebrating. After Lillie sent her marriage certificate to her father, the quartet took off for Denver, where they stayed at the plush Hotel Victor for five days, drinking nothing but champagne. Next on the agenda was the McFall House in Shoshone, Idaho, "for some hunting."

Unexpectedly, Carver and Kid Curry left and didn't return for five days.

"Where have you boys been?" Lillie asked with the indignation of a young, petulant bride when her new husband finally returned.

"Up the road," Carver replied.[12]

Maud and Lillie soon forgot their outrage when Carver and Kid Curry opened a suitcase, pulling out several bags of gold. Kid Curry opened a sack, took out a coin, and flipped it to Maud, who tested it with her elegant, strong teeth.

"There's lots more where that came from," he said.

The bridegroom and best man turned into big spenders. They splurged on dinners, champagne, fine buggies, and horses. And, of course, Lillie got not one but several hats with drooping ostrich plumes.

But the romance soon paled. Will Carver grew weary of Lillie's continual patter espousing the values of home and domesticity. She was an empty-headed young wench who cared only for clothes and sumptuous suppers.

Maud, who was prettier and more sensible, was soon dazzling both outlaws, which made Lillie furious with jealousy. After a loud exchange of words that threatened to reach the hair-pulling stage, Kid Curry told Carver he'd had enough of the women and was going back to Fort Worth to meet Butch Cassidy for their next strike.

"I'm going too," Carver said.

They called in both girls, gave each of them a few hundred dollars in cash, and told them to go back home. Will Carver, in answer to Lillie's tears, gave her a vague explanation of "going up the road." He also bought her a pair of $225 earrings, which dried her tears a bit while Kid Curry gave Maud $20 for a "fur sack."

Lillie returned to Palestine full of virtue and ostrich feathers. Dressed in her finest, she told her father and brother in the loftiest tones that she was now a married woman.

"But where's your husband?" her father demanded.

Lillie looked a little dazed. "Up the road," she replied.[13]

Neither Lillie nor Maud ever saw the boys again until the Pinkertons showed them a picture. It was Lillie who identified the bandits for Pinkerton. Later, she called on Fannie Porter and demanded that the madam tell her where her husband was.

Fannie brushed aside the question and tried to get Lillie to come back to work for her. The two got drunk, with Fannie becoming very maudlin. She wept for the "boys" and, through her tears, told Lillie she knew where she could get her hands on a cool $3,000.

"Where?" Lillie asked.

But Fannie, pouring another whiskey, shook her head.

"They'll kill me if I tell," she said.

Later, Fannie told one of her great secrets: "Maud Walker was really Beulah Phinburg . . . and her brother owned a dry goods store in St. Louis."

"And her putting on airs!" Lillie snapped.

Fannie also let slip that the handsome young man who had called on her several times was not her brother but her son, Morris. When Lillie tried to get more scandal for future reference, Fannie just shook her head.

A few days later, they learned that Maud had been picked up by detectives investigating the robberies.

"Why don't you sell your earrings and hire a lawyer for poor Maud?" Fannie asked.

"I told Fannie she should jump in the Rio Grande," Lillie recalled. "And furthermore, I don't care what they do with her. And I don't care what they do to Bill Carver, or Casey, as you know him. I'm going to stay right here [Cameron, Texas, where the Pinkertons found her], and you can find me any time."

As an afterthought, she added: "If I had known what kind of men they were I would have worked them for all they had. I didn't love Bill and I didn't marry him for love. I wanted to clear my name and show them at home I was married and respectable."

Following the interview, William Pinkerton told her to sign the statement, which she did. He tipped his hat and said goodbye. As an afterthought, he asked her if she was sure she would be in Cameron if they wanted her to make an identification in the future.

"I will," she said. Then, as Pinkerton turned to the door, she added, "Unless I take a notion to go to San Antonio."[14]

Pinkerton sighed and walked out.

*   *   *

The major robberies committed by the Wild Bunch during the Pinkerton era included the Union Pacific Train No. 3 at Tipton, Wyoming, on the evening of August 29, 1900, and the holdup of the First National Bank of Winnemucca, Nevada, from which they stole more than $30,000. The Union Pacific robbery allegedly netted them a bag of watch parts and $50.14 in cash, according to the railway's official report, although it was actually many thousands more.

By 1900, Butch Cassidy already realized that the Wild West as he had known it was quickly drawing to a close; the open range was gone, the manhunters were growing in numbers with every robbery, and the criminals' avenues of escape were shrinking. In the Denver office of the Pinkerton Agency, Superintendent James McParland, William Pinkerton, and US marshals had begun dispatching posses on flatcars to the nearest points where they could close off the famous horse-relay plan used so effectively in the Wild Bunch's escapes.

Then, at the turn of the century, either an operative or a Union Pacific detective discovered a group portrait of the Wild Bunch in the studio of John Swartz, 705 Main Street, Fort Worth. On a whim, the Wild Bunch had their photos taken while they were dressed in derby hats, sporting watch chains and suits. Kid Curry, who had recently traveled two hundred miles to kill a man, sported a boutonniere. In the photograph were Will Carver, Kid Curry, the Sundance Kid, Ben Kilpatrick, and Butch Cassidy. A copy of the print was rushed to Chicago, where Will Pinkerton ordered hundreds of wanted posters made from individual pictures chosen from the group shot. This was in addition to furnishing every bank in the country with a list of the serial numbers of the stolen bonds.

In Nashville, an alert teller spotted one of the purloined notes and notified the Pinkertons, who captured Kilpatrick and Laura Bullion. The Tall Texan and his girlfriend were later sent to federal prison. Meanwhile, the Pinkertons continued their pursuit of Butch, the Sundance Kid, and Etta Place. In February 1901, the three outlaws traveled to New York City, where they stayed for a while at an East Twelfth Street boardinghouse.

The Pinkertons later discovered that the outlaw trio had treated themselves to a grand holiday bash while in the city. They had celebrated Etta's birthday at a champagne supper, attended the theater, and bought the birthday girl a $150 watch at Tiffany's; then, she and Sundance, dressed in formal attire, had their portraits taken at the De Young Photograph Studio, *the* place for society photographs of the day. But by the time the Pinkertons had picked up their trail in New York, the two had set sail on the SS *Pioneer Prince* for Buenos Aires. The bowlegged Sundance Kid and the tall, stately Etta Place occupied the honeymoon suite.[15]

Nearly twenty years later, Pinkerton operative Frank Dimaio, then ninety years old, described how he had chased Butch, Sundance, and Etta from Buenos Aires to Chubut Province of Chubut, District 15 de Octubre, in the interior, where they staked out a homestead ranch. Dimaio was told that it would take months to reach the seaport nearest the place and that there would still be a fifteen-day ride to the outlaws' ranch. The fact that the rainy season had set in, he was told, made the trip impossible.

On instructions from Robert Pinkerton in New York, Dimaio had hundreds of posters made up in English and Spanish. He distributed them up and down the South American coast to banks, mining-supply houses, police stations, and steamship companies, requesting that information about the *bandidos* be sent to Buenos Aires chief of police Francis J. Beasley. At the time, Butch and Sundance were thought to have committed so many gold-train and bank robberies in Argentina that official protests were lodged with the ambassador in Buenos Aires who forwarded them to Washington. In Ambassador William Paine Lord's initial reports, Kid Curry was listed as among Butch Cassidy's riders in South America, a rumor still accepted as fact by some frontier historians, though unproven. According to official reports by the Pinkerton Agency, Cassidy and the Sundance Kid were later killed near San Vicente, Bolivia, by a detachment of Bolivian cavalry after Etta Place had returned to the United States and vanished.

The tenacity with which the Pinkertons insisted on chasing an outlaw even beyond the grave to confirm his identity is underscored in the nationwide manhunt of Kid Curry after he had broken out of the Knox County, Tennessee, jail shortly before his transfer to the federal penitentiary at Columbus, Ohio, to begin serving a life term.

Not long afterward, on June 7, 1904, three masked men held up the Denver & Rio Grande Express at Parachute, Colorado, and dynamited the express car but found the safe empty. That night, a posse cornered the trio in a gully near Rifle and wounded one. As a sheriff later said, "We heard one of them in the darkness call out, 'Are you hurt, Tom?' And the other answering, 'I'm all in, I'm going to end it here.' Then there was one shot."[16]

In the morning, the posse found that two of the train robbers had slipped through their lines, leaving behind a dead man identified as Tap Duncan, a drifter who had worked at some of the local spreads for over a year. He was known as a loner and a fast man with a gun. The town buried Duncan in a cheap pine coffin in the cemetery at Glenwood Springs. As was the custom, the local sheriff telegraphed the Denver office of the Pinkertons, giving a description of the dead man. James McParland sent the report on to Chicago, where it was circulated among the operatives working in the West. Lowell Spence telegraphed to William Pinkerton that the dead man was undoubtedly Kid Curry. When the Pinkertons released the story that the shabby cowhand in the obscure cemetery was the infamous gunfighter and outlaw, several railroad detectives publicly disputed Spence's account. To clear up the confusion, the State Department asked Pinkerton to confirm the identification of the body as that of Kid Curry (Harvey Alexander Logan) or Tap Duncan.

Accompanied by Chief Agent Canada of the Union Pacific, Spence went to Glenwood Springs and had the body disinterred. After close examination by a physician, it was photographed in the presence of both men. Spence took the pictures and sent the description to several Knox County jail guards, federal prosecutors, wardens, and even outlaws "no longer on the dodge" to confirm his suspicions. All agreed that the body in Glenwood Springs cemetery was that of Kid Curry. Spence said,

I was laughed at a number of times because of my identification, but I knew it was Logan's body. Mr. Canada only saw Logan but once and then behind bars in the Knoxville jail. I had seen and talked to Logan a dozen times. I had seen him awake and asleep in the jail, on the streets of Knoxville, going and coming from his trial and I had observed him for many hours as he sat in the courtroom. I have seen a number of reports that Logan was known to be here, there, everywhere, including South America, but I know his body is buried in Glenwood Springs, Colorado, marks, scars, old bullets holes and all.[17]

CHAPTER 4

The Death of Butch Cassidy

Joe Bush, Sheriff Tuttle of Emery county, Sheriff Allred of Carbon county and their posse, which for a week or ten days have been hunt-ing the Robbers Roost gang of outlaws, have scored a great victory and have, after a desperate battle, four of the gang to their credit, two dead and two alive. The two dead, Butch Cassiday and Joe Walker, are perhaps the most desperate characters of the crowd while the two captured alive, Lay and Thompson, are not far behind them in their records of crime.
—SALT LAKE HERALD, SALT LAKE CITY, UTAH, MAY 14, 1898

THROUGHOUT 1897, THE LARGEST OF THE CATTLE RANCHES IN THE tristate area of Colorado, Utah, and Wyoming suffered heavy losses at the hands of rustlers. Smaller ranchers, too, as well as farmers, freight haulers, and even ordinary travelers, felt the robbers' sting. The blame fell on wandering bands of organized thieves, whom the newspapers labeled the "Robbers Roost" or the "Hole-in-the-Wall Gang" or sometimes the "Powder Springs Gang."[1] Meanwhile, while rustlers in and around Brown's Park ignored their friends' herds of beef, many other cattlemen watched helplessly as their own herds steadily shrank in number.

Most of the beeves stolen in the northwestern corner of Moffat County, Colorado, found their way out of Brown's Park and down to central and southern Utah. The mystery surrounding the rustling grew as local ranchers puzzled over how the cattle could be driven out of the park without being spotted. And then some old-timers stepped forward to enlighten them: The thieves used the old "Shelf Trail."[2]

At the southernmost bend of the Green River two miles east of the Utah-Colorado line, a trail leading south from Wild Mountain appears to end sharply in a canyon on the north bank of the river. From a distance, the land seems to disappear at the edge of a cliff with a drop of several hundred feet to the water's edge and the jagged rocks below. Just beyond the rim lies a broad shelf sloping gently down toward the canyon bottom. From the top, the shelf also seems to drop off sharply into the river. But viewing the lower end of the ledge from down below reveals a termination point a few feet above a second shelf that slopes down in the opposite direction—a switchback, in railroad terms—leading to the river's edge. The rustlers had somehow managed to keep this hidden trail a secret for years. It may have been spotted by a few ranchers, but it was unlikely any of them believed that a skittish herd of cattle could be driven down it. But, according to the old-timers, the rustlers found a way to do just that. Once at the bottom of the canyon, they spurred the beeves across the river and headed them off to market.

Of course, not every head of cattle reached the bottom safely; more than an occasional misstep led to disaster. It wasn't until years later, when explorers began running the Green River on rafts, that the remnants of the Shelf Trail's boneyard were found among the rocks and eddies. By then, the trail had been discovered by the ranchers and rendered virtually worthless courtesy of a few well-placed sticks of dynamite.

The Shelf Trail was occasionally confused with the Brown's Park "Outlaw Trail" that paralleled the east rim of Lodore Canyon and ended at the Yampa River just shy of it joining the Green River north of Steamboat Rock. Outlaws used the Outlaw Trail as an exit from the east end of the park, but it was unfit for driving livestock until 1910 when local rancher Jack Chew and his sons used black powder, dynamite, picks, and crowbars to smooth it out enough to get their cattle off Douglas Mountain and onto a seemingly endless grazing range near Pool Creek.

In the mid-1800s, with law enforcement officers in northeastern Wyoming unable or unwilling to cope with the problem of rustlers, the cattlemen of the tristate area banded together to tackle the problem. In early March 1898, a group of cattlemen met in Denver with the governors of Colorado and Wyoming and a state official from Utah to discuss the situation. Secretly, the cattlemen longed for total extermination of the outlaws—legal or otherwise—but cooler heads suggested seeking help from the military, possibly a detachment of troopers from Fort Duchesne backed by a declaration of martial law.

But, even as the meeting was being held, news came from Brown's Park that confirmed what everyone already knew: Something had to be done.

On February 17, 1898, at the Valentine Hoy Ranch near Pine Mountain just north of the Wyoming-Colorado line, a hard-drinking cowpuncher and part-time rustler named Patrick Johnson shot and killed a sixteen-year-old boy, Willie Strang, because the boy had spilled some water down the front of Johnson's shirt. Johnson later claimed he was only trying to scare the boy, but he didn't wait around for the repercussions: He saddled up one of Hoy's horses and, accompanied by fellow rustler John (Jack) Bennett, fled to nearby Powder Springs, where the two had been hiding out.

Powder Springs, located just below the Wyoming line in Moffat County, Colorado, lay midway between Baggs, Wyoming, and Brown's Park and was a favorite stopover for outlaws and drifters traveling between the park and the Hole-in-the-Wall in northern Wyoming. One of two Powder Springs, the upper springs, about a mile south of the Wyoming-Colorado line, lay nestled among rocks and crevices in a bowl-shaped valley along Powder Wash. The lower springs, about two miles farther south, lay in the flatter, more rolling terrain, a tiny oasis in a bleak, sage-covered wasteland.

Sharing Johnson and Bennett's camp at Powder Springs were a pair of even worse desperadoes, Harry Tracy and Dave Lant, both of whom had escaped the previous October from the Utah State Penitentiary. Tracy and Lant had been on the run ever since, hiding out in Uintah County, southeast of Vernal near Naples, Utah. Lant, who once worked for the McCoy Sheep Company, was familiar with the Vernal area. The two outlaws had stolen a couple of horses in Ashley Valley, and when Uintah County sheriff William Preece gathered up a posse to run them down, the outlaws fled east through Brown's Park to the springs.

At first, the rugged wilderness of the springs area seemed a safe place to hide, but when Tracy and Lant learned about the death of the Strang boy, they began to worry that the law would be coming after Johnson. They were also facing a solid month of bitter-cold winter, when camping out in northern Colorado was no one's idea of a good time. The four men decided to pack up and head for the warmer climes of Robbers Roost country and the canyons of southern Utah.

But before they could make the trip, they needed to put in more supplies, so Jack Bennett, the only one without a bounty on his head, was elected to go to town. Before he left, the others decided that, while he was away, Johnson, Tracy, and Lant would move camp from Powder Springs down into the park at a spot near Lodore Canyon. That was a mistake. Before long, a posse led by Sheriff Charles Neiman of Routt County, Colorado, spotted the camp and quickly closed in.

The Routt County sheriff deputized Valentine Hoy, along with several other private citizens, to form a posse. After locating their man and the two escapees on the Green River, they approached cautiously, only to find all three men had fled on foot to higher ground on the rimrock shelf, abandoning their horses and provisions, which the posse seized before returning to town for the night.

The following morning, the men resumed their search for the subjects, who by then had climbed still higher up the mountain along a steep, narrow trail. As Deputy Hoy followed them through a tapered fissure, Tracy shot him in the chest, killing him instantly. Shaken by the death, the posse retreated to regroup, allowing the three fugitives to escape. However, Neiman's men later captured Jack Bennett as he rode back from town with the supplies he'd been sent to fetch.

Hoy's death confirmed in most people's minds that Brown's Park was an outlaw haven that couldn't be invaded without casualties. Still, the locals knew that something had to be done. Willie Strang, barely in his teens, and Valentine Hoy were respected members of the ranching community. Their deaths couldn't be downplayed.

Not surprisingly, Jack Bennett was the first to feel the community's wrath. The posse that had apprehended him took him to the Bassett Ranch for safekeeping, which was a big mistake. The following day, a handful of masked men rode out to the ranch, overpowered the deputy who had been assigned to guard him, and hanged Bennett from the crossbar of one of Bassett's gates.

The original posse led by Sheriff Neiman had consisted of nine volunteers, most of them unenthusiastic, but when word spread of Valentine Hoy's death, more than sixty citizens jumped at the opportunity to hunt down his murderers. It didn't take long. Four days later, on March 5, at a site about five miles south of Powder Springs, they cornered Tracy, Lant, and Johnson, nearly frozen to death; the trio surrendered without a fight.

When the three of them were brought to the Bassett Ranch, few bystanders would have wagered that they would live to see another sunrise, but that night, Sheriff Neiman reasoned with the crowd that had gathered at the ranch to help keep a lid on the powder keg. The next day, he turned Johnson over to federal marshals who took him back to Wyoming to stand trial. Neiman and one of his deputies then bundled up Tracy and Lant and hurried them off to the Routt County jail in Hahn's Peak.

But on March 24, when Sheriff Neiman walked into the outlaws' cell with a breakfast tray, he found himself staring down the muzzle of a gun.

"Get in," Tracy snarled. Neiman stepped into the cell slowly. "Get his gun, Dave," Tracy snapped. When Lant handed the six-shooter to Tracy, he swung it hard across the lawman's head, knocking him out. Tracy tossed his own "gun" aside—it was carved out of a piece of wood and covered with tin foil. As an added insult, Tracy robbed the sheriff of ninety dollars, locked him in his own cell, and stole his horses. But Neiman was a tough lawman:

After a deputy had pried off the lock, [Neiman] took up their trail. At Steamboat Springs he reasoned they were moving southwest and headed for the railroad. He took the stagecoach at Steamboat which headed southwest. Six miles out of town the two outlaws hailed the stage. They stepped into a shotgun pointed at their chests.

Neiman, after he had slipped on the handcuffs, relieved Tracy of his gun and his money.

"Who the hell would think anybody from Hahn's Point would be up this early," Tracy growled as they headed back to jail.

Tracy and Lant were later removed to the Aspen, Colorado, jail house [which was thought to be more secure] but a short time later they broke out again. Here they parted, Lant to return to Powder Springs, Tracy to the Northwest, where he would be hunted on land and sea; by the Army, the Coast Guard, and by the largest posse in the history of the Northwest.

At Rock Springs, Wyoming, Johnson was convicted and sentenced to life on the murder charge. But a higher court reversed the conviction and he was freed. Colorado, which took him into custody, sent him to the penitentiary for rustling. He was released after two years and vanished, never again to appear in the outlaw country.[3]

Although Butch Cassidy played no role in the apprehension of fugitives Tracy and Lant—which has come to be known as the Battle of Brown's Park—when Harry Tracy later became famous as a desperado, some writers falsely connected him with Butch and the Wild Bunch. With one exception, nothing suggesting such a connection has ever been proved. According to a historian, Kerry Ross Boren's grandfather, who was supposed to have known Butch, claimed that the Wild Bunch leader personally ordered Tracy to leave Brown's Park. Tracy's contact with other outlaws in the park area probably was limited to knowing Patrick Johnson and Jack Bennett. And while Johnson and Bennett themselves may have been acquainted with Butch, it is more than likely that they were never more than on the periphery of the Wild Bunch.

Although not involved in this series of events, Butch and the Wild Bunch nonetheless felt the sting of the killings of Willie Strang and Valentine Hoy. The uproar over their deaths brought about the beginning of a gradual decline of Brown's Park as an outlaw haven.

In mid-March 1898, the governors of Colorado, Wyoming, and Utah met at Salt Lake City to announce the formation of a unique multistate force: officers with special powers to pursue and make arrests in all three states. They also agreed to place a large reward on the head of each outlaw and encourage bounty hunters who were familiar with the area to work alone or in pairs. J. S. Hoy, brother of slain rancher Valentine, favored this approach, believing that one or two highly trained men could stick to the trail of an outlaw and succeed where a hundred men would fail.

Before they could implement a plan, though, their attention was diverted to a more significant problem: On April 24, the United States declared war on Spain. Even before the declaration, war fever had taken hold in Wyoming. Shortly after the sinking of the battleship *Maine*, lawyer and former Big Horn Basin rancher Jay L. Torrey, who once held the rank of general in the National Guard, proposed organizing a volunteer cavalry regiment made of Wyoming cowboys. US senator Francis E. Warren of Wyoming thought it was a promising idea and introduced a bill in Congress authorizing such a unit. Within weeks, the War Department allocated Torrey nearly $250,000 to raise and train troops.

The press praised the idea, urging Wyoming cowboys to volunteer and share in an opportunity "to make the earth tremble and win glory in some of the greatest cavalry charges of modern times."[4]

These patriotic pleas must have reached Butch and the Wild Bunch. What effect they had isn't clear. Some researchers suggest that some gang members gave serious thought to joining. As one story goes, Butch, Sundance, Harvey and Lonny Logan, and possibly Elzy Lay gathered with a half dozen other outlaws near Steamboat Springs to discuss signing up as a group. Although some writers have suggested that the meeting was the result of an outpouring of patriotism, it's more likely that the outlaws saw an opportunity to exchange their military service for amnesty from the law. Whatever the reason for the gathering—if there was one—nothing ever came of it.

Some outlaws probably did volunteer on their own. According to two separate accounts given by officers who served in the Philippines, several members of the Wild Bunch ended up in a detachment of muleskinners, whose job was to get supplies through an area infested with Moros, the fierce tribesmen causing trouble for American occupation forces. As the officers told the story, soon after the arrival of the Wild Bunch members and several disastrous encounters, the Moros backed off, finding their raids too costly in human lives.[5]

It is not known whether any of the Wild Bunch joined Colonel Jay Torrey's Second US Volunteer Cavalry. A few may have slipped in under aliases. If they did, they were most likely disappointed in the results. The regiment, which eventually reached a force of 1,100 men, failed to see action against the enemy, although it did suffer casualties. On June 26, at Tupelo, Mississippi, a train carrying the regiment to Jacksonville, Florida, was involved in a serious derailment. Five members of the outfit were killed and fifteen more were seriously injured, including Colonel Torrey, who suffered "badly crushed feet."[6]

Although little evidence exists as to how many outlaws joined the war effort, the conflict did remove from service some of the most experienced outlaw hunters, particularly from the ranks of deputy US marshals.

Whether or not Butch considered volunteering for military service, he never relented in his pursuit of fertile, ripe banks ready for plucking. Following the lead of several railroads and express companies, several Wyoming banks began putting pressure on Governor Richards to do more to protect them. During the first week of May 1898, the president of the First National Bank in Buffalo, concerned over the release of Wild Bunch bank robbers Tom O'Day and Walt Punteney, urged the governor to form a Wyoming strike force similar to the Texas Rangers to capture or drive the outlaws out of the state.

His request appeared to be misplaced. One week later, the Butch Cassidy problem was solved. Only days earlier, a posse led by Carbon County's newly appointed sheriff, C. W. Allred, had ridden out of Price, the county seat, with Pete Anderson, J. W. Warf, J. M. Whitmore, George Whitmore, Jack Gentry, Jim Inglefield, Billy McGuire, and Jack Watson. Although well armed and probably packing enough provisions to last for weeks, the posse was not bent on invading Butch Cassidy's hideout in Robbers Roost but rather on searching for some horses and cattle that had been stolen from the Whitmores.

As the nine men rode southwest along the winding Price River, the route the thieves were believed to have taken, they came to a spot west of the Book Cliffs called Lower Crossing. There, they found what they thought to be the rustlers' trail. Probably much to the posse's relief, the hoof prints led not toward but away from the Roost, northwest toward the cliffs of Range Valley. Before long, they knew they were on the right track when they came across several strays from the Whitmore herd. They also stumbled upon a horse that had apparently been left behind by the rustlers. Allred sent several of the men back to the Whitmore Ranch with the strays and instructions to catch up with the posse in the valley later.[7]

Allred pressed on to Jim McPherson's spread. McPherson denied having seen the rustlers, despite evidence to the contrary. In turn, Allred suggested the rancher accompany them as their "guide."

The posse resumed the trail, which turned southwest toward the Green River. Once across, Allred noted that the tracks entered a long, narrow series of canyons with craggy walls, offering dozens of hiding places—a perfect spot for an ambush. But it was the new sheriff's first big manhunt, and turning back empty-handed wouldn't reflect well upon him; therefore, he decided he and his men would wait for nightfall when they wouldn't make such easy targets for desperadoes armed with Winchesters.

As darkness settled across the canyons, the posse worked its way forward some fifteen miles. Still somewhere on McPherson's land, perhaps fifty miles north of Thompson Springs, they continued on well past midnight as they approached the canyon's end. Allred passed the word to his men that they were likely getting close. He ordered them to dismount and turn in until dawn.

An hour or so before sunrise the following morning, the posse mounted up again. Riding no more than a few minutes brought them to the outlaws' camp. The sheriff signaled to dismount and advance on foot.

Allred could see four men, asleep and wrapped in their blankets on a shelf of rock protected on one side by a deep ravine. After making sure that his men were set and their guns drawn, Allred called to them.

"Come out and surrender!" Pete Anderson and J. M. Whitmore added, nearly in unison, "You're surrounded by a hundred men!"[8]

As two of the outlaws threw up their hands, the other two grabbed their guns and opened fire. When their pistols had been emptied, they took off on a dead run. One managed to go around sixty feet before a volley of lead dropped him in his tracks. The second man hadn't made it that far. As Allred approached the first man, he recognized him as Joe

Walker, a member of Butch Cassidy's gang. When he turned over the second, he couldn't believe his eyes.

It was Butch!

Allred let out a whoop as his men handcuffed the two captured outlaws. Then they tied Walker and Cassidy to their saddles and started back to Thompson Springs, the nearest town with a Western Union office. There, on May 13, 1898, Marshal Joe Bush telegraphed Utah governor Heber Wells. The telegram was sent from Thompson Springs: "Came up with outlaws five this morning. Killed Joe Walker and Cassiday [sic], captured Lay and one man. Have prisoners and dead men here. Send message to my house please. Sheriff Allred and posse did nobly. J. R. Bush."[9]

The next day, Saturday, the posse rode into Price. As the town poured out into the street to see the dead men, a number agreed with Allred that the man laid out beside Joe Walker was, indeed, Butch Cassidy; others, though, weren't so sure. A makeshift inquest was held, and the "jury," relying mainly on the testimony of Allred and Emery County sheriff Ebenezer Turtle, decided that it was indeed Butch. As soon as the decision was announced, the bodies were prepared for burial. That night, they were placed in two wooden coffins, and the next morning, they were lowered into a hole and covered with dirt.

But even as the rustlers' remains were being interred, some bystanders expressed doubt over the second body. The two captured criminals, who gave their names as Thompson and Schulz, said that it wasn't Butch. They insisted it was some Wyoming cowhand named John Herring (or Herron). Someone suggested that Allred should get in touch with officials in Wyoming who had actually known Butch. He sent a wire to Sheriff John Ward at Evanston. Ward knew what Butch looked like from having briefly held him in jail following his arrest in 1892. Allred also summoned former Gunnison County, Colorado, sheriff Cyrus "Doc" Shores, who by then was working for the Denver & Rio Grande Railroad. On Monday, the body thought to be Butch Cassidy's was exhumed, and much to Sheriff Allred's dismay, both Ward and Shores stated that the dead man was definitely *not* Butch Cassidy.

Hearts sank. Spirits fell. The angels wept. Rumors had already begun circulating of some $15,000 in combined rewards available for Butch.

Adding to Allred's problems, his two captures, Thompson and Schulz, had to be freed for lack of evidence connecting them to the theft of Whitmore's cattle. There was a small reward for Joe Walker, and apparently it was eventually paid, but Sheriff Allred and his posse had to share it with Emery County sheriff Turtle and his group, so in the end there was barely enough for any man to buy a drink or two at the nearest saloon.

Interestingly enough, a story has circulated through history, bolstered by Charles Kelly and confirmed by Butch's sister in 1975, that, while passing through town, Butch actually stopped to pay homage to his "dead body," laid out for public viewing. Butch was allegedly on his way between Robbers Roost and Brown's Park when he learned of his own demise. He rode over to the cabin of a friend, Jim Sprouse, who lived just outside Price. Butch, thinking that it would be a great story to tell his pals, talked Sprouse into driving a wagon down the main street of Price with Butch hidden under a layer of straw. Through a crack in the sideboards, the outlaw leader saw the crowd milling around the entrance of the building where he was supposed to have been laid out. According to Butch's sister, he thought "it would be a good idea to attend his own funeral just once during his lifetime." He added that he was touched when he saw several women wiping their eyes.[10]

Charles Kelly provides a footnote to the story, which, if true, places Butch's Wyoming attorney, Douglas Preston, in a bad light. Kelly says that a mining entrepreneur named Finley P. Gridley happened to run into Preston sometime shortly after the report hit the newspapers that Butch Cassidy had been killed. When Gridley mentioned Butch's death, Preston allegedly threw back his head and laughed. When Gridley asked him what was so funny, Preston replied, "Nothing much, except that I talked to Butch just before I left Brown's Hole this morning."[11]

If the story is true, Preston was conducting dealings with a suspected criminal who was wanted by the law—a criminal offense on its own. Such things rarely bothered Preston, though. He considered his relationship with Butch Cassidy sacred because Butch, according to the attorney, had once saved his life.

Meanwhile, Sheriff Allred's excursion into Robbers Roost country and the death of Walker and Herring may have led Butch to reconsider just how safe the Wild Bunch was in the Roost. This incident, plus the threat of an all-out effort by the governors of Utah, Wyoming, and Colorado to rid their states of the Wild Bunch for good, may have persuaded the gang leader to abandon his favorite hideouts and head for distant climes.

It couldn't have been an easy decision. Robbers Roost and Brown's Park had been ideal sanctuaries, serving the Wild Bunch well for years. Butch had amassed an array of friends, both "straight" and outright criminals, upon whom he knew he could rely for help whenever he needed them. Even on the run, he was confident that he could rely on someone somewhere for a meal or a night. Among them were Ford Dejournette, a transplanted North Carolinian who had a sheep camp in southern Wyoming between Brown's Park and Rock Springs; Jack Edwards, who operated a spread near Powder Wash in Moffat County, Colorado; and John Sampson Hacking Jr., a large sheep rancher who ran his herd on Diamond Mountain in Uintah County, Utah.[12]

Although Butch may have regretted leaving the gang's favorite haunts, he knew the time was quickly coming. Exactly when it would arrive, he wasn't sure. But there was no doubt about it: The time was coming.

But before folding their tent, the Wild Bunch leader decided to head south, where he took a job working for the WS Ranch near Alma, New Mexico, where he would spend a brief, relatively peaceful, carefree period of his life as an ordinary citizen under the name of Jim Lowe.

But if there was one thing about Butch Cassidy that was true, he could never be considered *ordinary*.

CHAPTER 5

New York, New York

Then the United States government took a hand and the whole West laid for Etta and her gang. The West still is waiting. For the gang went East—almost openly—had its picture taken in group, and sailed from New York for the Argentine. There, in a hotel called the Sixteenth of October [sic], in the province of Shibaut, they settled down for a while. Meanwhile the United States was being combed for Etta and her fellows, and it was a severe jolt when their pictures were found in one of the most popular galleries of New York.
—WICHITA DAILY EAGLE, WICHITA, KANSAS, JANUARY 1, 1918

FOLLOWING THE TIPTON ROBBERY ON AUGUST 29, 1900, THE LOCAL constabulary formed a posse and set off to catch the robbers. The lawmen rode long and hard for three days straight before finally calling off the search for lack of clues. An article appearing in the *Salt Lake Herald* on September 17 reported the difficulties encountered in the search:

All hope of capturing the four men who held up, dynamited and robbed the overland express train at Tipton three weeks ago has been given up, and the crime goes on record as one of the most successful and daring robberies in the history of the west.

Not once has a glimpse of the outlaws been obtained since they mounted their horses and rode away in the darkness after securing the treasure contained in the safe of the Pacific Express company, and

their present whereabouts is a mystery to the railroad and express offi-
cials and the United States officers. The identity of two of the robbers
has been decided, however, and this may aid in their capture sooner
or later.

Deputy United States Marshal Joe Lefors of Cheyenne, who was
first on the trail of the bandits with a posse of men and who followed
the outlaws for several days through the bad lands south of Tipton
until their trail was lost in the sands of the desert, returned to Sara-
toga a few days ago from the chase and went on east to Cheyenne.
While here, he was interviewed as follows:

"I think I know most of the men that participated at the hold-up
of the Union Pacific train at Tipton, and they are not strangers to
the law, either. I also know that two of their number are none other
than the notorious Roberts brothers, the Ute half-breeds who have
terrorized the country from Arizona to Montana for several years,
and who are two of the three men who held up a train at Wilcox
over a year ago and who are still at large. [The reference was most
likely to George and Tom Dixon from Arapahoe County, Colorado,
whose mother was a Ute Indian and who, together, were known as
the Roberts brothers, although LeFors may also have been mixing the
brothers up with Harvey Logan and Sundance, who also referred to
themselves as the Roberts brothers on occasion.] There were six men
in the Wilcox affair. Lonny Curry was killed at Kansas City, George
Curry was killed north of Thompson's, Utah, and Bob Lee was sent
to the Wyoming state penitentiary for a term of ten years. The three
remaining members of the gang, the Roberts brothers and one other,
are still at large.

"I have personally been acquainted with these outlaws for many
years, as we worked the same round-up in Johnson county together.
At that time I knew they were bad men and because I would not
take part in their crimes they came to hate me. I saved my money and
invested in a small bunch of cattle. It was not long, however, until
they rustled every head I possessed and I was left without a dollar. I
made up my mind to rid the country of them and with some friends
worked to this end. When the bank of Belle Fourche was robbed, the

outlaws made straight for the Hole-in-the-Wall country and holed up for the winter after killing six beeves for a food supply. I wired to Cheyenne officers to assist me in running the robbers down as I knew right where they were located, but before assistance came a heavy snowfall made it impossible to push into the mountains and early the next spring the outlaws got away. A year ago last May I notified the Burlington, Northwestern and Union Pacific roads to be on the lookout for a holdup and in less than a month the Wilcox robbery occurred.

"The Tipton holdup and the Wilcox affair were managed in exactly the same manner and the robbery executed in precisely the same way. The escape was also effected in the same manner as the Wilcox hold-up. After the robbers left the scene of the Tipton hold-up they rode their horses out on the prairie a distance of seven miles and cooked breakfast. They were mounted on the very best of horses and led a pack horse. It was very evident they did not fear pursuit but they did fear running into an ambush as they took every precaution and avoided deep canyons and high rocks which might conceal anyone. After eating their morning meal, the robbers rode straight across the sandy desert for a distance of seventy miles without even halting their horses for water. They rode both day and night and from their manner of traveling they were directed by compass. After we followed their trail for several days a heavy rainstorm melted their tracks from the sand and we were unable to determine which direction the robbers had gone and were forced to give up the chase. The route of the robbers was well chosen and was through a wild and uninhabited country. I believe the outlaws have gone to Arizona where they will probably remain for a few months or until next spring when they will make their appearance again at some point along the line of one of the transcontinental railways."[1]

At wit's end, railroad executives turned to the Pinkerton Detective Agency for help. The Pinkertons dispatched Charles Siringo to track down the robbers. Harvey Logan (Kid Curry) was highest on the agency's list of suspects once they'd gotten a tip that Logan had vowed to raid the Union Pacific in revenge for the railroads' dogged pursuit of his brother Lonny.

Siringo launched the chase near Grand Junction, Colorado, where Logan and a "tall" companion—very likely Ben Kilpatrick—were thought to have been spotted. After a few false starts, Siringo picked up a trail that led south and then west into Utah toward Monticello and the Blue Mountains. Tracking outlaws, especially undercover, was Siringo's specialty. He had a knack for disguising himself as a hard case and persuading other hard cases to talk openly about the men he was pursuing. At the Carlisle Ranch near Monticello, a popular stop for outlaws on the run, he learned that he was only a little more than a day behind his quarry.

The trail grew cold, however, and Siringo had to guess where Logan and his tall companion were headed. He figured that was most likely Hanksville and Robbers Roost, so he headed out. He questioned Charlie Gibbons, the store owner who regularly sold supplies to Butch and the Wild Bunch while they were hiding out at the Roost. Gibbons swore that he had not seen Butch, but Siringo worked on him, convincing him that he was taking him into his confidence—no questions asked. Probably to protect his own hide, Gibbons finally admitted that shortly after the Winnemucca bank robbery, Butch had left a large amount of money with him for safekeeping. Naturally, Gibbons claimed that he knew nothing about the theft and that he had no idea he had been given stolen loot, which he said contained a generous amount of twenty-dollar gold pieces. When Siringo asked him what had happened to the loot, Gibbons replied that Butch had come to pick it up.[2]

While at Hanksville, Siringo received orders from the Pinkerton office in Denver to ride over to Circle Valley, where Butch Cassidy had been raised, to learn as much as possible about the outlaw's background. Afterward, he was to head south to Alma, New Mexico Territory, to follow up on a report that the Wild Bunch might be fortifying a ranch down there for their winter quarters. The instructions came from a man who should have known: Assistant Superintendent Frank Murray, the detective who, thanks to Butch, once barely made it out of the town of Alma alive.

At Circle Valley, Siringo spent a week nosing around, learning as much as he could about Butch from the Parker family's friends and neighbors. He had hoped to pick up some actionable clues; instead, he picked up family trivia and minutiae, such as the fact that Butch had been nicknamed "Sallie" as a child, which should have been enough to turn any self-respecting male into a hardened killer. Nevertheless, during his visit, Siringo got to know one of Butch's younger sisters and apparently developed a fondness for her. "I had to work hard to keep from falling in love with Miss Parker, the pretty young sister of Butch Cassiday [*sic*]. She was the deputy post-mistress in Circleville."[3] He later wrote the editor of *Frontier Times* regarding his trip to Circleville and fascination with Cassidy's sister: "There I made the acquaintance of the whole Parker family. I became attracted to George Parker's pretty black-eyed sister, who was deputy post-mistress in Circleville. From her I gained many important secrets of the 'Wild Bunch.'"[4]

True, Siringo uncovered a few interesting, if not necessarily pertinent, facts about the gang while in Circle Valley. One was that they had at one time kept in contact with one another through a series of hidden private postal drops they had established from the Hole-in-the-Wall in northeastern Wyoming to the Robbers Roost area and possibly beyond. According to Siringo, the drops were hidden in rocky crevices and hollow stumps and were used to deposit ciphered mail and occasionally newspaper items. The mail consisted of seemingly innocuous letters with coded messages in key words; by reading only every fourth word in a letter, the real message would be revealed. Butch's sister later learned of one such drop in a hollow tree near Linwood, Utah. The tree had a cavity that was hidden by a rusty metal band. Inside the opening was a bottle tied to a string. If the band was moved to one side, a person could reach through the hole for the bottle and place a message inside. Once lowered again, the bottle became invisible.[5]

On leaving Circle Valley, Siringo rode south to Panguitch, loaded food and water on his packhorse, and set out for the Arizona border. After several long, hard days of desert travel, he reached Gallup, New Mexico, where he renewed supplies for the final leg of his journey to Alma.

Posing again as a man on the run, Siringo chatted with cowboys who drifted in and out of the saloon until he learned the details of Frank Murray's earlier visit. The story that was given was basically the same as that reported by Murray to his superiors in Denver, except for one startling fact: The saloonkeeper, Jim Lowe, the man who had saved Murray's life, was actually the outlaw Butch Cassidy!

From Alma, Siringo rode north into the Mogollon Mountains, where he nosed around several mining camps. At Frisco, he found a local cowboy who claimed to have known former WS Ranch trail boss Jim Lowe. Not only did the cowboy know Lowe, but also he said that at that very moment Lowe was no more than forty miles away. Siringo immediately sent word to Frank Murray in Denver for instructions, but to Siringo's surprise, Murray ordered him off the hunt, instructing him to return to Denver. Murray said that Siringo's source must have been mistaken about Jim Lowe being Butch Cassidy because he had met Lowe, and Lowe was no outlaw.[6]

Siringo sold his two horses and caught the next stage to Silver City, the nearest town with a railroad. Along the road, he met a fellow passenger by the name of Blake Graham, who told him that he, too, knew the Jim Lowe who had worked for William French at the WS. Both Siringo and Graham had brought along a generous amount of whiskey, and before long, the liquor had loosened Graham's tongue: He told Siringo that Lowe was indeed Butch Cassidy and that Butch had once owned the saloon in Alma. Graham told him about Frank Murray's visit and how, not long after, Butch sold the saloon and left town with a fellow WS ranch hand named Red Weaver. Graham added that Butch himself had told him that he had once saved Murray's life because he just didn't have the heart to see him killed.[7]

Butch may well have been hiding in the Mogollon Mountains, as Siringo's source had said, but many sources allege that, on the heels of the Winnemucca bank robbery in September 1900, Butch and other members of the gang, including Sundance, Harvey Logan, Will Carver, and Ben Kilpatrick, headed for Fort Worth, Texas, for a little long overdue R & R.[8]

By the turn of the century, most cowpunchers who rode into Fort Worth at least occasionally sampled the lurid pleasures of the town's tenderloin district, aptly called Hell's Half Acre. Today, the forty square blocks that once made up the "Acre"—an area that now lies just north of Interstate 30 between Jones and Houston Streets—contains a respectable Hilton Hotel and the popular Tarrant County Convention Center. Back in 1900, though, the district was an embarrassment to upright civic leaders. Amon Carter, the founder of the *Fort Worth Star-Telegram*, was supposed to have maintained a long-standing policy that practically banned the name "Hell's Half Acre" from the pages of his newspaper.[9]

The Acre was home to Fort Worth's Big Three of madams: Mary Porter (not to be confused with San Antonio's Fannie Porter), Jessie Reeves, and Josie Belmont, all queens of prostitution who ran the best sporting houses in the city. They all stood within a block of one another and must have presented a quandary to visiting cowhands and criminals. The three houses operated as friendly coconspirators, all seeking out the better class of customers who frequented the district.

The Acre was also the home to a saloonkeeper named Mike Cassidy (no relation to Butch, of course), a debauched character who had staggered into Fort Worth in the late 1880s seeking work as a bartender. To his customers, he was known as convivial "Mikey Mike," everyone's good-time Charlie. But in reality, he was remarkably closed-mouthed about his past. Over the years, he operated several seedy saloons in the Acre, during which time he acquired a wife and a family and probably a long list of creditors. He also accrued a record of minor criminal offenses, but, at least locally, they were nothing more than violations of city liquor laws.[10]

The trip to Fort Worth in the fall of 1900 was not the Wild Bunch's first, but it was to be one of its most memorable. Gang member Will Carver was about to be married. His intended, Callie May Hunt, also known as Lillie Davis, was one of Fannie Porter's girls from San Antonio. Although the wedding ceremony was filled with celebrations, the marriage itself may have been a sham, because no official record of it exists.[11]

The party following the Carver-Davis "ceremony" was apparently an elaborate dress-up affair, which most likely culminated in the famous group photo of the "Fort Worth Five": Butch, Sundance, Logan, Carver, and Kilpatrick, all spiffed up in their best Sunday-go-to-meeting suits and jaunty derby hats. The photo was taken by John Swartz, a prominent

Fort Worth photographer who ran his own gallery and studio, the Swartz View Company, at 705 Main Street. Swartz's enterprise was located only a few blocks from where the Wild Bunch decided to make their headquarters in the Acre.

Another reason given for the photo was that it was Butch's idea of a joke, while still another includes a decision ascribed to Sundance, who loved to dress up and show off. Author Anne Meadows probes a little deeper into the outlaw psyche and speculates that they might have been poking fun at the wealthy class they professed to despise but really envied, or perhaps they were acting out their fantasies of how life might have been had they stayed on the straight and narrow.[12] Regardless of the explanation, the photo turned out to be a disastrous idea. Photographer Swartz was so proud of his work that he put a print in the window of his gallery. Somebody recognized it for what it was, had another print made, and sent it to the authorities.

The man given credit for spotting the photo in Swartz's window was Fred Dodge, a special agent for Wells Fargo. But Dodge himself never mentioned it in his memoirs, so it might not have been true. Whoever *did* notice the picture in the window, if that was how it was discovered, made sure it found its way into the proper hands. Finally, authorities had a photo of all five members of the inner circle of the Wild Bunch. Detectives converged on the Acre district, but by then, Butch and his pals had disappeared.

Some writers credit the portrait of the "Fort Worth Five" as the cause of the Wild Bunch's eventual downfall. It's true that, for the first time, law enforcement agencies throughout the West could circulate wanted posters displaying the faces of Sundance, Harvey Logan, Ben Kilpatrick, and Will Carver, but Butch Cassidy's photo, taken when he entered the Wyoming State Prison in July 1894, was nothing new. Sketches based on his prison mug shot had appeared in newspapers nationally as early as the summer of 1899.[13]

The Swartz photo was probably the one the Pinkertons sent to George S. Nixon, head cashier of the National Bank of Winnemucca, Nevada, in an attempt to determine if Butch or any of the others in the portrait were the robbers there. For years, a large print of the photo has hung in the lobby of the Winnemucca bank and may have given birth to a legend that, in a display of bravado, Butch had sent a print of it directly to Nixon. In another version of the story, Butch sent a copy to young Vic Button, the boy at the WS Ranch to whom Butch gave his white horse. While many doubt this tale, it supposedly was confirmed by Button's daughter.[14]

Some writers believe that, upon leaving Fort Worth, Butch and Sundance headed for San Antonio and Fannie Porter's house of delights. If so, it was one more bad move, because the Pinkertons weren't far behind.

At the time, San Antonio had its own Hell's Half Acre, and Fannie Porter was the undisputed queen of the madams there. She offered to her customers the best services in luxurious surroundings. She particularly catered to select members of the Wild Bunch who sometimes stayed for weeks at a time. And unlike many sporting-house operators, Fannie never discouraged her girls from becoming romantically involved with their clients. She even encouraged it, at least where the Wild Bunch members were concerned. That's one of the reasons conjecture is strong that Etta Place worked for Fannie's house before becoming a significant part of the lives of Sundance and, to a lesser degree, Butch.

Of course, of all the people closely involved with the Wild Bunch, Etta remains the most obscure. Although she was the best-looking of the gang's molls—some would even say she was beautiful—she received far less scrutiny than nearly anyone else. But what exactly was she like? A photograph taken with Sundance in 1901 reveals a small, shapely woman with a warm, intelligent face and a quiet elegance—not the kind of woman you'd expect to find playing the role of sidekick to a hardened outlaw. But where the analysis begins is nearly where it ends, for virtually nothing else is known about the real-life Etta Place.

Researchers have managed to deduce quite a bit by piecing together tertiary evidence, historical contacts, and actual places where Etta is known to have appeared. We know that her name was most likely not real. Ed Kirby, a Sundance biographer, claimed he uncovered undoc-umented evidence that Etta's mother was actually named Emily Jane Place of Oswego, New York; that she was related to Sundance's mother, Annie G. Place; and that Etta and Sundance had known one another in Pennsylvania before Sundance left for the West.[15]

Author Donna Ernst, "a tireless researcher," claims that Etta's first name was really Ethel (a name she used in early 1901) and that the name Etta came as a result of her later visit to South America. There, Ernst claims, the Spanish pronunciation of "Ethel" would have come out sounding like "Etta." Dan Buck agrees about the pronunciation, although he suggests that the name Etta most likely resulted from a clerical error in the Pinkertons' file.[16]

Another popular theory suggests that Etta was actually Ann Bassett of Brown's Park, the early girlfriend of Butch Cassidy. She and her sister Josie competed for Butch's affections. But although Ann had numerous opportunities to substantiate the story over the years, she never did.

Another rumor suggested that Etta's real name was Laura Etta Place Capel, the daughter of George Capel, a man also known as George Ingerfield. According to the legend, Capel was killed in 1892 while living in Arizona, and Etta, barely sixteen, ended up at Fannie Porter's "sporting house" in San Antonio, where Butch Cassidy met her. Believing she deserved a better life, he took her with him to Price, Utah, where he placed her with a "good Mormon family" named Thayne. There, Etta took the name of Ethel or Hazel and, prior to her involvement with the Sundance Kid and the Wild Bunch, taught school "for a while."[17]

The Capel theory led to another tale that surfaced in 1970 when a man claiming to be Harry Thayne Longabaugh, the son of Harry Alonzo Longabaugh, went around insisting to the world that Etta Place was actually a woman named Hazel Tryon, half sister to his mother, Anna Marie Thayne. He said that, after he was born in 1904, Etta (Ethel) took up with his father (Harry), eventually deserting her own children and running off with him to South America. The younger Longabaugh also said that Etta had been married two times before, once to a "Johnnie" Johnson, and later to a man named Smith. He said that in later years, Etta attempted to locate her two children but was unsuccessful. He claimed that Etta finally settled in Marion County, Oregon, where she died in 1935.[18]

Still another theory from Fort Worth newspaper editor Delbert Willis alleged that Etta Place was a Fort Worth prostitute whose real name was Eunice Gray. Willis, who had interviewed Gray many times, said that she told him she had come from Missouri. Gray lived to be eighty-one and died in a hotel fire in Waco, Texas, in January 1962. Although Willis apparently was convinced that Eunice and Etta were one and the same, he never managed to produce concrete evidence to back his beliefs. Willis's theory was pursued by Fort Worth historian Richard F. Selcer for his book on the Hell's Half Acre district of that city, but Selcer, too, came up empty-handed.

Then there was the story of the woman from Wisconsin named Fish who reported that she was sure Etta was her father's second cousin. According to Mrs. Fish, her father told her that the girl, who was from Door County, Wisconsin, "got mixed up with a bad crowd." Not only that, said Mrs. Fish, but the girl's father (Mrs. Fish's uncle) was found murdered in 1894, and it was rumored that the guilty party was none other than Sundance.[19]

In the early 1990s, Wild Bunch researcher Jim Dullenty thought he may have had a promising lead on Etta Place when he received a call from an outlaw enthusiast named Jesse Cole Kenworth who had what Dullenty believed was actionable information on Etta's identity. According to Kenworth, Etta could be traced to Florence, Arizona. Dullenty was ready to pack up and meet Kenworth for a trip to Florence when Kenworth broke off contact.[20]

Some researchers believe that Etta eventually ended her life in Denver, Colorado. Gail Drago even supplied an address: 619 Ohio Street. The late F. Bruce Lamb felt that Etta might have come from the Denver area. Following these leads, Donna Ernst combed the census and other public records in that city but found nothing. If Etta Place had lived out her life in Denver, city officials never knew it.

Another rumor tied Etta to the Parker clan in Utah, where she was supposedly Butch's cousin, Amy Parker, who was born in Kanosh, Utah, in 1879 and grew up in the town of Joseph in southern Sevier County. This would have made Amy about the same age as Etta, and there was some physical similarity between the two. Joseph, Utah, is fifty miles from where Butch lived in Circle Valley. The story alleges that he knew her when they were growing up and, in fact, introduced her to Sundance years later.[21]

An offshoot of *this* story is from Salt Lake City researcher Steve Lacy, who claimed to have information that Etta was a schoolteacher who married a relative of Butch's and later resided in Leeds, Utah. He says that Etta's last name was Harris and that she lived until January 1959, but, again, the details and historical facts don't bear this out.[22]

One of the most tantalizing tales of Etta's roots came from additional digging by Donna Ernst. At least one Pinkerton detective who had been assigned to find the Wild Bunch alluded to Etta's parents living in Texas. Ernst searched the 1900 census records for every Ethel born between 1873 and 1880 who lived in or near Fort Worth or San Antonio (two of Sundance's favorite haunts). Ernst also studied old city directories and marriage, death, and tax records. She eliminated from consideration women named Ethel with large families, eventually crossing out all of the Ethels who had popped up . . . except one. And she was a near-perfect match.

Her name was Ethel Bishop, and she lived in San Antonio with four other women—all young and single—at 212 South Concho Street, a bordello just around the corner from Fannie Porter's pleasure den. In one of the directories, Ethel had described herself as an unemployed music teacher.[23]

Ernst then conducted a nationwide census search, but it turned up little additional information. She did find two Ethel Bishops in the 1880 census for West Virginia, both of whom roughly matched the San Antonio Ethel. In writing to women who were named Bishop and living in West Virginia, Ernst was encouraged by a letter from a man who wrote, "The past is best left in the past anyway," and included a confusing family tree on the back of his letter. But before Ernst could probe the matter further, the man died.

Utah outlaw writer Kerry Ross Boren has suggested that Butch may have had stronger feelings for Etta than is generally believed. Boren claims that his source for this information was his own grandfather, Willard Schofield, who supposedly knew Butch. According to Boren, sometime shortly before Butch, Sundance, and Etta fled to South America, Butch spent an evening in the saloon at Linwood, Utah, where his grandfather tended bar. Boren says that his grandfather recalled that

Butch talked quite a lot about Etta that night. "He talked about her like he thought an awful lot of her. He didn't come right out and say anything, but I could tell that he was anxious to tell someone about it and he spent nearly an hour just telling about things she did."[24]

Whatever Etta's budding relationship with Butch may have been, by late fall 1900, she had clearly paired up with Sundance and was his companion at both Fort Worth and San Antonio.

By 1900, it appears that Sundance had also replaced Elzy Lay as Butch's closest friend in the gang. Whether or not Butch and Sundance ever shared the same lover is debatable, but they undoubtedly shared several other commonalities. Unlike Harvey Logan, they were not killers, at least not as far as they had been put to the test. They also probably shared the belief that things were getting out of hand, that in their escape from Fort Worth they had cut it too close, and that it was only a matter of time before the gang had to call it quits.

Butch later described his uneasiness that year as restlessness, a feeling that, as vast as the West was, it was getting too small for him.[25] He may have been right. In one of his favorite hideout areas, desolate Grand County, Utah, which in 1900 had fewer than 750 residents, not only telegraph but suddenly *telephone* lines began popping up to link the towns. Butch later remarked to another friend that the law had become so familiar with the Wild Bunch's practices that it was only a matter of time before all the members of the gang were killed or captured.[26]

Charles Kelly suggests that Butch's uneasiness that year was an indication of his uncanny intuition about such things: Butch usually knew when the game was played out and when it was time to toss in his cards. But predicting a possibly bleak future for the Wild Bunch would not have been that difficult. The West was beginning to tackle its crime problem. Robbing trains was becoming increasingly difficult. In the early years, it was relatively easy to crack open an express car like a ripe melon and scoop up the meat inside. But once the railroads had entered the steel-car era, the cars became virtually impregnable.

Also, train crews were beginning to stiffen their opposition to robbers. A train robbery was a stain on a crew's reputation. Even if the fault didn't rest solely with them, every misstep, delay, and error in judgment could be a black mark against a crew and affect its individual members' chances for corporate advancement.[27]

Not only were train crews getting more hardened, but also the federal commissioner of railroads had recommended that extra guards be put on trains carrying valuable express shipments. The guards were to be armed with repeating shotguns and enough rounds of buckshot to dissuade any brigands. Rumors floated around that extraordinary new devices were being explored by express company and railroad line officials to thwart thievery. These included Gatling guns and searchlights; globular steel cars with revolving turrets; battery-powered, electrically charged steel floor plates near express car doors that could cook an intruder alive; messengers armed with hand grenades that could be thrown out of express car windows; hoses connected to the locomotive boiler from which scalding steam could be sprayed over attackers; and devices designed to pour burning oil on would-be robbers.[28]

But surrendering the life of an outlaw? Was that actually possible? Butch figured it was, and he also thought the time was as good as any. No one knows how the Wild Bunch loot had been split up during the previous several years, but if Butch and Sundance had managed to hang on to their share of it, they had probably accumulated sizable stakes.

Still, one question remained: If the two decided to start life anew, where would they begin? The West was no longer safe: Fort Worth had proved that. The East was out because living there was too costly; their money would be used up in no time, and then what would they do? They were used to working the range: They weren't used to toiling away as dirt farmers or city laborers.

Canada was no longer an option: Sundance had been there and knew what it was like—too much law and order. The word was that it was nearly impossible to be a successful outlaw north of the Canadian border, thanks to the damnable efficiency of the Royal Canadian Mounted Police. On the other hand, there was always South America. It had its share of steaming hot jungles, it was true. But it was a big enough continent to have mountains and prairies and wide-open ranges, too, similar to those of the American Southwest. So, South America was a distinct possibility, especially for Butch. He felt he had seen all of the West that he "thought was good" and wanted to see more of the world.[29]

Still vacillating, Butch had his mind made up for him when he spied someone who looked suspiciously like an undercover agent on the streets of Fort Worth. He and Sundance decided then and there to separate, agreeing that they would meet again in New York City to further discuss the possibility of traveling south—at least until the heat died down. But before they did, Sundance took a few days off for a side trip to Fort Worth and a quick visit to Etta.

Even though no wedding license has ever been found, Sundance told his family and friends that he and Etta were married; in fact, later, everyone in Argentina would know them as husband and wife, Mr. and Mrs. Place. Even the Pinkertons began referring to her as Mrs. Longabaugh. Believing that she was from Texas, the agents wrote to J. H. Maddox, chief of police in Fort Worth, and asked him "to try to learn through some of your acquaintances in Texas who this woman is and where she came from."[30]

After what one can only assume were a pleasant several days together, Harry got together again with Butch to begin laying plans for their trip to South America. That's when Sundance told Butch that Etta would be joining them. At first, Butch didn't like the idea. According to his sister, Butch felt such a rugged land was no place for a woman. Eventually, though, he relented, most likely after Sundance reminded him that they would need a reliable cook and housekeeper.[31] According to Charles Kelly, Butch also tried to persuade Harvey Logan to join them, but he declined.[32]

So the two *bandidos* decided on settling down in South America, more specifically Argentina. Butch or Sundance may have read about the country in a magazine. *National Geographic* had run several articles on Patagonia back then, with its vastness that stretched between the Andes Mountains and the Atlantic Ocean. Or perhaps the two had met someone who had recently been to Argentina or someone who *knew* someone who had.

It was not an illogical choice. Turn-of-the-century Argentina was poised for an economic boom. A hoof-and-mouth disease outbreak in England placed a ban on importing live cattle and sheep from Europe, so

Argentina expanded its own industries, not only growing enough meat-on-the-hoof for its personal consumption but also for export to the rest of the world. Both local and foreign investors found that to be a sound reason for sinking money into the local economy.

Once the leaders of the Wild Bunch had reached a decision to leave the States, Butch severed one of his last ties to Wyoming: He sold the remaining interests he held in the ranch that he and Al Hainer had acquired in 1889.

The acreage containing Butch and Hainer's cabin was acquired by a couple from Iowa—Francis B. Nicol and his wife. The Nicols had come to Wyoming in 1891, where Francis held a US Mail contract between Fort Washakie and Dubois. According to one source, Nicol improved the land with an irrigation ditch that diverted water from Horse Creek. He and his wife held the property until 1919 when they sold it to the Dubois Mercantile Company.

Another conflicting source says that Gene Amoretti Jr. purchased the property directly from Butch and Hainer in 1900, although this reference may have been to additional land that Butch and Hainer had acquired later. According to local history, Amoretti operated a hunting lodge for tourists called the Ramshorn Lodge in the Rockies. In promoting the lodge, Amoretti advertised that "there were more deer, elk, bear, bobcats, and mountain sheep in the area than anywhere else in the world."[33]

So, in winter 1901, Sundance and Etta left for New York, but when they arrived, they found the Eastern Seaboard locked in by snow and frigid temperatures. They were ready to celebrate, but New York wasn't ready to provide them with the venue; rather than fight the snow and freezing cold, Sundance booked a quick trip to the more pleasant clime of New Orleans. After spending several weeks there, the couple, using assumed names, boarded a train headed northeast for a visit with Sundance's family. They arrived in Pennsylvania at the same time as the Phoenixville Railroad Depot from which young Sundance had departed in 1882: He was making his first visit home in nearly twenty years.

The couple's first stop in Pennsylvania was at Mont Clare, where Sundance's sister, Samanna, and brother-in-law, Oliver Hallman, were high on his list of family members to visit. By then, both of Sundance's parents had died. His brother, Elwood, lived in California, while his other sister, Emma, lived in Philadelphia. Another brother, Harvey, was in nearby Flourtown.

The visit, according to family records, turned out to be anything but tranquil: By then, the Pinkertons had discovered Sundance's Pennsylvania roots and periodically surveilled the Hallman home, and Sundance and Etta had to be alert and ready to move at a moment's notice. At some point during the visit, Sundance mentioned his plans to buy a ranch in South America, and Samanna was ecstatic to think that her brother might be going straight. Things weren't quite as cozy between Sundance and sister Emma, though, who frowned upon her brother's occupation and the resulting shame it had heaped upon the family name. In fact, she was so disturbed by his notoriety that she changed the spelling of her last name to Longabough. She may have been wise to do so. Having a wanted outlaw for a brother wasn't propitious for her seamstress business.

While in Pennsylvania, Sundance mentioned that he was having trouble with an old gunshot wound in his left leg. Just before departing for New York, Samanna or Oliver may have suggested he pay a call to a specialist in New York. Sundance scheduled an appointment with a doctor named Weinstein, who recommended he pay a visit to a specialist in upstate New York.

The Buffalo physician, Ray V. Pierce, operated what would today be called a clinic but was known in 1901 by two names—Dr. Pierce's Invalids Hotel and Dr. Pierce's Medical Institute. The institute, an impressive, five-story brick building with a stained-glass entry and lush paneled walls, was located at 653 Main Street in Buffalo. Among other things, it offered its guests/patients Turkish baths and holistic remedies for "chronic diseases—specifically those of a delicate, obscure, complicated or obstinate character."[34]

Although the Pinkerton files reveal that both Sundance and Etta checked in to Dr. Pierce's hotel, no records have ever been found that disclose the medical reason for their visit. While Sundance may have sought treatment for his leg wound, some have speculated that, since Etta checked in with him, their problem may have been venereal in nature, a disease Etta likely contracted during her time as a prostitute in Texas. On the other hand, spouses and patients at health spas often shared accommodations in those days.

It's also feasible that Sundance may have been suffering from a lung disorder. According to Elton Cunningham, a friend of the Wild Bunch and a saloonkeeper in Mogollon, New Mexico, Sundance was a "lunger," plagued by a disease known commonly as consumption (tuberculosis), often spitting blood when he coughed. This seems unlikely, however, since a condition as severe as consumption would have attracted the attention of the family, who never mentioned it; but Sundance was known to have suffered from acute "catarrh," which today would be called chronic sinusitis.

Whatever the reason for their stay at Dr. Pierce's, when they left, Sundance and Etta were feeling well enough for a side trip to Niagara Falls before returning to New York. The hospital, unbound by today's commonly accepted patient-doctor privilege, sent a brief report about Sundance and Etta to the Pinkertons: It remains the best description of both Sundance and Etta available. Dated May 1902, it reads,

> *Harry Longbaugh [sic] alias Harry A. Place. About 35, 5 ft 9, 185 or 190. Med Comp. Brown eyes, Lt Bro hair. Lt Bro or Sandy Mustache, feet Small, not bow legged—both feet turn in walking, face much tanned with the Sun. Mrs. Harry A. Place age 23 or 24—5 ft 5. 110#. Med Comp medium dark hair Blue or gray eyes regular features. No marks or blemishes.*[35]

Back in New York on February 1, 1901, Sundance and Etta checked in to Mrs. Catherine Taylor's boardinghouse at 234 West 12th Street, taking the best second-floor suite she had available. They paid cash in advance for a three-week stay and signed the guest register as Mr. and Mrs. Harry Place. According to census records, the Taylor house was larger than an average home and boasted twenty rooms. Mrs. Taylor employed a chef and two servants to help with the guests. Mr. Taylor had recently died, and Mrs. Taylor's thirteen-year-old son, John, helped her run the house, which held up to twenty-five boarders. Throughout their trip, Sundance called himself Harry A. Place, while Etta referred to herself as Ethel. Harry told Mrs. Taylor that he and his wife were cattle buyers from Wyoming.

A third guest from Wyoming also signed in. Butch Cassidy, using the name James Ryan, had caught up with the pair and informed Mrs. Taylor that he was Ethel Place's brother.[36] For the next three weeks, Butch, Sundance, and Etta painted the town red. According to witnesses later interviewed by the Pinkertons, the trio took in the popular vaudeville shows of the day and frequented the city's numerous taverns and nightspots, among them Connelly's Bar at 3rd Avenue and 23rd Street, Pete's Tavern at Irving Place and 18th Street, and Joe's Bar on Union Square. After carousing late into the night, they returned to their boardinghouse, a little unsteady and probably a little too noisy for Mrs. Taylor's liking.

Among their shopping stopovers, the trio visited Tiffany's, which was then located at the corner of 15th Street and Union Square and was already renowned for its fine jewelry. There, one of the boys purchased for Etta a fancy gold lapel watch worth $150, most likely for a Valentine's Day present. Later, Sundance, all spruced up in fancy Eastern duds and sporting the diamond stickpin he'd purchased for himself, and Etta, in a sweeping full skirt, high collar, and lace, had their photograph taken at De Young's on Broadway, one of the city's top photography studios. Sundance sent a print of the picture to a friend from his cowpunching days in Wyoming's Little Snake River Valley, a clerk who worked at Robert McIntosh's General Store in Slater, Colorado. Along with the photo, according to author Ernst, he included a letter "from New York City, with a picture of him and his wife, saying he had married a Texas lady he had known previously."[37]

Presumably, he also mailed a copy of the photo home to his family; however, it never arrived in Pennsylvania. Within sight of Samanna's Mont Clare home, a clerk at the post office kept close tabs on the mail and notified the Pinkertons of all communications traveling to and from the house. The family believes the clerk confiscated the photo and turned it over to the agency. A notation in the Pinkertons' file on Sundance states, "We have ordered copies of a photograph which Longbaugh [*sic*] had taken of himself and the woman . . . said to be his wife and to be from

Texas." That picture soon appeared on wanted posters plastered around the West.[38]

Naturally, the trio's New York shopping and sightseeing spree didn't pass totally unnoticed by the Pinkertons. An angry William dashed off a memo to his brother Robert, complaining about the agency's "looking for them in the mountains and wilderness" while the outlaws were instead acting like "tourists in New York."[39]

The trio paid another visit to Tiffany's on February 4, 1901, where Butch purchased a beautiful gold watch for $40.10, serial number 68210-1685, possibly as a "wedding gift" for Sundance and Etta. An acquaintance of the trio in South America later claimed that Sundance had "a very fine Tiffany gold watch that his partner Butch Cassidy had purchased on his way thru New York City en route to South America."[40] The date of purchase suggests that it could not have been the lapel watch worn by Etta in her photograph on February 3.

A review of the Pinkerton files shows that Sundance, before leaving for South America, took treatment with Dr. Weinstein in New York City that year. The 1900 and 1902–1903 New York City directories list Dr. Isaac Weinstein's office at 174 Second Avenue. Weinstein's name is also found in the 1896 and 1897 directories of the Public Medical Society for the County of New York. He is listed as a physician at St. Marks Hospital, the New York Eye and Ear Hospital that was located across the street at 177 Second Avenue. Sundance may have been seeking treatment for his catarrh. Interestingly, one of Dr. Weinstein's partners trained at the University of Buffalo, suggesting that Sundance may have received a recommendation for Dr. Weinstein during his stay at Dr. Pierce's Invalids Hotel in upstate New York.[41]

On February 13, the trio witnessed a phenomenon that had New Yorkers chattering for years. A sudden warm front caused massive chunks of ice that stretched from shore to shore to break up and flow down the Hudson River and into the harbor. As these chunks rounded the Battery and met a sister ice floe from the East River, the two merged, paralyzing harbor traffic for days. Gale-force winds of more than sixty miles an hour amazed spectators, even as the wind devastated shipping. At one point, a witness said he counted sixty-two vessels caught in the sea of ice, while another man claimed he counted twice that number.[42]

Despite the weather, Butch, Sundance, and Etta continued frolicking in Manhattan for another three weeks. With their fun-filled days drawing to a close, Sundance and Etta Place finally boarded the British ship *Herminius*, which sailed from New York Harbor the following morning. The destination: Buenos Aires, Argentina. The couple traveled together as Mr. and Mrs. Harry Place. Although some researchers believe that Butch returned West for one final robbery, catching a later sailing to Argentina, others claim that all substantive evidence available from South America suggests that he departed with them under the name of James Ryan.[43] It's also possible that Butch had initially planned on sailing with Etta and Sundance but had a change of heart when he learned of a lucrative strike to be made out West—one too good even for a man on his way to South America to pass up.

Lending some credence to the latter theory, the *Herminius* docked in Buenos Aires, Argentina, on March 23, 1901,[44] and Mr. and Mrs. Harry Place disembarked, temporarily settling into the Hotel Europa, a fashionable and popular hotel in the center of the thriving city. Sundance visited the London and River Plate Bank, where he deposited £2,000 in gold notes, worth about $12,000 at the time. He gave his residence as the Hotel Europa, employing the alias "Harry Place."

CHAPTER 6

Harry Alonzo Longabaugh

Local officers who have had much to do with the "Hole-in-the-wall"
and "Robbers Roost" gangs of outlaws in this State during the past
five years and who are acquainted with every member say they are
almost certain that the man under arrest in St. Louis for attempting
to pass bank bills taken by the men who robbed the Great North-
ern train at Wagner, Mont., in July last, is no other than Harry
Longbaugh [sic].

—OGDEN STANDARD, OGDEN, UTAH, NOVEMBER 18, 1901

PAUL D. ERNST, IN THE INTRODUCTION TO HIS WIFE'S BOOK *THE*
Sundance Kid: The Life of Harry Alonzo Longabaugh, wrote:

> *As you enter the public library in Phoenixville, Pennsylvania, near*
> *where I live, your attention is drawn to two exhibits across from*
> *one another. They display the lives of two well-known native sons—*
> *Samuel Pennypacker, one of Pennsylvania's early governors, and*
> *Harry A. Longabaugh, my great-great-uncle, better known as the*
> *Sundance Kid. Most people might say the governor was the more*
> *important citizen, and I agree. But being related to an outlaw has*
> *been a lot more fun and exciting.*[1]

But Sundance wasn't always so notorious. Having sprung from a
family of humble beginnings, he might not have achieved any notoriety

at all. But he did, and the groundwork was laid before the outset of America's War of Independence.

In the 1770s, two German immigrant brothers named Conrad and Baltzer traveled separately from their homes to the American Colonies, arriving just in time to participate in the Revolutionary War. Neither one could read or write, and upon arrival—Baltzer in Baltimore and Conrad in Philadelphia—their surnames underwent the predictable transformation. To the officials checking Baltzer in, his last name sounded like Langenbaugh, so that's what it became. To the officials welcoming Conrad to America, his name sounded to them like Longabaugh, and thus he was christened. From that day on, they became two branches of the family—Baltzer Langenbaugh and Conrad Longabaugh. "Today," according to Ernst, "there are about a dozen spellings of the original name, but our immediate lineage has always and only used two variations— Longabaugh and Longabough."[2]

Although they lived miles apart, the brothers remained in touch with one another. Baltzer's line tended to move frequently, but Conrad's family has lived in the Phoenixville, Chester County, area since the arrival of its patriarch in 1772.

Across the Schuylkill River and the canal from Phoenixville lay the quaint village of Mont Clare, in Montgomery County, where Sundance was born and raised. The two towns are located thirty miles from Philadelphia on the canal and railroad line. The primary industries of steel production, agriculture, and transportation gave the area its start. Within five miles, the fields and meadows of Valley Forge, where Washington and his men trained and regrouped during the harsh, war-torn winters of 1777 and 1778, call out the names of their fallen warriors.

Today, many of the houses, schools, and buildings that Sundance knew before he left in 1882 still exist. Each June, the communities of Phoenixville and Mont Clare celebrate "Canal Days" in commemoration of their collective history. The canal and river are still essential parts of the community, although today they're used for small boating and recreation instead of transporting the large, mule-fueled barges overflowing with coal and ore.

In this conservative and still predominantly spiritual setting, Sundance must have had a family-oriented childhood. Back then, two sisters and two brothers meant money was a huge problem plaguing the Longabaugh family, so Harry worked for farmers and attended school between harvesting and planting. The family rented the farm where his father, Josiah, worked.

But living on a canal with barges passing on their way to and from Philadelphia instilled in the young boy a wondrous determination to someday explore distant parts of the country. Harry's elder brother, Elwood, set off on his own around the same time that young Harry did. Harry left home to pursue life as a whaler before eventually making his way to San Francisco. According to Ernst,

> As a child, I wasn't aware of my connection to the Sundance Kid. Sometimes a comment was made by my grandfather, William H. Longabough, to his son Bill in reference to having a wayward relative; but then Grandpop would just smile and change the subject when asked for details. In his final weeks of life, Grandpop developed dementia, probably from his medication. He died in March of 1976 without sharing anything he knew about his outlaw uncle; perhaps he was too embarrassed, since his relationship was so much closer than mine is today.
>
> We found out our family's connection to Sundance almost by accident later that year. My uncle, Bill Longabough, Grand-pop's son, was at a church dinner. While waiting in the traditional buffet line, a friend said she wasn't going to stand near him because he had to be related to that outlaw, Harry Longabaugh. After all, it was such an unusual last name that they had to be related. In fact, Longabaugh was my mother's maiden name, and that triggered a series of events and discoveries that for us eventually explained Grandpop's rambling statements.
>
> When Uncle Bill asked what she meant, she explained that she had read an article by Robert Redford on the Outlaw Trail in the National Geographic. Redford had portrayed Sundance in the popular 1969 movie Butch Cassidy and the Sundance Kid. And in

the movie, Redford mentioned that Sundance's real name was Harry Longabaugh. Unfortunately, no one in the family had seen the movie; thus no one had heard that line. But Redford also wrote the name in the article.[3]

Suddenly, the family moniker triggered a wealth of memories in Ernst, who recalled his father's comments about being called Sundance as a child and hearing tales of an uncle who had robbed banks and trains and died somewhere in South America. His grandpop also insisted that Sundance was like Robin Hood; he stole from the rich and gave all of his gains away to the poor. It didn't take long for Ernst to recognize that his grandfather was nowhere *near* accurate on *that* one.

According to Ernst,

Next, Uncle Bill called my wife, Donna, who is the family genealogist and historian. While almost out of breath with excitement, he told her what he suspected. At the Federal Archives, with just a little research in the 1870 and 1880 census, Donna discovered that Sundance appeared on our family tree.

What I quickly discovered truly amazed us all. Sundance and Grandpop's father, Harvey, had been brothers! Furthermore, we had cousins with whom our family branch had lost touch but who knew the family history concerning Sundance. By contacting other family members, particularly the grandson of Sundance's sister Samanna, we started to fill in the missing details.[4]

All at once, the family was able to put names to four-year-old Sundance with his father Josiah; the heavy-set woman, Annie Place (Sundance's mother); the unidentified but quaint tea-party picture of Butch, Sundance, and his wife Ethel in Argentina; and much more. Ernst learned from family records that a young Sundance left home and traveled west to Illinois and then to Durango, Colorado, with a cousin, George Longenbaugh. George was a horse breeder, and Sundance loved working with horses. His knowledge of fast and reliable mounts would serve him well in years to come. After he left Phoenixville on August

30, 1882, Sundance occasionally wrote the family, although he never returned for a visit until 1900, after his parents had died.

In 1985, Ernst took his wife and three daughters on their first "Sundance" trip out west. Along the way, they got hooked on the stunning scenery and Rocky Mountain majesty in locales long ago haunted by Sundance—places he lived, worked, and robbed.

Reading books such as Charles Kelly's Outlaw Trail *and James D. Horan's* Desperate Men *sparked our interest to learn more. That began over 20 trips to every place that Sundance rode through. I finally suggested to Donna that she write a book.*

The end result was Sundance, My Uncle, *which was published in 1992. However, in the 16 years since Donna's first book was published, much new information has come to light about the Sundance Kid. These new revelations helped to complete the story of Sundance.*

As we did more and more research, we were astonished at the incomplete accounts and major inaccuracies of the early writings. By using newspapers and first-hand accounts, we were able to fill in many missing pieces within the United States and Canada. Our friends, historians Dan Buck and Anne Meadows, have uncovered the details of Butch and Sundance's South American lives and 1908 deaths in Bolivia. Donna has been able to use information from Anne's book, Digging Up Butch and Sundance *(1994), to detail Sundance's life in South America.[5]*

At the time, the Pinkertons, the railroads, and many banks accused the Wild Bunch of nearly every robbery that took place. If someone wore a bowler hat, he had to be Butch or Sundance. Gang members were often accused of holdups that occurred when they were actually days away from the site or even out of the country. Ernst wrote,

The Wild Bunch, a loose-knit group made up mostly of cowboys, robbed a lot of banks and trains for a living. Butch and Sundance, the gang leaders, preferred outracing a posse rather than having a

gunfight. Not until the final shootout in 1908 [in Bolivia] is there any evidence they ever killed anyone.

Many of the early Wild Bunch writers didn't travel out west or authenticate the stories being reported of Butch and Sundance. By researching the Pinkerton Detective Agency Archives, and visiting museums and libraries out west, Donna has written a more complete and more accurate biography of Sundance's life.[6]

Some examples of new finds and corrections in Sundance's life story concern the location of the Wilcox, Wyoming, train robbery in 1899. The year following the holdup, the Union Pacific rerouted and straightened the tracks thirty miles to the south, so the original site is today no more than an elevated bed cutting its way across the prairie. Donna Ernst also located payroll records in Wyoming, showing that Sundance worked as a cowboy shortly after leaving Colorado and before he embarked on his career of crime. Letters from Dave Gillespie, a Wyoming friend, show that Sundance could not have participated in the Belle Fourche bank robbery of 1897, although he was later captured with the real robbers and falsely accused.

Ernst continues:

Donna discovered other information in Canada, describing Sundance's two years there before returning to the States to rob a train in Montana. We found a note in the Pinkerton files that clears Sundance and Butch of the Tipton, Wyoming, train robbery of August 1900. At that time, they were well on their way to Winnemucca, 600 miles away, where they made their biggest heist. That money enabled them to prepare for a new life in South America. As for the Winnemucca, Nevada, bank robbery, our detailed following of the escape route found the Idaho ranch, store, and cabin where Sundance stopped. It looks the same today, right on down to the old hitching post.

Although we like to say that we have uncovered the complete story of Sundance's life, the identity of his wife, Ethel Place, remains a mystery. We have many theories and possibilities, but nothing absolute. She originally came from Texas and apparently met Sundance there,

possibly in the late 1890s. They were husband and wife, through the
good and the bad, until 1906, when she disappeared from history.[7]

From cattle rustling to bank robberies and train holdups—this often
seemed to be the natural progression of events for cowboys-turned-
outlaws in the late nineteenth century. The gangs shared in the stolen
money and excitement found along the Outlaw Trail, a series of hideouts
and safe houses scattered across the Old West.

The Wild Bunch was one of the best-known outlaw gangs in Western history, well trained and experienced in travel along the Outlaw
Trail. Their name came about as a result of their frequent wild behavior
in towns along the Wyoming, Colorado, and Utah borders. They shot
up saloons and hurrahed main streets in celebration, earning themselves
recognition as a "wild bunch" of cowboys in the local newspapers. The
name stuck.

The Wild Bunch had a swinging-gate membership of about twenty-
five men, but any given robbery seldom involved more than two or three
of the same outlaws from any other holdup. Their advantage over the
law was their skill in keeping their identities uncertain, their use of good
horseflesh and relays, and their ability to lie low in one of the hideouts
between heists. The gang's core group consisted of only five men.

The leader of the gang was Robert LeRoy Parker, alias Butch Cassidy.
The oldest of thirteen children, Butch was born April 13, 1866, in Beaver,
Utah, to a pioneering Mormon family. His early mentor was Mike Cassidy, a hired hand and part-time rustler from a neighboring ranch. When
the need to pick an alias became apparent, Parker chose "Cassidy." Except
for his penchant for stealing money, Butch adhered to a rather strict code
of conduct. He never killed anyone until the end; and historians say that
he never stole from regular folk, only banks and railroads.

The editors of *Police in America* attempted to describe the gang in
their 1906 annual report to the International Association of the Chiefs
of Police:

One of the most notorious bands of train robbers and bank "hold-ups"
who operated in the West and Southwest, from Wyoming to Texas,

from 1895 until 1902, was known as "The Wild Bunch." They made their headquarters in the South in various small cities in Texas, after their robberies they hid in the North in the "Hole in the Wall" country in Wyoming.

This band originally comprised:

- *"Tom" Ketcham, alias "Black Jack," leader, hanged at Clayton, New Mexico, April 26, 1901, for killing Sheriff Edward Farr, of Whalensburg, New Mexico, who was attempting his arrest for a train "hold-up."*
- *William Carver, alias "Bill" Carver, second leader, killed April 2, 1901, while resisting arrest in Texas for a murder committed at Sonora.*
- *"Sam" Ketcham, died June 24, 1900, in the Santa Fe, New Mexico, penitentiary, of a wound inflicted by a posse of officers attempting to arrest him for the robbery of the Colorado and Southern R. R. Co., at Cimarron, New Mexico.*
- *Elzy Lay, alis [sic] McGuinness, now serving a life sentence at the Santa Fe, New Mexico, penitentiary for participation with "Black Jack" Ketcham in the Cimarron train robbery.*
- *Lonny Logan, and Harvey Logan, alias "Curry brothers." Lonny was killed at Dodson, Mo., February 28, 1900, while resisting arrest.*
- *George Curry, alias "Flat Nose George," third leader, killed near Thompson, Utah, April 15, 1900, resisting arrest by a Sheriff's posse.*
- *"Bob" Lee, alias "Bob" Curry, now serving a ten-years' sentence in the Rawlins, Wyoming, State penitentiary, for the robbery of the Union Pacific train at Wilcox, Wyo., June 2, 1899.*

When the Southern end of this band was practically wiped out by death, arrest and conviction of the members, a new band was formed, under the leadership of Harvey Logan, alias "Kid" Curry, which was

*composed of O. C. Hanks, alias "Camila" Hanks, alias "Deaf Char-
lie"; George Parker, alias "Butch" Cassidy; Harry Longbaugh, alias
"Sundance Kid"; Ben Kilpatrick, alias "The Tall Texan." A part of
this band on September 19, 1900, at the noon hour, robbed the First
National Bank, of Winnemucca, Nev., a member of the American
Bankers Association, of $32,640.00 in gold, holding up the officials
with rifles and revolvers.*

    *Logan, Cassidy, Longbaugh, "Will" Carver, "Ben" Kilpatrick,
"Deaf Charlie" Jones, alias Hanks, at Wagner, Montana, July 3,
1901, "held-up" a Great Northern Express train, stealing therefrom
$40,500 of unsigned bills of the National Bank of Montana, and
the American National Bank of Helena, Helena, Mont., for which
"Ben" Kilpatrick, alias "The Tall Texan" was arrested by the police
in St. Louis, Mo., Nov. 5, 1901, having a number of the unsigned
stolen bills in his possession. He was sentenced to fifteen years in the
Columbus, Ohio penitentiary, and has since been transferred to the
United States Penitentiary at Atlanta, Georgia. When Kilpatrick
was arrested, the police found a room key of the LaClede Hotel on him.
When they arrived at the hotel, they found Laura Bullion, companion
of Kilpatrick, leaving with a satchel containing a number of unsigned
bills. She was arrested as an accomplice and sentenced to two years
and six months in the Missouri Penitentiary, at Jefferson.*

    *On December 13, 1901, a stranger got into an altercation with
two others over a pool game at Knoxville, Tennessee, resulting in
a pistol fight. Two policemen came in to quiet the disturbance. The
stranger shot both, "held-up" the occupants of the saloon, backed out
of a rear door and jumped thirty feet into a railroad cut, but was
eventually traced and arrested in an exhausted condition from cold,
exposure and injury from his thirty-foot jump. We subsequently
identified this man as Harvey Curry, alias Harvey and Southwest
[sic]. Logan was taken to Knoxville, Tenn., tried and convicted for
uttering forged bank notes and sentenced to a term of twenty years in
the United States Penitentiary at Columbus, Ohio, on November 29,
1902. While awaiting transfer to that institution, he made his escape*

by holding up the guards in the jail and fleeing to the mountains on horse-back. He has not been recaptured.

O. C. Hanks, alias "Camila" Hanks, of Texas, another one of this band, attempted to pass some of the unsigned notes in Nashville, Tennessee, on October 27, 1901. Circulars describing these stolen unsigned notes had been sent by us to every city, town and hamlet in the United States, with the request that the local authorities notify their merchants. When Hanks offered one of these stolen notes at Nashville, the merchant became suspicious and notified the police by telephone, who responded quickly, but Hanks, observing what occurred, quickly drew a revolver, "held-up" the officer temporarily, jumped into an ice wagon and forcing the driver out of the wagon drove rabidly [sic] down the street; intercepting a man in a buggy, he abandoned the wagon and captured the buggy, forcing the driver therefrom at the point of a revolver and in this escaped through the marshes to the Cumberland River, where he forced two negroes to row him across in a boat and was lost trace of.

On April 17, 1902, he was killed by officers in the streets of San Antonio, Texas, while resisting arrest. In 1892 Hanks and Harry Longbaugh "held-up" a Northern Pacific train in Big Timber, Montana, for which he was convicted and sentenced to ten years in the Deer Lodge Penitentiary, from which institution he was released April 30, 1901, rejoining his old companions in "hold-up" robberies.

"Butch" Cassidy with Harry Longbaugh and Etta Place, a clever horse woman and rifle shot, fled to Argentine Republic, South America, where they, it is said, have been joined by Logan. During the past two years, they committed several series of "hold-up" bank robberies in Argentina. We advised the Argentina authorities of their presence and location. They became suspicious of preparations for their arrest, fled from Argentine Republic and were last heard from on the Southwest coast of Chile, living in the wild open country.

This is the last actual band of railroad train and bank "hold-up" robbers who have operated in the United States. Etta Place, the alleged wife of Harry Longbaugh, it is said, operated with the remnants of this band in male attire in their bank robberies in South America.

> *When the band was not committing robberies in S. America, they*
> *were engaged in cattle raising on a ranch they had acquired and were*
> *expert ranchmen. Their ranch was located on a piece of high table land*
> *from which they commanded a view of 25 miles in various directions.*
> *Owing to this their capture by the South American authorities was*
> *made almost impossible.*[8]

Some additional information provided by Ernst about the main group of the Wild Bunch is that Harvey Alexander Logan, alias Kid Curry, was born in 1867 in Tama County, Iowa, the third of six children. After the deaths of his parents, he and his three brothers homesteaded in Landusky, Montana, where they made a living rustling cattle and horses. But ranching and rustling were too mild for Logan's temperament. He was the wildest member of the gang, having murdered nine men. Although short-tempered and vicious, he deferred to Butch's leadership in the running of the outfit.

Benjamin Arnold Kilpatrick, the "Tall Texan," was born in 1874 in Coleman County, Texas. His family of twelve moved to a ranch in Tom Green County, Texas, where Kilpatrick and his brothers quickly earned a reputation as the delinquents of the day. Two of his earliest acquaintances were Sam and Tom Ketchum, fellow Texans and future outlaw leaders.

William Richard Carver, alias Will "News" Causey, was born September 12, 1868, in Wilson County, Texas. Formerly a member of the Texas-based Ketchum Brothers Gang, he joined the Wild Bunch only after the Ketchums began to break up. Will was probably the only member of the Wild Bunch who could hold his own against the marksmanship of Sundance.

Harry Alonzo Longabaugh was born in the spring of 1867 in Mont Clare, Pennsylvania, the youngest of five children. In 1887, he was sentenced to eighteen months in jail for stealing a horse in Sundance, Wyoming. Having earned an outlaw's reputation and the alias "the Sundance Kid," he quickly became proficient at both bank and train robberies. He and Butch became partners and eventually tried to go straight together in South America.

And they succeeded.

For a while.

By today's standards, Sundance's family seems dysfunctional. Saying this, however, does not in any way pardon or excuse the decisions the gunman made throughout his life. Whatever he made of his early years on earth was done purely for excitement and easy money, and he paid dearly for his choices. But his upbringing may help explain them.

The Longabaugh family lived along the Schuylkill River and Canal in the neighboring towns of Mont Clare, Montgomery County, and Phoenixville, Chester County, Pennsylvania. Their ancestor, Conrad Langenbach, emigrated from Germany as an indentured servant, arriving in Philadelphia on December 24, 1772, aboard the brig *Morning Star*. Conrad's debt was released early, just in time for him to serve with the Northampton County Militia during the Revolutionary War. At the end of his service, Conrad settled in eastern Pennsylvania, some thirty miles north of Philadelphia. By the time he married Catharina in 1781, his surname had been through a variety of spellings and was phonetically Anglicized to Longabaugh. The Longabaugh union was blessed with seven children, the last one named Jonas Isaac, born in 1798 in Pennsylvania.

Jonas Longabaugh married Christiana Hillbert in 1821, and they had five children—Josiah, Nathaniel, Michael, Mary, and Margaret; a sixth baby was stillborn. Josiah, the oldest, was born June 14, 1822, in Montgomery County, Pennsylvania; he married Annie G. Place, the daughter of Deacon Henry and Rachel (Tustin) Place, on August 11, 1855, in Phoenixville. They also had five children—Elwood Place, born June 21, 1858; Samanna, born April 22, 1860; Emma T., born in 1863; Harvey Sylvester, born May 19, 1865; and Harry Alonzo, born in the spring of 1867.[9]

Josiah was not particularly ambitious; he never owned property or held a job for any length of time. He was drafted for service in the Civil War and was later granted a pension for "general debility," a politically correct way of saying he had hemorrhoids.[10] Annie, however, worked hard to make a home for her family; she was very religious and extremely strict.

For years, the family moved from one rented house to another, almost annually. They seemed to relocate each time Josiah changed jobs, from day laborer and carpenter to farmhand; but they always stayed in the neighboring towns of Mont Clare and Phoenixville. When Harry was born, the family was living in half of a duplex located at 122 Jacobs Street in Mont Clare. The duplex backed up to the Schuylkill Canal, where Josiah was then working.

The towns of Phoenixville and Mont Clare were solidly blue-collar with a broad mix of Italian, Irish, and German immigrants. Phoenixville, the home of the Phoenix Iron Company, was a typical mill town. The company board members also served as officers of the Iron Bank. They donated a large tract of land for a town park; they underwrote a general store for employees only; they bought out a failing nail-manufacturing company to save local jobs; and they donated free family housing to workers who volunteered to serve in the Union Army.

In contrast to the working-class mix of laborers was the impressive leadership at the Phoenix Iron Company, which included future politicians such as Governor Samuel Pennypacker; inventors, including John Griffen; and military men. Beginning in 1861, the Phoenix began manufacturing "the Griffen wrought iron cannon, an arm made by welding together bars laid longitudinally, transversely and spirally, and which, on trial in the field, proved to be peculiarly durable and effective. About twelve hundred of these guns were supplied" to the US government. As the Griffen gun "gained the reputation of being the best arm of the kind in the service and were more generally used in the light artillery than any other" weapon, it also reflected well upon the town of Phoenixville. Both the town and the company prospered.[11]

Although it's doubtful that any of the Longabaugh family members worked for the Phoenix, the atmosphere in such a company town influenced everyone. Half a mile away, across the covered bridge from Phoenixville, the village of Mont Clare was a boatman's community. While a few of the local residents walked over to the mills, the majority worked along the canal. Because Josiah worked along the waterway, the entire Longabaugh family was strongly influenced by life on the canal. Originally built to facilitate the shipping of coal from upstate Pennsylvania to Philadelphia, the canal also serviced local communities in the shipment of farm products and iron.

Harry's uncle, Michael, who owned a large home in Mont Clare, had his own canal boats and merchandised the products he shipped out of a small store in Phoenixville. His boats often carried coal and other local products to ports as distant as Boston, New York, Erie, and Scranton. At one time, each of the Longabaugh brothers, including Harry, worked for Uncle Michael, prodding the mules along the canal and poling the boats on the river.

According to the 1880 federal census records, by the time Harry and his brother Harvey were teenagers, Josiah had sent them out of the home to work as hired servants, boarding with their employers. Samanna had already married and was out of the house, but Elwood and Emma were unemployed and still living with their parents. No one today seems to know why the older siblings never worked while the two younger boys were earning their keep in the outside world.

The census records indicate that Harry, age thirteen, was boarding with the Wilmer Ralston family in West Vincent Township, Chester County, about ten miles from his parents' home. Ralston owned over one hundred acres of farmland and raised horses. It was at the Ralstons' ranch that young Harry first learned to work with horses, a trade that proved quite useful in later years.

By 1882, Harry had moved back home with his parents, who were then living at 354 Church Street in Phoenixville. He attended the First Baptist Church there, where the family worshipped and where his maternal grandfather, Henry Place, was a respected deacon. He attended the nearby Gay Street School just three blocks away. Despite only sporadic schooling, Harry was well read. He owned his own library card, purchased at the price of one dollar and issued on January 31, 1881. He probably began reading novels at about the time that his oldest brother, Elwood, left home in 1882 and became a whaler aboard the *Mary & Helen* out of Maine, bound for California, most likely via Cape Horn. Elwood was based out of the San Francisco Bay area, and the Pinkerton Detective Agency recorded that, in later years, Harry and Elwood were in frequent contact with one another.[12]

Samanna, Harry's oldest sister, married Oliver Hallman, a self-employed wrought-iron worker who had apprenticed under John

Griffen, and they had already begun a family. In his youth, Sundance had developed a close and long-lasting relationship with Samanna; she was the sibling who stayed most in touch with him over the years. In fact, the Pinkerton Detective Agency recorded her home address in their files and paid a postal clerk to open her mail and watch her home from the Mont Clare post office a few doors away.

Using his new agency, Pinkerton worked closely with the railroads to capture holdup men and to organize a guard force onboard the trains. During the 1850s, he made a name for himself doing undercover work. Then, in February 1861, Pinkerton discovered a plot to assassinate President-elect Lincoln. Soon thereafter, President Lincoln asked Pinkerton, using the alias of Major E. J. Allen, to close the North Western Police Agency and set up a Union spy system for the government. In later years, this same system became the Federal Secret Service, which in turn served as a primary concept for the Federal Bureau of Investigation.

After the Civil War, Pinkerton opened a new agency, named Pinkerton's National Detective Agency, which used an open eye for its logo along with the motto "We never sleep." He took fierce pride in his work and the agency's accomplishments and once wrote, "I do not know the meaning of the word 'fail.' Nothing in hell or heaven can influence me when I know that I am right."[13]

Ironically, it was this very unwavering preoccupation with success that put Pinkerton's methods in question. With Pinkerton's death in 1884, his sons William and Robert stretched their legal practices to the limit. In a 1921 letter, William A. Pinkerton wrote, "We did have to do with the breaking up of the 'Wild Bunch' and the killing off of a number of them." Another unsigned letter stated, "We hope someday to apprehend these people in this country or through our correspondents get them killed in the Argentine Republic."[14] They became desperate in their cause; they wanted these outlaws at any cost.

Expenses for the Pinkertons were usually paid by the American Bankers Association, the Union Pacific Railroad, the Great Northern Railroad, and other large companies. However, "on one occasion at the agency's expense . . . [the Pinkertons] sent an official from the New York Office to the Argentine Republic to endeavor to get information and locate the remaining members of this band. . . . The American Bankers Association would not permit the expense. And therefore we have been keeping a run on these people in our own way."[15]

"In their own way" meant hiring undercover detectives and paying informants themselves. The informants included postal clerks whose jobs included opening mail and forwarding information to the agency. One of their best undercover agents, Charlie Siringo, managed to infiltrate the gang in the guise of a fugitive from Texas. This provided him with information from Harvey Logan's family in Montana and from Sundance's friends in Wyoming. His reports became part of the dossiers that the agency opened on each Wild Bunch outlaw.

Sundance's sister Emma was also listed in these Pinkerton files. She had become a successful businesswoman in a day when women's rights and independence were rare. By the 1890s, she owned a seamstress business, McCandless and Longabaugh, which did piecework for the well-known John Wanamaker's Department Store in Philadelphia. Family members recalled Emma as a spinster and the most austere member of the family. In time, she changed the spelling of her name to Longabough because having an outlaw for a brother was not good for business. But the Pinkertons knew where she lived and worked and entered the information into their growing dossier on her brother, no matter how she spelled her name.

Sundance's brother Harvey was a day laborer and a carpenter like their father, and his business sign is still owned by the family today. In 1902, according to Pinkerton Detective Agency records, Sundance visited a beach resort in Atlantic City, New Jersey, at a time when Harvey was doing carpentry work on the now-famous boardwalk.

Years earlier, at the age of fourteen, Harry traveled by canal boat with his Uncle Michael to find a new job. His sister Samanna kept her husband's business books and made occasional personal notations among the purchase orders. She wrote, "Phoenixville June 1882—Harry A. Longabaugh left home to seek employment in Ph. [Philadelphia]. And from their [sic] to N.Y.C. from their [sic] to Boston and from their [sic] home on the 26 of July or near that date."[16]

However, Harry was apparently unsuccessful because Samanna's next entry reads, "Phoenixville Aug. 30th 1882 Harry A. Longabaugh left home for the West. Left home at 14 [years old]—Church St. Phoenixville below Gay St."[17] Harry boarded the train at the Phoenixville depot less than a mile from his home. He traveled alone, past Horseshoe Curve in western Pennsylvania, and headed for the West he had read about so often.

Harry landed a job helping his distant cousin, George Longenbaugh, who, with his pregnant wife and young son Walter, had moved west from Illinois to Colorado by covered wagon. According to descendants, George originally moved his family to Durango, Colorado, where he worked with the town's new irrigation system before being drawn to homesteading land fifty miles west, near Cortez, Colorado. Harry helped George and his family work the ranch until early 1886, also working occasionally for Henry Goodman, the foreman of the LC Ranch in nearby McElmo Canyon. During Harry's time with his cousin, he became a horse wrangler and learned how to purchase and breed good horseflesh, trades he would put to good use after leaving the Longenbaugh ranch.

During his stay in Cortez, Sundance met some of his future outlaw partners. The Madden brothers lived in Mancos, within a day's ride from the ranch. Bill Madden partnered with Sundance for a train robbery in Malta, Montana, in 1892. Outlaw Tom McCarty had a hideout less than a mile from the Longenbaugh family ranch.

Cortez, situated some seventy-five miles from Telluride, played home to both Willard Erastus Christianson, later known as Matt Warner, and Robert LeRoy Parker, alias Butch Cassidy. Together, Butch, Warner, and McCarty often raced horses for money in McElmo Canyon and Telluride.

Although no one knows when or where young Harry actually met these outlaws, there were at least two possible occasions when it might have happened near Cortez, while Harry lived there with his cousin George. While working for the LC Ranch, Harry often had reason to ride herd over the sprawling lands of McElmo Canyon. Since horse racing was common there, he likely attended at least one or two such events.

Another possibility may have involved a squabble between Henry Goodman's ranch hands and the herders working for the rival Carlisle

Ranch in nearby Monticello, Utah. Harry was working for Goodman at the time, and Dan Parker, Butch's younger brother, was working for the Carlisle. Some Goodman sheep were stolen and slaughtered, and the hides were hung out to dry; one report claims Parker was to blame. When Carlisle happened upon the skins, he ordered his foreman, Len Scott, to hide them out of sight in an old cabin in town.

Later, a Goodman ranch hand, in town for a local dance, noticed the skins and reported the theft to Goodman. However, Parker reportedly saw what was happening, and he quickly switched the Goodman hides for some with the Carlisle brand. When Goodman arrived on the scene to investigate, he saw only Carlisle skins and immediately ordered their return, bringing the confusing situation to an end. Both Harry and Dan Parker may very well have been involved, and Harry could have met Dan and his brother Butch then. Regardless, by that time, Harry had already embarked upon a trail destined to clash with the law, and he knew it.

For outlaws on the run, there were no better places to cool their heels than Hole-in-the-Wall, Brown's Park, Powder Springs, and Robbers Roost, all major hideouts spread out along what came to be called the Outlaw Trail. Connected by a winding, meandering cattle way running from Canada to the Mexican border, the hideouts provided safe harbor between jobs and over winter. For the most part, they were well known by outlaws and too well defended for the law to approach.

The Hole-in-the-Wall was initially used by rustlers for herding stolen cattle and horses. Located sixteen miles from Kaycee, Wyoming, and named after the KC Ranch owned by rustler Nate Champion, who was killed during the Johnson County Cattle War of 1892, the Hole was strewn with remote cabins. While there was no actual town there, there was in fact no real hole either, only a narrow notch through which horses and cattle could be driven. Outlaws could see for miles in any direction from the top of the wall, and a mere handful of men could hold off a posse of a hundred or more for days.

George Sutherland "Flat Nose" Currie headed a small gang of cattle rustlers who worked out of the Hole-in-the-Wall. He was part of the Red Sash Gang that headquartered in Kaycee, but he soon turned to holding up banks with Harvey Logan and other lesser-known Wild

Bunch members. It was in the Hole-in-the-Wall that Sundance probably met Flat Nose, and he almost certainly spent time there with Harvey Logan and Butch.

In her history of the Hole-in-the-Wall, local historian Thelma Gatchell wrote, "Longabaugh like Cassidy was happy-go-lucky, courageous and liked by all who knew him. He was also tall, good looking and dark complexioned with a smart mustache, very temperate in his drinking, and never a killer. It was said that Cassidy, Logan, and Longabaugh were the 'Big Trio' of the Hole-in-the-Wall gang."[18]

A two- or three-day ride south from the Hole opens up to Brown's Park, a forty-mile by six-mile valley that straddles the tristate corners of Wyoming, Colorado, and Utah. Located on the Green River, it's surrounded by Douglas, Diamond, and Cold Spring Mountains, and it was already a populated valley during the era of the outlaws. Offering mild winters, good grazing, and state lines that raised invisible barriers against pursuing lawmen, the area provided seasonal ranch work with friendly families living in the park. Most of the outlaws were welcomed as long as they behaved. One local story recounts the Outlaws' Thanksgiving dinner around 1895, during which Sundance, Butch, and a few other roustabouts played host to the community, serving a complete, traditional turkey dinner. The local families brought their finest linens, dishes, and silver for the meal and even arrived dressed in their Sunday finery!

Sundance greeted the guests at the hitching post of the Davenport Ranch on Willow Creek. Once the locals had all arrived, he and Butch put on white butcher's aprons and served their guests an elegant dinner. The party lasted until midmorning and included local entertainment comprised of music and dancing. Ann Bassett, a young teen at the time, later claimed that Sundance was tall, blond, and handsome and that he had the young girls thoroughly enchanted the entire evening.[19]

Another favorite outlaw layover was just over Douglas Mountain at the homestead of Willard Erastus Christianson, alias Matt Warner, one of the men who held up the bank in Telluride in 1889. His land bordered the Wyoming hideout known as Powder Springs. Sundance knew the area well because he spent two years working less than forty miles away for Al Reader of Savery, Wyoming. Even closer was the Reader Cabin

Draw, where Sundance kept the Reader herd during the winter months. A local newspaper wrote, "Reader's outfit left last Monday for the lower country for the winter. Bert Charter, Harry Alonzo, and Mr. Filbrick were with the horses."[20]

While Powder Springs remained a safe haven for local rustlers, Butch and his Wild Bunch overstayed their welcome in the late 1890s, and the law turned up the heat on the area. The hideout is made up of the upper and the lower springs, both of which once housed outlaw cabins. It was in an ideal location, according to author Donna B. Ernst, because,

> *In addition to its ideal location between the Hole in the Wall and Brown's Park, Powder Springs also offered a visible marker of safety. Powder Springs happens to be within sight of Wyoming State Mile Marker no. 223, which was placed along the forty-first parallel when the boundary between the Territory of Wyoming and the future state of Colorado was surveyed in August of 1873. That five-foot marker provided a clear definition of safety to those hiding at the springs; it meant the law could not reach them. The Springs became much more popular with the [Wild Bunch] gang after the law invaded the Hole in the Wall in July 1897.[21]*

The last major hideout along the Outlaw Trail was Robbers Roost, located in the high desert canyons of Utah midway between Moab and Hanksville. Aside from the Green and Colorado Rivers that border the Roost, the area suffers from a severe lack of water. The Roost's intimidating and twisting canyons protected the outlaws by discouraging the law from entering.

One lawman whom the Roost *didn't* faze was Sheriff Tom Fares, who followed Tom McCarty, Matt Warner, and Butch Cassidy into the Roost before losing his way in a maze of dry-wash canyons. Warner got the drop on him, took his gun, and gave him a water canteen before heading him out of the Roost. Unfortunately, Fares mumbled something about returning to get his man, which made Warner angry. The outlaws took Fares's saddle and pants and sent him riding bareback toward Hanksville in just his underpants.[22]

With its proximity to his cousin's home in Cortez, Sundance most likely knew of the Roost before learning of the other stops along the trail. Certainly, Butch Cassidy's mentor, Mike Cassidy, must have run his rustled beeves through the Roost more than once.

One of the less popular places to hole up along the Outlaw Trail was near Malta and Culbertson, Montana, just south of the Canadian border on the N Bar N range. Both Sundance and Harvey Logan had run with a local gang of rustlers there years earlier.

Dutch Henry Ieuch was the leader of a gang who often joined the Nelson-Jones Gang under the leadership of Frank Jones. The headquarters for both bands was just north of Culbertson, which was convenient for frequent raids into Canada. Years later, Sundance often used the name Frank Jones as an alias. In June 1900, J. D. B. Grieg, an informant from Malta, Montana, and editor of the *Harlem Enterprise*, wrote the Pinkerton Detective Agency to inform them about some outlaws operating nearby.

> *About Culbertson there are a couple of fellows, ex-cowboys . . . [who] formerly worked for the N-N outfit that are outlaws and fugitives from justice. There is another party named Logenbough [sic] who was supposed to have been implicated in the holdup which occurred at Malta a number of years ago. Some people here think he is one of the Jones or Roberts boys. . . . They rustle cattle and horses, do many misdeeds and either hide in Canada or across the border.[23]*

The Outlaw Trail included one final stop near the Mexican border, a favorite locale for outlaws on the run. Although not officially part of the trail, the WS Ranch in Alma, New Mexico, run by Captain William French, served the same purpose. French didn't realize that a number of his ranch hands were wanted men and members of Butch Cassidy's Wild Bunch. He knew only that when Jim Lowe (Butch) was around, his herds weren't disturbed and his ranch ran smoothly. Grateful for the superb job Lowe had done, French was happy to hire any of Butch's friends who came along looking for work.

One day in 1899, following the Wilcox train robbery, Pinkerton agent Frank Murray showed up on the trail of the stolen loot. Captain French was shocked to learn that one of his best hands was actually an outlaw, but it certainly explained the almost constant comings and goings of Butch and his other ranch "hands."

The WS Ranch was a perfect hideout for outlaws on the run. The rail line and nearby state boundaries provided quick, effective escape routes from the law. So, after leaving his cousin's ranch in Cortez, Sundance drifted north through Colorado and into Wyoming, taking whatever work he could find. Spring was a good time for experienced wranglers to hire on. Horses needed to be broken, and cattle had to be rounded up, counted, and branded. Harry did all that and, for his expertise, was paid well.

On April 20, 1886, Harry was hired for thirty-five dollars a month by the Suffolk Cattle Company of Crook (now Weston) County, Wyoming. The ranch was located thirty miles northwest of the town of Lusk, where another of Harry's distant cousins resided.

Ellsworth Eugene Longabaugh (most often called E. E.), Harry's fourth cousin, had the same grandfather as George Longenbaugh and was a good friend of the town's founding father, Frank Lusk. Together, E. E. and Lusk had worked the local mines and laid out a town in 1886. E. E. hung out his shingle, advertising himself as a lawyer. However, an incident involving Harry may have hastened E. E.'s departure for the growing city of Sheridan, Wyoming.

According to a letter written by Sam W. Mather, a coworker at the Suffolk Cattle Company at the time, Harry was a hotheaded youngster:

In the eighties I was working for the Suffolk Cattle Co., of Wyoming. Their ranch, the AV, was located on the Cheyenne river at the mouth of Lodge Pole. . . . A boy about 18 years old, came to the ranch hunting work; he said his name was Harry Longbaugh [sic] and that he was from Colorado. Our foreman, J. B. Crawford, put him to wrangling horses, and the first week on the round-up he whipped three horse wranglers about the best grazing ground for our remuda, and came very near whipping our Dutch cook for calling him Longboy. After *that the cooks and horse-wranglers did not step on his toes. He got on fine until we got back to the ranch, when the sheriff from Lusk, Wyoming, arrested him for robbing an old man of $80, but he got away that night.*[24]

Although Mather's letter says that Harry worked for the Suffolk Company for a few weeks, records show that Crawford issued Harry a check for $1.25 for a single day's work on April 21, 1886. Although no explanation was given for Harry's impromptu departure, robbery would undoubtedly have provided justification for his dismissal.

The Home Land & Cattle Company, known as the N Bar N, began operations on September 15, 1885, as a Missouri company owned by brothers William F. and Frederick G. Niedringhaus. Their move into the exploding cattle business came on the heels of profits taken from their St. Louis enamelware manufacturing company and Utah silver-mining ventures, making them men for all seasons.

The brothers used their proceeds to buy out the Anchor THL Ranch, located near Miles City, Montana, from Major Thomas H. Logan of Fort Keough, Wyoming. The brothers then chose their initials of N-N as their primary brand to signify the close relationship between the two. N-N quickly translated into N Bar N.

The N Bar N began with nearly six thousand head of cattle that grazed on the open range between Wolf Point and Rock Creek in northern Montana, stretching south to ranch headquarters at Miles City. The company eventually owned ranching spreads from Saskatchewan, Canada, to Clayton, New Mexico, all under the banner of the N Bar N Ranch. Soon a third brother, H. L. Niedringhaus, joined the business to oversee the purchase of both horses and cattle. By the end of 1886, the N Bar N reported an amazing 65,000 head of cattle on their northern range.

During that 1886 expansion, a drive of seventeen thousand cattle trailed north from Perico Creek, New Mexico, to Little Dry Creek, Montana. On the employment records of the N Bar N at the time: a man named Harry A. Longabaugh.

But Harry's timing was terrible. The brutal winter of 1886–1887 became known as "the Big Die Up." The N Bar N lost between twenty thousand and forty thousand head of cattle to the freezing ice and snow, and several cowboys were laid off, including Harry. The Niedringhaus brothers hung on but barely.

After leaving that job, Harry drifted to South Dakota's Black Hills, where he worked for food and shelter and little else.

> *I have always worked for an honest living; was employed last summer by one of the best outfits in Montana and don't think they can say aught against me, but having got discharged last winter I went to the Black Hills to seek employment—which I could not get—and was forced to work for my board a month and a half, rather than to beg or steal. I finally started back to the vicinity of Miles City, as it was spring, to get employment on the range.[25]*

They were beautiful, inspirational words, but when Harry headed back to the N Bar N in hopes of obtaining a better job, he ran into trouble on the Triple V Ranch. That trouble would mark him for the rest of time.

The Triple V was situated in the northeastern corner of Wyoming, where it bumps shoulders with South Dakota and Montana. The road Harry traveled between South Dakota's Black Hills and the N Bar N crossed right through the heart of the Triple V.

The ranch's horse camp and winter quarters were located on Crow Creek in an area of canyons and wide-open range just north of the town of Sundance, Wyoming. During the winter and spring of 1887, the ranch, also known as Western Ranches Ltd., was owned by a group of English investors under the management of John Clay and his assistant, Robert Robinson. Clay was very respected and influential in the area—a member of the exclusive Cheyenne Club and president of the well-known Wyoming Stock Growers Association.

On February 27, 1887, as Harry headed back to the N Bar N, he stole a light gray horse branded "Jon" on its left shoulder. He also filched a revolver and a saddle rig from Alonzo Craven of the Triple V Ranch. He continued northwest toward Miles City, while the employees of the ranch began a search for a "smooth-faced, grey-eyed boy" in possession of the stolen goods.[26]

After searching and failing to find food for two weeks, James Widner, an employee of the Triple V, rode into Sundance, Wyoming, the Crook County seat. Because the ranch sat on the border of Montana, South Dakota, and Wyoming, Widner opted for the closest county seat. On March 15, 1887, he filed charges with Sheriff James Ryan on behalf of himself and Alonzo Craven.

Ryan soon received word that Harry had been picked up outside Miles City. According to the *Sundance Gazette*, "Sheriff Ryan has gone to Miles City after the kid who stole Jim Widner's horse, on the head of Crow Creek in this county. He was caught there some time ago."[27] Ryan filed arrest papers in Miles City, resulting in the arrest and temporary incarceration of Harry Longabaugh in the small jail located on the north side of the new courthouse at Main and Seventh Streets.

On April 12, for reasons still not known, Ryan took young Harry to St. Paul, Minnesota, nearly seven hundred miles away, aboard the Northern Pacific Railroad. Even the newspaper commented on how unusual such a trip was. "Sheriff Ryan departed with the prisoner this morning bound for Sundance. The route taken by the sheriff would seem to be a long one; Miles City to St. Paul. St. Paul to the railroad terminus in the Black Hills and thence by stage to Sundance, a distance in all of nearly 2,000 miles. Sundance is less than 300 miles across country from here."[28] It seems logical that Ryan may have had personal business to conduct in the Twin Cities and, since Harry was in his custody, took him along under guard.

Regardless of the rationale, shortly after the two reached St. Paul, Ryan and Harry turned around and headed west to Rapid City, South Dakota, traveling again by train. But somewhere near Duluth, Minnesota, while Ryan was in the bathroom, Harry picked the locks of his shackles, slipped out of his handcuffs, and jumped off the moving train. Some researchers suggest that he may have had an accomplice; some go so far as to finger Butch Cassidy, who happened to be in the Miles City area at the time. Harry, though, was quite capable of picking locks to effect his escape without any help from others.[29]

After learning of the escape, Ryan summoned the conductor to stop the train and searched each car and the surrounding terrain, all to no avail. When he arrived back in Wyoming, he immediately posted a $250 reward. Ryan was undoubtedly frustrated, but not for long. Harry soon returned to the Miles City area, where Deputy Sheriff Eph K. Davis and stock inspector W. Smith caught up with him on June 6 on the N Bar Ranch in Powderville, Montana. The N Bar, owned by the Newman brothers, was a neighbor of the Niedringhauses' N Bar N, which Harry knew well. According to the *Big Horn Sentinel*, "Lombaugh [*sic*], the man who escaped from Sheriff Ryan of Sundance . . . [was] arrested at the Newman ranch, on Powder river."[30]

Davis and Smith handcuffed Sundance, shackling him to the wall of an N Bar line shack while they awaited the next stage. The regular route between Miles City and Deadwood ran past the line shack. It was there, on the N Bar Ranch, according to the newspaper, that Harry again picked his locks, giving birth to the story of Davis "playing possum."[31]

On Saturday Deputy Sheriff Davis, together with Stock Inspector Smith, made a most important arrest . . . near the N-bar ranch on Powder river. . . . After his escape from Sheriff Ryan he [Longabaugh] made his way back to Montana. . . . After Mr. Davis had made the arrest he took three six-shooters from the bold young criminal and shackled him and handcuffed him with some patent lock bracelets which were warranted to hold anything until unlocked by the key and which the manufacturers offered a premium if they could be opened otherwise. Eph Davis had heard a good deal of Longabaugh's prowess in effecting escape, and after taking all due precautions when night closed in upon them he lay down in one corner of a shack and Mr. Smith another, the kid between them. Smith was tired out and soon fell to sleep and Davis played "possum," keeping an eye on the prisoner. Soon as he thought everyone was asleep the kid, shackled and manacled as he was, managed to free himself and rising stealthily approached the window and raised it and was about to make a break for liberty when sly old Eph thought it was time for him to take a hand and raising on his elbow with a cocked six-shooter in his hand he said in a quiet tone of voice, "Kid, your [sic] loose, ain't you?" and then called to Smith. The kid dropped back as though he was shot and it is needless to add that the officers did not sleep at the same time during the rest of the night.[32]

Taking offense at the extent of the newspaper's accusations, Harry wrote a letter to the editor, who published his complaint on June 9.

In your issue of the 7th inst. I read a very sensational and partly untrue article, which places me before the public not even second to the notorious Jesse James. Admitting that I have done wrong and expecting to be dealt with according to law and not by false reports from parties who should blush with shame to make them, I ask a little of your space to set my case before the public in a true light. In the first place I have always worked for an honest living; was employed last summer by one of the best outfits in Montana and don't think they can say aught against me, but having got discharged last winter I went to the Black Hills to seek employment—which I could not get—and was forced to work for my board a month and a half, rather than to beg or steal. . . . I am aware that some of your readers will say my statement should be taken for what it is worth, on account of the hard name which has been forced upon me, nevertheless it is true. As for my recapture by Deputy Sheriff Davis, all I can say is that he did his work well and were it not for his "playing 'possum" I would now be on my way south, where I had hoped to go and live a better life.

Harry Longabaugh[33]

Sheriff Ryan arrived on June 19 to reclaim possession of his prisoner. The road that ran past the N Bar line camp was the old stage line throughway between Montana's Miles City and Deadwood, South Dakota. This time, Ryan and Harry traveled by stage. A local newspaper reported that "Longabaugh was securely shackled and handcuffed, the shackles being made of steel and riveted with steel rivets, and as they got aboard Ryan informed the kid that he was going to land him or his scalp in Sundance jail. The kid gave him fair warning that he intended to escape and told him to watch him but not to be too rough on him."[34]

They arrived in Sundance, Wyoming, on June 22, and Harry was placed in the new jail behind the courthouse, where he was held on a charge of grand larceny. Court records show that he listed his home state as Pennsylvania, his occupation as cowboy, his height as six feet, and his age as twenty-six, although he was only twenty. But the clerk who wrote down the information had a sloppy hand and often wrote his zeroes to look like sixes. The records further show Harry claimed no living parents. His mother, Annie, did die the month before, although curiously enough, his father, Josiah, was still alive.[35]

True to his word, Harry continued his attempts to escape while awaiting trial. He and fellow inmate William McArthur managed to remove a bolt from the hinge of their cell door, but it was discovered before they made their escape. Finally, on August 3, 1887, Harry Long-abaugh was indicted on three counts of grand larceny:

True Bill # 33—Indictment for Grand Larceny. One horse of the value of Eighty Dollars ($80.00) of the personal goods and Chattels of Alonzo Craven then and there being found, then and there feloniously did steal, take and carry away, ride away, drive away and lead away contrary to the form of the Statute in such case made and provided and against the peace and dignity of the Territory of Wyoming.

True Bill # 34—Indictment for Grand Larceny. [The details and description are missing.]

True Bill # 44—Indictment for Grand Larceny. One Revolver of the value of thirty Dollars of the personal goods and Chattels of James Widner, then and there feloniously, did steal, take and carry away contrary to the form of the Statute in such case made and provided and against the peace and dignity of the Territory of Wyoming.[36]

The prosecuting attorney in the case was Benjamin F. Fowler, who later became a US attorney for Wyoming from 1890 to 1894 and the state's attorney general from 1895 to 1898. On August 4, Judge William L. Maginnis appointed attorney Joseph Stotts to represent Harry.

On August 5, Harry pleaded not guilty. But Stotts convinced him to reverse one plea—the one to horse stealing as defined in indictment no. 33—in exchange for the other two indictments being dropped. A transcript of his court appearance states,

The defendant Harry Longabaugh was this day again brought before the court, and having been asked by the court if he had anything to say why judgement and sentence should not be pronounced against him upon the plea of guilty in this cause says he has nothing to say; the court thereupon pronounced sentence upon said plea as follows: the sentence of the court is that you HARRY LONGABAUGH be confined in the place designated by the penitentiary commissioner of the Territory of Wyoming as a penitentiary for the term of eighteen months at hard labor.[37]

Because of Harry's young age, his place of confinement was changed from the penitentiary at Laramie to the county jail in Sundance, Wyoming.

Naturally, in keeping with his free-spirited nature, Harry wasn't convinced he would serve out his sentence. On May 1, 1888, he and a fellow prisoner assaulted the jailor in an attempt to escape. The *Sundance Gazette* reported,

Just before 6 o'clock, as Jailor Daley was taking supper to the prisoners in the county jail, he was suddenly assaulted in the hallway by Jim O'Connor and Harry Longabaugh, two of the prisoners who had effected their escape from the cells. Mr. Daley grappled Longabaugh (the "kid") and succeeded in overpowering him and returned him to his cell. . . . Longabaugh, or "the kid" is the slippery cuss who gave Sheriff Ryan so much trouble, while bringing him to this place from Miles City. He is serving out a sentence of 18 months for stealing a horse on Crow creek two years ago.[38]

O'Connor succeeded in escaping but was soon apprehended and returned to jail.

Despite Harry's escape attempt, H. A. Alden, then Crook County prosecutor, wrote to Governor Thomas Moonlight and to Colin Hunter, the secretary of the Board of the Prison Commission, requesting a pardon for Harry. The January 22, 1889, letter said, "We have forwarded to the Governor a petition for the pardon of Harry Longabaugh whose term will expire on the 5th of February. I should have sent it to you but fearing that you might be away from home and not get it in time I forwarded it directly to him. The Sheriff tells me that you will assist in obtaining a pardon so that the boy may be restored to his civil rights."[39]

On February 4, just one day before his scheduled release, Harry was granted a full pardon by the governor. "He is still under 21 years of age, and his behavior has been good since confinement, showing an earnest desire to reform. . . . Therefore, I do hereby grant unto Harry Longabaugh a full and complete pardon."[40] However, because of the short time between the signed pardon and his release, it is not known whether Harry ever learned of it.

On February 8, 1889, the *Sundance Gazette* wrote, "The term of 'Kid' Longabaugh expired on Tuesday morning, and the young man at once hired himself to the Hills, taking the coach for Deadwood."[41] While this should have been the last the town of Sundance ever heard of young Harry, it wasn't. According to the *Sundance Gazette*, Buck Hanby, a cowboy from nearby Newcastle, Wyoming, was wanted for murder by authorities in Greeley County, Kansas. He had recently returned from Nebraska, where he'd been exonerated of another murder indictment. On May 17, 1889, Sheriff E. B. Armstrong and Deputy Sheriff James Swisher of Crook County located Hanby in a dugout on Oil Creek, about thirty-five miles south of Sundance, with three other young men, including Harry Longabaugh. When Hanby was ordered to surrender, he reached for his gun and was killed by Swisher and Armstrong. On May 18, Swisher swore out a complaint against Harry because he feared retaliation for Hanby's death. The warrant was filed on May 24, and Harry was arrested, although there's no indication in the records of any trial, so he either escaped or skipped bail.[42]

At last, Harry Alonzo Longabaugh had made the final transition to outlaw. He was officially known as the Sundance Kid. Denver's

Rocky Mountain News headlined its lead story, "The Robbery of the San Miguel Valley Bank of Telluride on Monday by Four Daring Cowboys." It reported that "the four rode over to the bank, and leaving their horses in charge of one of the number, two remained on the sidewalk and the fourth entered the bank."[43]

One of the robbers was very likely Harry Longabaugh, the Sundance Kid. Another was Robert LeRoy Parker, aka Butch Cassidy. Thus was born the criminal duo of Butch Cassidy and the Sundance Kid. Whether or not Harry had already met and worked with Butch is unknown. What is absolutely clear, however, is that the two were bound together by their personalities, their values, and their goals: They were born to become robbers. And soon enough, they would prove to the world just how true this was.

CHAPTER 7

Robert LeRoy Parker

Mr. Max. Parker, who lives about one and a half miles from the town of Circleville, east of Beaver, was returning home about 3 o'clock Tuesday morning from a social gathering held in Circleville. He had his wife and a two year old child with him in his buggy. The night was dark and it seems that as the team was jogging along one wheel of the vehicle struck a rock, thus throwing Mrs. Parker, who also held the child, out of her seat. As she went out of the buggy she threw the little one, which, by the way, was not injured in the least.
—BEAVER SOUTHERN UTONIAN, BEAVER, UTAH, APRIL 20, 1888

ETTA PLACE WAS STILL A YOUNG CHILD OF SIX OR SEVEN WHEN ROBERT Parker prepared to leave his Circleville home in Utah. She would have liked the young man—his devotion, dedication, work ethic, and cheery disposition, not to mention his innate sense of morality—but she was still years away from meeting the man who would lead the last and, in many ways, the most notorious band of outlaws the American West had ever seen.

Young Robert's mother was like any other Mormon mother, only more so. She did her best to raise her son well, to educate him in the dogma of the church, and to prepare him for that fateful day when he would grow up and leave home to start a family of his own—Mormon, naturally.

But even as she knew that day would come, she still dreaded it. Little Robert was her firstborn. And when at last he turned eighteen in 1844 and had grown into a fine young man, he was still a small boy in his mother's eyes. As he would always be.

After making sure he had warm clothes and a blanket, plus enough foodstuffs to see him through a week or more out on the trail, she tied together his bedroll filled with provisions. As she watched him cinch it to his animal and pause to kiss her goodbye, she fought back her tears. He, too, tried to hide his emotions with less than admirable success.

Finally, his mother slipped a copy of the Book of Mormon into his saddlebag and stepped back to watch as her son climbed aboard his mare, Babe, and grabbed the lead of his colt, Cornish. With that, he turned the horses toward the road, and soon they were little more than a speck of dust on the horizon.

According to sister Lula, Robert first "left home at 13 and went to Rock Springs, Wyo, where he worked in a butcher shop for a spell. That's how he come onto the nickname Butch."[1]

Utah rancher Patrick Ryan, who hired Bob Parker in 1879 as a hired hand when the lad was still only thirteen, said the boy could already do a man's work around a ranch. Although Ryan thought young Bob was a little impatient with the horses, the boy was otherwise quiet and inoffensive. Ryan found him to be smart and dependable but, most of all, family oriented. Bob knew his parents needed whatever money their son could earn at the ranch to help raise the family. He got along well with his employer, and the rancher was sorry to see him leave two years later when Bob found work at a ranch closer to home.[2]

Bob's parents, Maximillian and Ann Gillies Parker, had moved their brood of six children from Beaver, Utah, to near Circleville the year Bob turned thirteen. At the time, the town consisted of little more than a few stores and a schoolhouse, nestled against the convergence of Cottonwood Creek and the Sevier River in what is now southern Piute County. The Parker property, all 160 acres, lay three miles south of town at the mouth of Circleville Canyon near the southern edge of the valley, which was then a rural conclave of hardworking Mormons struggling to make a living from crops and cattle on parched Utah land that never ceased crying out for water.

Butch's grandfather, Robert Parker, had been a weaver in Preston, England. Educated and successful, he must have felt his life missing something, because he often invited Mormon elders to stay at his home. Before long, he'd been converted to the new faith by missionaries who preached an earthly land of opportunity, as well as a new religion. To the men of limited opportunities in England, the pitch must have been too good to resist.

Robert Parker sold his home and set out with his family for the new Zion early in the spring of 1856. Besides their son Maximillian, the Parkers had a five-year-old son named Dan, a seven-year-old daughter, and a baby girl. They came with the Second Handcart Company aboard the ship, *Enoch Train*, named after its owner, and after a seven-week ocean voyage, they went by train to Iowa City, where they set out for Utah, more than one thousand miles away, pushing a handcart. According to author Pearl Baker,

> *The first group left early in the spring and came through in pretty good shape, men, women and children walking all the way. The Parkers were in the Second Company, arriving in Salt Lake City in September. The Gillies family came in a wagon train late that year, arriving in Utah probably in December. . . . They settled in Woods Cross, and the Parkers moved to American Fork, where Robert Parker taught school. The next spring both families were called by the Church leaders to move to Beaver—Robert Gillies to help build the houses of the new community as he was a carpenter and cabinet maker, and Robert Parker to help set up a woolen mill in Beaver.*
>
> *A few years later Parker was called to Washington, Utah, where the mild climate of Utah's "Dixie" produced cotton and mulberry trees upon which silkworms were being nourished. He was to set up a cotton mill, which would also take care of the silk production. After the dream of a cotton empire faded because it cost three times as much to raise cotton and process it as to ship the cloth in, Parker was put in charge of the co-op store, which had run into difficulties. He was an organizer and businessman, and soon had the store running profitably.[3]*

Max Parker and Ann Gillies met in America sometime in the early 1860s and were married in 1865. Robert LeRoy, their first child, was born on April 13 of the following year. During their early married life, Max carried the mail on horseback from Beaver south to Panguitch, Utah, along the Sevier River. During those runs, his route took him through Circle Valley. It was rough country and still only sparsely settled, but the few homesteaders who were there were friendly and honest people. Someday, Maximillian must have known, the valley would make an excellent place to raise a family. For him, that day finally arrived in the spring of 1879 when he and Ann packed up the children and what few belongings they had and headed south.[4]

The Parkers squeezed their family into a two-room log cabin that the former owner had built at the base of a small hill. That first year, Max cleared enough brush to plant a crop of summer wheat before the scorching days of July and August settled in. But soon after the planting, high winds destroyed everything in their path. Max planted a second crop, and it, too, was blown away by the biting gusts that roared in from the west over the northern edge of the appropriately named Hurricane Cliffs. With the loss of Max's second planting, only a few days remained before the grueling summer temperatures would end any chance of a growing season, but Max persisted in planting a third crop, and his efforts paid off.

With the wheat finally sprouted in the ground, Max went off to look for work, leaving Ann to care for the children and tend the Circle Valley Ranch. Most of Max's jobs consisted of temporary employment with mining companies. The 1880s were an erratic period in Utah's mining history, filled with promising strikes and overnight booms followed by inevitable busts. One of Max's first jobs was cutting and hauling wood at the Silver Reef Mine in the Pine Valley Mountains northeast of present-day St. George.

Pine Valley was nearly one hundred miles from Circle Valley, which allowed Max only an occasional Sunday visit home. Silver Reef, a town created by a non-Mormon mining company, was fierce and violent, soon grown famous for its drunken brawls and killings. But, for the most part, the Mormons who had moved in were recognized as hard workers and treated with respect by the gentiles, as the Mormons referred to them, who paid them better-than-average wages.

When the Silver Reef job played out, Max found similar work in the San Francisco Mountains at Frisco, a silver camp sixteen miles west of Milford, where New York financier Jay Cooke was building a new leg of the Utah Southern Railroad to reach a mine at Squaw Springs, which he had recently added to his investments' portfolio. Max again found himself a long way from home, but he was not far from Hay Springs, where Bob was helping out at Pat Ryan's ranch. For a while, Max also worked in nearby Pioche, Nevada, where he hauled wood for charcoal burners.

That fall, with Max's income and the pay that Bob brought home from his ranch work, the Parkers were able to buy a few head of cattle. But then came the winter of 1879, one of the worst in Utah in a decade, and all but two head of the Parker herd perished.

The loss of the cattle set the family back considerably, even as they continued to expand to include seven children—four boys and three girls. And there were more to come—fourteen children in all. Large families were common among Mormons, especially in southern Utah. Not only were they essential for rural families to scrape together a livelihood from the nearly barren earth, but they also fell in line with church doctrine, which proclaimed that a woman's highest glory in life was to honor her husband by giving birth to as many children as possible. The church, further deviating from the Christian fundamentals it claimed, decreed that a man's family went with him to the Hereafter and that a man's glory in Heaven would be dependent in part on the progeny that he could gather around him, seated beside him along with the other gods.

Desperate to make ends meet, Max attempted to homestead a second parcel of land, but his claim was challenged by another settler. The dispute ended up in the hands of the local Mormon bishop who, in the absence of civil law and according to church dictum, mediated the matter. The outcome was not favorable to the Parkers. While Ann was a devout member of the Latter-day Saints and attempted to raise the children according to Mormon law, her husband had occasionally wavered from official church doctrine. He had a poor attendance record at services. He also took up smoking and light drinking, both strictly prohibited by

Mormon teachings and frowned upon by the congregation. When the bishop decided against the Parkers on the homestead claim, Max was furious, convinced that his family was being punished for his own lax attitude toward the teachings of the Saints.

While the bishop may well have been prejudiced in his decision, the reason may not have been so cut-and-dry. Max, in the bishop's mind, had become too "land-wealthy." He already owned 160 acres, which was not a small parcel of land for a Circle Valley family at the time. By Mormon tradition, farming in the early 1880s was meant to be a small-scale, family operation. The bishop may have merely been following the dictates of Brigham Young, who had insisted that no man should own more land than he could cultivate personally.[5]

So, with the tides turned against them, Ann sought work with a neighboring rancher, Jim Marshall, operating his small dairy farm. Marshall also hired young Bob as a hand, which worked out well for the boy. The Marshall Ranch, located in what is now the northern edge of the Dixie National Forest, was much closer to the Parker home than Pat Ryan's ranch had been at nearly a day's ride from Circle Valley. Working Marshall's spread meant that Bob could live at home.

Ann was pleased to have her son back within the fold. While working for Ryan, the boy had run into trouble with the law. He had ridden into town to buy a pair of overalls. After a long, hot, dusty day on the trail, he found the store closed. Looking around, he discovered an open entryway, located the overalls he wanted, and left his name and an IOU for the owner. But when the owner opened the store the next morning, he was neither satisfied nor amused with the boy's persistence and filed a complaint with the town marshal. The matter was eventually settled, but not without a good deal of embarrassment to the Parker family.[6]

Another incident, according to Parley P. Christensen, who served thirty years as sheriff of Juab County, Utah, resulted in Bob's arrest for stealing a saddle. It happened in what is now Garfield County, probably between 1879 and 1884, although no records of the charges have been found. Christensen claimed that, while Bob was in custody awaiting a hearing, he had been mistreated by the authorities. The saddle's theft was subsequently confirmed in an interview with Pat Ryan by the *Salt Lake City Tribune* and the *Eastern Utah Advocate* on May 19, 1897.[7]

The mistreatment by the Garfield authorities and the impact on the family of the Mormon bishop's apparently biased decision in the dispute involving Max Parker's homestead claim ingrained within young Bob a disdain for the impartiality of the law. This may have instilled in him a desire to formulate his own rules of ethics regarding right and wrong.

Regardless, Bob's burgeoning problems with the judicial system came as a surprise, since he had been far from an unruly child. Still, while Ann tried to raise her children in the church, most of the boys followed in their father's footsteps, sidestepping the Saints' strict social and moral covenants whenever possible. Even before moving to Circleville from Beaver, young Bob found numerous reasons not to go to services, and eventually his mother gave up trying to force him.[8]

Meanwhile, Ann Parker's work running the dairy at the Marshall Ranch kept the family in milk, cheese, and butter while it brought in some much needed extra income, but her early morning, eight-mile ride to the ranch had become a problem. After discussing the matter with her employer, Ann decided that the practical thing to do was to move to the ranch, at least during the summer months, so she could get an early start on her daily chores. Bob was already working for Marshall as a hand, and Marshall agreed to hire two of Bob's younger brothers to help their mother with the dairy while allowing all four Parkers to live in a small house there. Naturally, Max wasn't overly thrilled with the idea, but he conceded in time that his daughters could keep house for him and that the extra money was worth whatever inconveniences the family might have to endure. With Max's tacit approval, Ann and the three boys moved to the Marshall Ranch in the summer of either 1881 or 1882.

Beginning as early as 1883, Bob Parker again ran up against the strong arm of the law, but this time, it was *with* his family's encouragement. A unique aspect of social life in early Mormon Utah was the church-sponsored practice of plural marriage, begun secretly by the Mormons before their migration west. In 1852, polygamy was officially sanctioned by church leaders as a moral right and a sacred responsibility. The practice, though, was not universally accepted, even among

Mormons, with some men unable to afford to take on more than one wife and extra mouths to feed. Among church leaders, though, the practice was widely accepted, even if conducted with a wink and a nod toward the leader's first wife.

Unfortunately for the church, polygamy in the United States had been declared illegal. In 1882, Congress passed the Edmunds Act, which pronounced the practice a felony punishable by up to five years' imprisonment and/or a $500 fine. Aimed specifically at Utah, which was then still a territory struggling to gain statehood and enhance the Mormon presence in the West, the law disenfranchised polygamists and rendered them ineligible for public office or even jury duty.

As a result, polygamous Mormons adopted various measures to elude federal officers, including constructing ingenious hiding places for their extra wives and children in their homes and on their lands. In rural southern Utah, they frequently escaped to hideouts in nearby canyons or were harbored by friends and neighbors until investigating marshals moved on. Polygamists formed "underground railroads" throughout the territory, complete with their own communication systems, secret codes, and warning devices.

Parker's family members may well have assisted in operating a branch of an underground railroad, temporarily concealing fleeing "polygs" before arranging for their eventual escape into Mexico. According to Utah writer Kerry Ross Boren—whose great-grandfather was supposed to have made use of the escape route through Circle Valley—young Bob Parker played an integral role in the operation.

Ann Parker and her sons had been boarding at the Marshall Ranch for nearly two years when owner Jim hired a new hand by the name of Mike Cassidy. Although only a few years older than Bob Parker, Cassidy had most likely drifted from ranch to ranch for some time. An experienced horse wrangler and skilled livestock handler, he and Bob struck a friendship, much to the dismay of Bob's mother, who saw in Cassidy a hardened cowboy who had been set out on his own too early and no doubt had acquired vices she preferred to keep from her son. On the other hand, Bob Parker saw in Mike Cassidy the man he'd always wanted to be—unrestrained and free to drift in any direction he chose whenever the whim struck him.

As suspicious as she was of the newcomer, even Ann likely underestimated Cassidy's history. By the time the wrangler had signed on at the Marshall Ranch, he was already an experienced livestock thief. Rustling was an ongoing problem in and around Circle Valley, especially when it came to picking off mavericks, or unbranded calves separated from their mothers, which rustlers would whisk away from the herd as soon as they could survive on their own. Worse still, when ranch owner Jim Marshall was not around, Cassidy and his cronies brought strays back to the ranch and rebranded them right there in Marshall's own corral—and young Bob most likely helped with the task. But as Bob's sister later commented, their mother accepted the fact that her responsibility ended at the dairy barn, and she could do little about what occurred on other parts of the ranch. But it was especially difficult for her when Cassidy went so far as to give her son a six-gun and taught him how to use it.[9]

Ann knew that lecturing Bob would be futile—he was old enough to do what he pleased—but she felt it might help if she could arrange to put some distance between Cassidy and her boy. So, in April 1884, she moved back to the Parker ranch in Circle Valley, hoping that Bob would follow. He didn't. Instead, the boy announced that June that he would be leaving Circle Valley and probably Utah. When Ann asked where he was going, he said he wasn't sure—perhaps to Colorado to work the mines in the mountains above Telluride. His reasons were endemic to Circle Valley families: "Ma, there's not much for me here. No future. Low pay. Maybe twenty or thirty dollars a month with board—and the board's not much to brag about! There's no excitement around here. I'm not a kid any more. Gotta be thinking about my future."[10]

Ann reminded her son that he was only eighteen, but he was ready for that gambit. He replied that most of his friends of the same age were out on their own, and many had already taken wives. Concerned that he might be roaring off on some desperado's spree with Cassidy, she confronted her son, and he told her that Cassidy had already left the ranch, most likely headed to Mexico. Bob emphasized that he and his friend, Eli Elder, would most likely ride over to Telluride together.[11]

When Bob announced his plans to leave, his father was still away and not expected back until the following evening. Knowing that Max would be disappointed to have missed seeing his son off, Ann tried to get the boy to postpone his trip by a day or two. But Bob knew that his father would understand his need to leave. After all, Max Parker had experienced those very feelings himself as a young boy and acted upon them. He had left his parents' home to guide Mormon emigration trains from St. Louis through the treacherous Rocky Mountains when he was no older than Bob. A few years later, he had married and gone to work dodging Ute arrows while carrying the mail along the rugged banks of the Sevier River. And only months after that, he was fighting alongside his fellow Mormons in Utah's Black Hawk War, the culmination of an ongoing dispute with the Utes over the occupation of their traditional hunting grounds.

Although for much of Bob's life Max Parker was away from home for weeks at a time, he always returned to be with his wife and family whenever he could. He never was ill-tempered with them or laid a hand on them in anger. His children had great respect for him, and when he spoke, they listened.

Nevertheless, young Bob was insistent: He should have left already and absolutely had to depart first thing the following morning. Although Ann must have wondered about Bob's hurry, she didn't question him as to why he was traveling so "light," with no pack animal or even a camp outfit to accompany him cross-country. But if Ann Parker failed to find it unusual that her son could not wait one more day to tell his father that he was leaving his house, others did not. There has been speculation, and some fact bears it out, that Bob Parker had good reason for a quick departure. He may have originally planned to work in the mines in Telluride as he said, but he most likely had a totally different job in mind while he prepared for his departure: to help deliver a herd of stolen horses to Telluride for notorious rustler Cap Brown.

Brown had drifted into southeastern Utah sometime in the 1870s, making his headquarters somewhere in the desolate Robbers Roost area, eastern Utah's high desert country of twisting canyons that lay between the Henry Mountains to the west and the La Sal Mountains to the east.

The area roughly formed the shape of a parallelogram: one border stretching southeastward along a line from the town of Hanksville to the place where the Dirty Devil River enters the Colorado. Another border runs northeasterly up the Colorado to the Green River. A third follows the Green River for fifty miles or so northwest to the San Rafael, while the fourth runs southwest across the San Rafael Desert back to Hanksville.[12]

Brown may not have been the first rustler to operate out of the Roost, but he was one of the most successful. Early in his career, he found profit in supplying horses to the mining communities of Colorado by raiding herds and capturing strays in southern Utah. At first, Brown operated mostly alone; in time, he recruited local wranglers in crews of three and four, mostly young cowboys eager to bolster their lowly pay. One cowboy whom Brown recruited was probably Mike Cassidy and, in time, another was more than likely Bob Parker.

Parker and Brown met around 1882, perhaps introduced by Cassidy at the Marshall Ranch, where Brown often stayed overnight during forays of hustling horses into Circle Valley and around the northern edge of what is now Dixie National Forest. They may also have met the following year when Bob worked as a cowhand for Charlie Gibbons of Hanksville on a ranch Gibbons owned near the Henry Mountains.

Several old-timers familiar with Robbers Roost suggest that a local rancher had hired Bob in the spring of 1884 to run twenty horses from Kingston Canyon six miles east of Circleville to nearby Hanksville, where Brown had a one-room shack. Brown was supposed to guide Bob and the herd east across Robbers Roost country toward the San Rafael Desert. From there, Brown was to take the herd across the Green River to Moab alone. If the Colorado River was swollen, he'd press on to owner Lester Taylor's ferry and cross the La Sal Mountains to the north before veering southeast to Telluride.[13]

According to Matt Warner, who later rode with Bob and joined him in the bank robbery at Telluride in 1889, "Bob was anxious" to leave his family in Circle Valley that night to keep his rendezvous with Cap Brown's hired men in Kingston Canyon. He was also anxious because he most likely had stolen some horses from a neighbor, Jim Kittleman, "earlier that day."[14]

Legend says that two lawmen, probably deputy marshals, caught him with Kittleman's stolen horses. Bob offered no resistance, but to play it safe, the officers handcuffed him before placing him in his saddle for the trip back to Circleville, which was the better part of a full day's journey. Around noon, the men stopped to rest and grab a bite to eat. While one deputy built a fire, the other went to a nearby creek for water. Seeing his chance, Bob sneaked up on the deputy by the fire and grabbed his gun. Catching the other man by surprise when he returned from the creek, Bob disarmed him, took his keys, and unlocked the handcuffs. In less than a minute, he had mounted up and was on his way, leading the stolen ponies and the lawmen's horses. But after riding only a short distance, he noticed the lawmen's canteens still tied to their saddles: he had left them without water for the long walk back to town. Bob turned around and rode back, tossed them their canteens, and bid them goodbye once more.[15]

To find out whether or not it happened just that way, Utah writer Kerry Ross Boren claims his grandfather, Willard Schofield, who had close ties to the Parker family, asked Bob about the story years later. Bob insisted it was true. According to Boren, Bob told his grandfather, "I've done a few things in my time, Willard, but I wouldn't leave nobody to die like that. Besides, a man don't know when he might need a favor himself someday."[16]

Kittleman *did* lose several horses that day, which he eventually recovered once Bob had departed Circle Valley. Although Bob was a suspect, his sister, Lula Parker Betenson, proclaimed her brother's innocence, saying, "Bob would as soon have stolen from his own father as from Jim Kittleman," who was a close friend, adding that one of Bob's "most outstanding virtues was his loyalty to friends and family." Lula admitted that Bob had ridden west to Kingston Canyon after leaving Circle Valley, but not to join forces with the rustlers. She said that he had told his mother "he met his friend, Eli Elder, who was to join him on his ride to Telluride to look for work together."[17]

The Kittleman horse theft was far from the only cloud hanging over Bob once he left Circle Valley that June. The following day, Max Parker was in Circleville and heard gossip that two local boys, identified only as Charley and Fred, were suspected of stealing cattle.

Ethel "Etta" Place posing for a studio portrait with her Tiffany's birthday watch, 1901.
LIBRARY OF CONGRESS

Harry A. Longabaugh De Young Photo Studio Portrait.
LIBRARY OF CONGRESS

Harry A. Longabaugh and Etta Place
posing for "wedding photo," c. 1900.
LIBRARY OF CONGRESS

Robert LeRoy Parker mug shot,
Wyoming Territorial Prison in
Laramie, WY.
AUTHOR'S COLLECTION

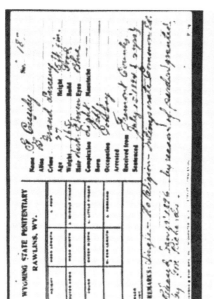

Butch Cassidy Wyoming State Penitentiary I.D. card, c. 1894.
AUTHOR'S COLLECTION

Wild Bunch Gang at Ft. Worth, Texas. Left to right: Harry Longabaugh (Sundance Kid), Will Carver, Ben Kilpatrick, Harvey Logan (Kid Curry), and Robert LeRoy Parker (Butch Cassidy), c. 1900.
AUTHOR'S COLLECTION

Unidentified visitors at Hole in the Wall, Wyoming, looking south toward Colorado.
LIBRARY OF CONGRESS

Earliest Wild Bunch gang members. Left to right:
Kid Curry, Bill McCarty, Bill (Tod) Carver, Ben
(Tall Texan) Kilpatrick, and Tom O'Day, c. 1892.
AUTHOR'S COLLECTION

Atlantic City Boardwalk, 1900, where Etta and Sundance frolicked on one of their trips to the East Coast.
AUTHOR'S COLLECTION

Tiffany Building, New York, c. 1900–1906.
LIBRARY OF CONGRESS

$5,000 Reward

WILL BE PAID FOR THE CAPTURE DEAD OR ALIVE OF

Harry Longabaugh

Age, 35 to 40 years

Complexion, dark
(looks like a quarter breed Indian)

Eyes, Black.

Features, Grecian type.

Height, 5 ft. 9 inches.

Nationality, American

Build, Rather slim

Color of Hair, Black.

Mustache, Black.

Occupation,
Cowboy, Rustler

ALIAS

"The Sundance Kid"

Harry Longabaugh, alias The Sundance Kid, served 18 months in jail at Sundance, Cook Co., Wyoming, when a boy, for horse stealing. In December 1892, Longabaugh, Bill Madden, and Harry Bass "held up" a Great Northern train at Malta, Montana. Bass and Madden were tried for the crime, convicted, and sentenced to 10 years and 14 years respectively. The Sundance Kid escaped and since has been a fugitive.

Harry Longabaugh, aka The Sundance Kid, $5,000 "Wanted" poster for train robbery, c. 1892.

AUTHOR'S COLLECTION

Generic Butch Cassidy and The Sundance Kid, $5,000 each "Wanted" poster.

AUTHOR'S COLLECTION

Pinkerton detective Charles A. Siringo, seated with a gun and a cane, c. 1900.
AUTHOR'S COLLECTION

Dr. Pierce's Invalid's and Tourist's Hotel in Buffalo, NY, where Etta and Sundance went for an unspecified treatment, c. 1878–1881.
AUTHOR'S COLLECTION

Robert LeRoy Parker, aka Butch Cassidy, $3,500 "Wanted" poster for robbery of First National Bank of Winnemucca, Nevada, c. 1900.
AUTHOR'S COLLECTION

Allan Pinkerton, of the Pinkerton Detective Agency, 1819–1884.
LIBRARY OF CONGRESS

William A. Pinkerton with special agents Pat Connell and Sam Finley.
LIBRARY OF CONGRESS

Annie Rogers and Harvey Logan, aka Kid Curry.
LIBRARY OF CONGRESS

Laura Bullion, member of the Wild
Bunch gang, 1893.
LIBRARY OF CONGRESS

Tom O'Day was one of the original
hard-core members of the Wild Bunch,
c. 1900.
LIBRARY OF CONGRESS

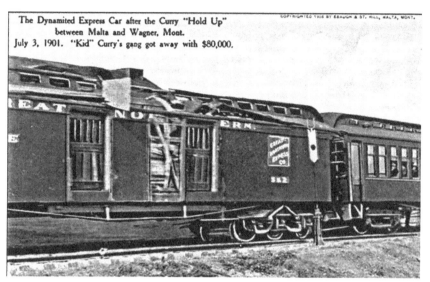

The Dynamited Express Car after the Curry "Hold Up" between Malta and Wagner, Mont. July 3, 1901. "Kid" Curry's gang got away with $80,000.

Kid Curry robbery, showing dynamited express car, July 3, 1901.
AUTHOR'S COLLECTION

Tom "Black Jack" Ketchum (1863–1901).
AUTHOR'S COLLECTION

Ann Bassett Willis, "Queen of the Outlaws," c. 1904.
AUTHOR'S COLLECTION

WANTED: Armed Robbery

Laura Bullion November 2, 1893

Generic Laura Bullion "Wanted" poster, put out by the Pinkerton's National Detective Agency for distribution throughout the West, c. 1893.
AUTHOR'S COLLECTION

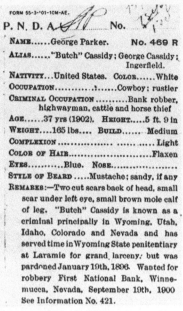

Pinkerton's National Detective Agency I.D. card for "George Cassidy," aka Butch Cassidy. For some reason, officials at the Wyoming State Penitentiary also used the first initial of "G" in identifying Cassidy for earlier state penitentiary records.
AUTHOR'S COLLECTION

Harvey Logan in Death.
LIBRARY OF CONGRESS

The ship, S.S. *Seguranca*, on which Etta and Sundance set sail for South America, c. 1910.

The ranch that Etta and the boys called home for years in Cholila.

Madame Tussauds Wax Museum, Hollywood, CA.

Dave Atkins, one-time member of the
Wild Bunch, c. 1895–1905.

"When confronted," according to author Richard Patterson, "the boys, both friends of Bob, produced a bill of sale bearing the name Robert LeRoy Parker, thus suggesting that Bob had owned the cattle and had sold them to the two suspects. Furious, Max sought out the town constable, James Wiley, for an explanation. Wiley's response only angered Max further: the constable admitted that Bob had probably signed the bill of sale simply to help his friends. Wiley's answer implied that Bob could afford to take the blame since he had already left Circle Valley, while Charley and Fred, both of whom were married, were not in a position to do likewise."

Because the cattle had already been returned to the owners, Wiley decided to drop his charges against Bob. But Max, like any good father, complained that even if the charges were dropped, his son would carry the stigma of "horse thief" within the community. Wiley countered by reminding Max that, if he insisted on making trouble, the issue would likely need to go before the local LDS [Mormon] bishop for resolution. Since Max's record with the bishop was far from sterling, he was advised to drop the matter. Besides, there was no way to locate Bob to participate in his own defense, so "Max grudgingly accepted Wiley's advice."[18]

* * *

In spring 1858, the town of Telluride, Colorado, was booming. Rich strikes of gold and silver put the village on the map overnight. With such sudden notoriety came sudden needs. Food, for one. Good horses, for another. Reliable horseflesh was hard to come by. In this respect, Telluride was no different from a dozen other towns that had sprung up in western and central Colorado. The fever spread as far as southeastern Utah and even west to Circle Valley, but hopes for fatty deposits in Utah's canyon country went unrealized. All along the La Sal and the Blue Mountains and up the San Juan River, prospectors staked out their claims and picked and panned their way from one promising-looking site to another, but mostly they came up with little or nothing for their efforts.

But Colorado? That was a different story. A mini-rush arose when a grizzled prospector and recluse named Cass Hite leaked information that gold had been found in the gravel-lined streambeds and along the banks of the Colorado River. As the newspapers ran the story, fortune seekers by the hundreds poured into Glen Canyon and the nearby mountains. To their dismay, they discovered little gold.[19]

Despite the rumors, residents of Circle Valley were slow to join in. Mormon leader Brigham Young exhorted his flock to search for more utilitarian commodities, such as lead, iron, and coal. Still, when economic hardship set in, several Circle Valley pioneers tossed their hats into the ring and set off for Telluride—Bob Parker's father and brother among them.

But not everyone who left for the boomtown of Telluride went in search of gold. The mountain settlement boasted other attractions as well. One Utah cowboy who must have felt he'd accidentally wandered into Sodom recalled being stunned by the saloons, gambling dives, dance halls, and board sidewalks, where thousands of strange, crazy people "pulled amazing scads of money out of their pockets and tried to gamble it off or throw it away on drinks and dance hall girls as fast as they could, and who tricked, robbed, shot, and stabbed each other to an amazing extent."[20]

The town of Telluride lies in a steep-walled, flat-bottomed gorge called San Miguel Valley. Roughly six miles long, it's home to the main fork of the gravelly San Miguel River that wends its way parallel to town from east to west. Telluride lies at the east end of the gorge, below the beginnings of the river, which is formed above by streams that drain Blue Lake and Ajax Peak. Near the western end of the park, the land drops off sharply, plunging the San Miguel into a cascade of whitewater fury past Keystone Hill and Skunk Creek toward a junction with the river's south fork.

The first mining claims around Telluride were filed in the mid-1870s, with the most promising lodes located at 11,000 feet or higher, where snow limited operations to five or six months out of the year. By the 1880s, placer-mining companies were sliding enough gravel down chutes to the San Miguel and its tributaries that the area was being touted as one of the most up-and-coming mining districts, if not environmental disasters, in the state.[21]

When founded, Telluride was called Columbia, and it carried that name on many official records well into the 1880s. But when an application for incorporation was made in 1878, the Post Office Department in Washington, DC, rejected the name because there was already a Columbia, California. The postal authorities believed that, with the state abbreviations then in use—"Col." and "Cal."—the risk of misdirected mail was too high. A new name was sought, and someone suggested Telluride, a name derived from the ore of tellurium, the half-metallic element related to sulfur and selenium and one of the most important found in combination with gold.

Although the amount of tellurium pulled from the ground around its namesake proved to be minuscule, there was still enough gold and silver extracted from the mountains around Telluride to create a population explosion. By 1880, the town had constructed twenty-six buildings, with more on the way. On June 21, 1881, the *Solid Muldoon*, a newspaper published in neighboring Ouray, reported that every available lot in Telluride had been sold, and the burgeoning town boasted of seven saloons and a dance hall. The following September, a toll road between Telluride and Ouray was completed. Telegraph wires soon followed, connecting the area to other mountain lines that eventually stretched all the way northeast to Denver. The new lines of communication created even more interest in the area. By early 1883, the state legislature split Ouray County into two districts—Ouray and San Miguel Counties—and Telluride became the new county seat.

Into that town in the spring or early summer of 1884 rode an eighteen-year-old Mormon cowhand named Bob Parker. Amazed at Telluride's urbanization, he found the town a wide-open, rip-roaring, anything-goes metropolis exploding with adventure.

Bob paid a rancher on the San Miguel River west of town to put up his horse and colt while he hired out to pack ore down the mountains by mule. The work was grueling, but the money was good, and he was even able to send some cash home to his family, probably with a reassuring note that everything was going well. In the evenings, he joined his fellow hands at one of the town's saloons.

When winter came, the mining activities slowed to a halt, and Bob most likely had to seek employment elsewhere. According to one source, he wandered as far north as Burnt Fork, Wyoming, and perhaps to western Nebraska, where he worked for the Coad Brothers Cattle Ranch on the North Platte River.[22] By early summer 1885, though, he was back in Telluride, once again seeking his fortune.

When Bob's colt, Cornish, turned three, his master took him out of the pasture to begin breaking him, which struck the pasture owner wrong. He may have coveted the colt, or Bob may have owed the man money for overwintering and feed. Whatever precipitated the argument, Bob eventually rode off without paying his demands, and the rancher filed a complaint against him.

Sensing trouble, Bob headed out of Telluride, nosing his way northwest, most likely along the old road that skirted the San Miguel River (now State Highway 145). He had followed this route when he first rode into Telluride, and he may have been heading back to Utah. But he made it only as far as Montrose County, Colorado, where he was picked up and taken to the county jail in Montrose. When his friends back in Telluride found out where he was, they sent a wire to his family in Circle Valley.

Although once more in jail, Bob was treated substantially better this time. In fact, when his father arrived to pay the boy's fine, he found his son sitting in the cell with the door wide open. When asked about it, Bob replied that the authorities knew he wouldn't try to escape. "They know I haven't taken anything that wasn't mine," Bob reportedly said. "I plan to stay right here until I get my horse."[23]

Bob eventually was vindicated and released. After checking his son out of jail, Max tried to persuade him to return to Utah, but Bob was adamant: He would return only after he'd made his fortune. Bob's sister, Lula, recalled years later that "Dad rode over on his horse to see what it was all about and tried several times to get Butch to straighten out and come home, but he never did."[24]

Afterward, Bob's family lost track of him. They'd heard rumors that he'd drifted up to Wyoming. If so, Bob was probably affected by the severe drought of 1886, which forced many of the large ranchers to move their herds farther north. He likely spent some time in Miles City, Montana, and he may have worked for a while on a ranch on the Yellowstone River across from Forsythe.

The following year, he returned to Telluride, finding the town had grown even more massive than he'd left it. History fails to record how he earned a living there, although he made enough money to enjoy an occasional evening out at some of the area's better saloons. It was in one of those establishments, most likely during the summer of 1887, that he made a new acquaintance by the name of Matt Warner.

Warner was a fellow cowboy from Utah not much older than Bob, and he shared Bob's Mormon upbringing. At fourteen, Warner (whose real name was Willard Christianson) beat up a rival in a fight over a girl and ran away from his home in Levan, Utah. Warner was sure he had killed his adversary and believed he was wanted for murder, so he fled Levan and never looked back. While on the run, he fell in with a shady bunch of wranglers and was soon earning a living rustling cattle and horses. When Bob and Matt Warner met, Warner had temporarily given up rustling for horse racing, which was a favorite local pastime, attracting hundreds of spectators. Mostly quarter- or half-mile stretches on straight tracks, the races triggered thousands of dollars in bets, sometimes on a single run.

In the early 1880s, residents of Saguache, a small town in the San Luis Valley west of the Sangre de Cristo Range, got so excited over one match between a legendary runner named Red Buck and an unknown long shot from New Mexico that they wagered more than $12,000, nearly all of the cash in town. When Red Buck lost, the town struggled to keep from going bankrupt.

Warner's horse-racing operation was centered in the southwestern corner of the state near Durango. Warner traveled a circuit of small towns looking for citizens who believed their horses could beat his prize mare, Betty. It was on his first trip to Telluride that he crossed paths with the future Butch Cassidy.

In town to match Betty against a local horse known as the Mulcahy Colt, Warner had celebrated with a whiskey after setting up the match when he spotted at the bar a friendly looking cowboy who seemed as if he wanted to talk. He and Bob hit it off from the start, particularly after learning they'd both come from Utah.

When Warner told the boy why he had come to Telluride, Bob said he knew about the Mulcahy horse and warned him that it was fast—*damned* fast. Faster than Warner's horse could ever hope to run. Warner was not impressed and challenged Bob to a bet. By then, with both of the Utahans well lubricated, they decided to bet everything they had, including their horses and rigs—saddles, bridles, and spurs—on the outcome.

According to custom at the time, an entry in a match race was allowed to select one of the judges. Warner chose Bob, saying that since he was a virtual stranger in town, he would be unbiased, knowing that at least he'd get an unbiased call from a fellow Utahan.

So the race was run, and the Mulcahy Colt charged through the course like greased lightning, but Warner's mare managed to outrun him. Afterward, Bob showed up with his saddle and tack, but Warner shook him off. Impressed by the young man's honesty, he made Bob a full partner in his racing business, setting up matches throughout Colorado until the weather turned too cold to run. Bob loved the opportunity to show off the fastest horse he'd ever seen, which certainly beat packing sluggish, ore-laden mules down from the mines!

From the beginning, the venture was a success. Warner and Bob had no trouble getting matches, and Betty was rarely beaten. The two men quickly doubled their money, although precious little of it ever left town. In Warner's words, "We threw our money away or gave it away as fast as we won it. After we had won a race . . . we would trail around to every saloon, gambling dive, and dance hall in the town and treat the whole population till the community just about had all of its money back."[25]

Later that summer, following a match in Cortez, Colorado, Warner recognized a dapper-looking man in the crowd. In his mid-forties, he was slim and smallish with a lean face. He apparently knew Warner, and they waved. When he came over, Warner introduced the man to Bob as Tom McCarty, another former Utahan and the husband of Warner's sister, Teenie.

Tom McCarty's early career is sketchy. He had been a rustler for some years and perhaps much worse. Although he and his brother, Bill, who also rode on the wrong side of the law, had come from a well-to-do family, Tom had a particular weakness for gambling, which made turning bad easy. He and Bill operated around the Utah towns of Nephi and Manti, stealing horses, cutting cattle out of herds, and selling both to whomever would overlook the doctored brands.

McCarty's preferred method of rustling was to buy a few cows and start driving them toward a railroad siding where a shipper would be waiting for him. While pushing his small herd, he'd pick up other ranchers' beeves along the way. Depending on the distance he had to travel, his little herd of eight or ten cows would grow to four or five hundred. With beef in such high demand, few shippers bothered to check the cattle for brands. After getting paid, McCarty loaded the beeves quickly and went on his way before anyone was the wiser.

Tom McCarty was still wanted by the law when he and Bob Parker met that day in Cortez, although he told Bob he'd gone into the mining business. Some researchers, though, believe it was McCarty who introduced Bob and Matt Warner to the fine art of express-train robbery. In the early morning of November 3, 1887, an eastbound Denver & Rio Grande passenger train was stopped by a pile of rocks on the tracks five miles east of Grand Junction, Colorado, along a curve near the Gunnison River at a spot called Unaweep Switch. The Denver & Rio Grande locomotive, which was fitted with a traditional front-end cowcatcher, most likely could have plowed through the barrier, but the engineer chose not to take the chance. After coming to a stop, three men stormed the express car, but the feisty express messenger stood his ground, insisting that only the stationmasters along the route knew the combination to the safe. The bandits, eventually convinced, collected a paltry $150 and a few pieces of registered mail.

According to the law, five men were involved in the robbery; outlaw historian Charles Kelly believes that three of them were Tom McCarty, Bob Parker, and Matt Warner. Nevertheless, four different men were eventually captured, tried, and convicted of the crime.[26]

Tom McCarty, though hardly averse to relieving an express-car safe of its contents, decided that fall to join Matt Warner and Bob Parker in their racing venture. McCarty was no stranger to horse racing, having ridden in matches in Cortez, Colorado. By then, though, word had spread that Warner's mare had beaten nearly every horse she'd gone up against, so finding matches was becoming difficult. Before long, having squandered their money and run out of competition, the men put their racing escapades on hold.

Bob, broke once more, picked up work with rancher Harry B. Adsit, owner of the Spectator Ranch, a sprawling spread forty miles west of Telluride. The ranch's main camp was at the base of Lone Cone Mountain, but it covered nearly thirty square miles, stretching from the San Miguel south to the Dolores River. Lone Cone itself was a towering dome of over twelve thousand feet, but around its base below the timberline was some of the best grazing land in the area. Adsit's cattle herd numbered upwards of five thousand head, and he also grazed range horses, which he sold to the mining companies.

As Adsit told the story, Bob and another cowboy—most likely Matt Warner—rode up to his ranch one day in 1888 looking for work. When he saw how skilled they were at cutting out cattle and breaking broncs, he hired them on the spot. Adsit recalled that Bob had "piercing eyes and a rapid-fire way of talking" and that he didn't seem to care much for liquor or cards, although "he occasionally held the candle while the boys played poker on a saddle blanket in the open." Adsit added that one night while they were camped out with the herd, he and Bob were talking when Bob told him someday he "would make his mark in the world." Adsit said Bob and Warner worked for him for a year before they quit, saying they planned on visiting their families back in Utah. Adsit paid them off and, as a bonus for their hard work, gave each of them the horses they'd recently broken. Bob's was a dappled-brown colt.[27]

Sometime during the late winter or early spring of 1889, Bob and Warner met with McCarty in his cabin near Cortez to make plans for their future—if you could call it that. As Warner described the scene, "We had spent our winnings as fast as we had made 'em, and now at McCarty's cabin we didn't have a thing to do but talk about our next move."[28]

As the three discussed their options, they quickly realized that any type of "honest work" would allow them barely enough money to scrape by. To latch on to some real cash, they were going to have to do something else. As McCarty described it, "Having been quiet for so long a time, my restlessness began to annoy me. Times being now rather dull and becoming acquainted with men that had no more money than myself, we thought it time to make a raid of some sort."[29]

It's not clear just what kind of raid McCarty had in mind, but it could have been a unique endeavor to extort $21,000 from a Denver bank. On Saturday, March 30, 1889, bank president David Moffat of Denver's First National welcomed into his private office a well-dressed gentleman he assumed was a local businessman and potential customer. Moffat could not have been more wrong. In minutes, the shocked banker realized that he was dealing with what appeared to be a totally deranged man. The stranger began babbling that Moffat's bank was going to be robbed; then, to the banker's astonishment, he added, "I am the man who is going to rob your bank." With that, the stranger drew a revolver from his coat and began waving it about, shouting that he desperately needed money. He then withdrew a bottle from his jacket and held it up with a trembling hand. Moffat saw that it contained some kind of clear liquid; he swallowed hard when the stranger said it was nitroglycerin and that he would blow up the place if Moffat did not follow his instructions.

Moffat was told to write out a check for $21,000, call in his cashier, and order him to exchange it for cash. Nearly petrified, Moffat did as he was told. The cashier could see that something was wrong, but when he questioned the request, Moffat insisted; the cashier reluctantly cashed the check and returned to his duties. Moffat gave the money to the stranger, who turned and departed the office into the lobby where he met another man standing by the door. Both men then left the building, walking in opposite directions.

Local sources attributed the crime to Tom McCarty and Matt Warner. Two separate old-timer tales that have circulated for years seem to support the idea. According to the first, as the cashier was exchanging cash for Moffat's $21,000 check, he slipped in a $10,000 bill, perhaps assuming that if a crime were being committed, the guilty party would have difficulty disposing of a bill of that size, leading to some merchant's suspicion and the robber's capture. To make the note even easier to trace, he tore a small piece off of one of the corners.

The second story involving Warner and McCarty occurred later that year. In the fall of 1889, the two turned up in Star Valley, Wyoming, using the names Matt Willard and Tom Smith. Brandishing plenty of cash, they purchased a log cabin on the outskirts of Afton and stocked it with groceries. To make the oncoming winter a bit easier to endure, they built a bar at one end of the cabin, loaded it with a generous supply of liquor, and let it be known to their new friends in the community that one and all were always welcome to stop by for a drink or two. For years, the old-timers in the area attested to the fact that tacked up on the wall behind the bar in Matt and Tom's cabin was a $10,000 bill.

McCarty later denied being in on the Denver bank incident, saying he had never met the banker, Moffat. If true, Warner and Bob Parker may have been the participants. Warner didn't mention the robbery in his memoirs, but his daughter, Joyce, said years later that both her father and Bob admitted to her their involvement in the crime.[30]

Regardless of who was in on that caper, little doubt remains about the holdup of Telluride's San Miguel Valley Bank that took place that summer. The participants included Warner, McCarty, Bob Parker, and perhaps two or three others.

With Telluride still booming from the lush strikes nearby, the San Miguel Valley Bank was a "target-rich environment." A small, false-front wooden building typical of its day, it was short of impressive on the outside, but to an experienced cowboy such as Matt Warner, the inside shone with the kind of prosperity designed to attract the moneyed gentry. "I didn't know before that there was any place in the world with such rich trimmings and furnishings as the inside of that bank," Warner later recalled.[31]

The bank's owner, Lucien L. Nunn (L. L.), was an eccentric local lawyer-entrepreneur. After earning a law degree back East, he opened a restaurant in Leadville, Colorado, where he generated extra income by renting out his tin bathtub to dirty miners on Saturday nights. When the Leadville restaurant folded, Nunn moved to Durango, where he scratched out a living as a carpenter. Upon his arrival in Telluride, he lived in a tent, ate a diet of oatmeal, and supplemented his meager lawyer's income by shingling roofs. It was rough going, but as the town grew, so

did Nunn's prosperity. He saved every penny he earned and began invest-
ing in the construction of small tract houses to rent and sell. Real estate
did the trick, as Nunn soon progressed to dabbling in some of Telluride's
more significant commercial ventures along Colorado Avenue. In 1888,
he purchased control of the San Miguel Valley Bank.

In writing of those days, Matt Warner recalled that young Bob
Parker was as eager as he was to rob the place, but Tom McCarty
remained cautious. He pointed out that nearly every able-bodied man in
Telluride carried a gun and would probably be shooting at them before
they could clear their saddles to ride out of town. Warner refuted this
argument by pointing out that banks were being robbed all over the West,
so it couldn't have been that difficult. In the end, McCarty's natural sense
of caution won out.[32]

In a somewhat different story, McCarty was the one who came up
with the idea of robbing a bank, and Bob Parker pointed him to the San
Miguel Valley Bank because, having worked in Telluride, he was familiar with the bank's routine. Still another source suggests that Bob was
stationed in Telluride for several weeks to learn when the mine's payroll
arrived at the bank. Mrs. John Hancock, a local resident who had once
lived in Torrey, Utah, and knew Bob on sight, recalled seeing him there
for a month or so before the robbery. He used to pass his time training
his horse to stand still while he charged it and leaped up into the saddle.[33]

While Bob was occupying himself in Telluride, Matt Warner and
Tom McCarty rode over to the Carlisle Ranch some five miles northwest
of Monticello, Utah, near the Colorado border. The foreman recalled seeing the two men making buckskin bags that would have been ideal for
carrying stolen bank loot. Warner and McCarty may have stayed at the
ranch while planning their escape route and arranging for relays of fresh
horses along the way. Bob's younger brother, Dan, may also have been
working there at the time.[34]

The Carlisle spread had a reputation as a safe haven for outlaws.
Brothers Edmund and Harold often put them on the payroll to discour-
age rustling and to scare off their arch enemies, the sheepmen. One story
alleged that, after some of their own cattle had been rustled, the Carlisles
hired the most hardened criminals they could find. A newspaper editor

once quipped that to work for the Carlisles, "a man had to have robbed at least three trains."[35]

This wasn't too far from the truth. The Carlisle brothers' reign over the area was undisputed. When the town of Monticello was settled in the mid-eighties, the brothers told everyone they were against it. Worried about water rights, they ordered their hands to dam up the stream that flowed to the town and then encouraged them to ride through the streets, yelling and firing their revolvers wildly in the air. Several hands even shot up the schoolhouse while the children were attending class. But the Monticello settlers were made of stern stuff and refused to leave.

While Warner and McCarty hung out at the ranch during the summer of 1899, plans for the bank robbery were slowly solidifying. Ranch ramrod W. E. "Latigo" Gordon, a tough, colorful character who kept a rein on his crew of hard cases by being tougher than they, had a streak of wildness himself. Gordon, described as a "good-looking, intelligent, and ordinarily kind and peaceable" man, threw all that to the wind when someone broke open a fresh "keg of red-eye." He had lost the fingers on his right hand to a rope loop while throwing a steer, and rumors persisted that he proudly bore several bullet holes in his body. According to one acquaintance, Gordon got the wounds from a shootout at the Carlisle Ranch headquarters, probably in a showdown with one of his hired hands. After the shooting, a doctor told Gordon he had only a week to live. The gutsy foreman is said to have replied, "God damn you, I'll be riding the range when you are dead." Two years later, the doctor was dead, and Gordon was still riding the range.[36]

Later, Gordon, too, admitted to seeing Warner and McCarty making buckskin bags at the ranch, setting the stage for action. The performance began right on time.

It started outside the San Miguel Valley Bank when several men rode into Telluride on Saturday, June 22, 1889. They put up their horses at Searle's livery stable and headed for the saloon. Although Warner claimed they had only recently become flat broke, they must have scraped together *some* cash (perhaps as much as $21,000, courtesy of Denver banker David Moffat) because witnesses later recalled them drinking and spending money that entire weekend, lending the impression of several recently paid cowhands who had shaken off the trail dust and were out for a good time. According to Warner, it was all part of their plan: "We dressed up top-notch, cowboy style, like we was going to a dance instead of a holdup. . . . There was policy and protection in it. . . . We would be just some more cowboys riding into town to see the girls."[37]

Even though the bank may have been open that Saturday, the boys decided to wait until Monday to make their play because they believed more money would be on hand then. They were right.

In Matt's account of the holdup, he mentions only himself, Bob Parker, and Tom McCarty as participants, although researchers suggest that one to three others were also involved. Warner may not have wanted to identify the others since they weren't known criminals at the time, and their families had no idea of what they were up to.

According to witnesses, on the morning of the robbery, four strangers checked their horses out of the livery stable and spent the next few hours in one or more of three saloons located near the bank, probably eyeing the bank customers as they came and went. Around noon, Charles Painter, the bank cashier and San Miguel County clerk, left to collect some money, leaving only a single teller in the bank. As Painter rode off, the four men left the saloon and either rode or led their horses over to the front of the bank. Two of the men stayed with the horses while the other two went inside.[38]

The fourth man may have been Bert Madden, the half brother of Bill Madden, a Mancos, Colorado, saloonkeeper. Bill eventually rode with the Wild Bunch after Bob Parker became known as Butch Cassidy. According to one account, Warner, Parker, and McCarty offered Bert, a spirited soul always on the lookout for adventure, the job of holding their horses.

Another possibility is that the fourth man was Harry Longabaugh, the Sundance Kid, a theory advanced by Donna Ernst, wife of Longabaugh's great-nephew, Paul Ernst. Harry Longabaugh lived in the area in the late 1880s and could have been acquainted with Warner, Parker, and McCarty, but Warner never mentioned Harry being involved, and as far as anyone knows, he had no reason to hide the fact if it were true. Harry Longabaugh was well known as the Sundance Kid and already a famous outlaw when Warner told his story in 1937.

It's also possible that the fourth man at the Telluride heist was Dan Parker, Butch's brother. For years, researchers believed Dan may have been one of the horse-tenders at the various relay points along the outlaws' escape route. Vouching for this notion, researchers recently learned that a lawman involved in the chase following the robbery had positively identified Dan as one of the four outlaws he had pursued.[39]

According to the bank teller, one robber came in and asked to cash a check. As the teller bent over to examine it, the man grabbed him around the neck and pulled his face down to the desk, telling him to remain silent or endure the "pain of instant death." The robber called to his partners on the sidewalk, saying, "Come on boys, it's all right." The men rushed into the room and quickly rifled it of all the cash. When they were through, they left the building, and the robber holding the teller released him, where he "fell in a heap on the floor." The robber looked down at him and murmured that he should have shot the man for being such a coward. Instead, he turned and walked out the door, after which, according to the teller, the group saddled up and "rode leisurely away." Bank officials reported to the newspapers that the robbers made off with between $20,000 and $21,000.[40]

Information about the robbery was taken from eyewitness accounts, including that of the teller. Matt Warner offers a slight variation, saying that, on entering town, he and Bob Parker dismounted "casual-like as we could," leaving McCarty to watch the horses. Inside, when they reached the teller's cage, they saw "a lot of money . . . stacked up in piles in front of him." The teller smiled and asked what he could do for them. Warner replied by shoving the barrel of his gun under the teller's nose. As Bob filled a sack with money, Warner noticed that the vault was open and told Bob to check it out. Within minutes, Bob emerged with what appeared to be "bales of greenbacks and a lotta gold."[41]

According to Warner, he and Bob then herded the teller out of the bank ahead of them "with his hands sticking up in the air," which would have been unlikely since such a spectacle would have drawn undue attention to the robbers before their getaway. In his own account, McCarty says nothing about taking the teller outside but instead warned him to remain where he was or "pay the penalty."[42]

Warner contends that, once they had exited the bank, he expected to see the town "explode in our faces any minute with everybody in creation shooting at us,"[43] but the onlookers did nothing, as though they were paralyzed with fear.

One of the witnesses who relayed the story of the robbery later said that, as the robbers left the bank, one of the gang shot at the feet of the teller to make him stand still (assuming he was outside), but the shot frightened the robber's horse, causing the rider to lose his hat and nearly get bucked off.[44] According to other witnesses, the robbers rode casually for a few blocks before suddenly spurring their horses, letting out a yell, and firing their revolvers into the air. One shot just missed a youngster named Edward Weller who was standing on the sidewalk. This version of events corresponds with McCarty's account, which said they fired their pistols "in different directions to intimidate the people we would meet."[45]

Although Warner denied it, some sources say that the robbers probably had established a relay of horses along their escape route. Several years after the robbery, an anonymous local man claimed that McCarty had hired him to set up the relay in return for a payment of $1,600. The unnamed man called himself "Rambler," saying that he and McCarty had met the previous fall in Cortez at a dance hall called French's. He and McCarty had hit it off, and Rambler spent part of the winter at McCarty's Bar-X Ranch at Aztec Springs south of Cortez. There, McCarty was wintering a considerable number of horses that he had picked up in Utah during the raids of 1888. Sometime the following spring, Rambler said McCarty asked him if he would "like to go in cahoots" with him and "open up a bank." Rambler thought McCarty was joking, but he indicated his willingness. Surprised to learn that McCarty had been serious, he decided to join in.[46]

Instead of being paid from the proceeds of the holdup, Rambler said that McCarty wrote out a note as a bill of sale under which Rambler was supposed to have sold sixty head of horses to McCarty for $1,600, for which he hadn't been paid. Following the robbery, Rambler was to present the bill to the sheriff at Cortez, obtain a legal "attachment," and proceed to McCarty's Aztec Springs ranch to "repossess" the stock. Rambler said the scheme worked just as McCarty had planned, although local county officials took their "generous fees" for assisting in the process.[47]

To earn his $1,600 worth of horses, Rambler was to set up the robbers' relay stations along their escape route. He said that McCarty wanted fresh horses posted at Keystone Hill, Hot Spring, West Fork, Johnston's Horse Camp, and Mud Springs. These locations imply that their escape route was probably west out of Telluride, past San Miguel City to the south fork of the San Miguel River, down the south fork to Ames at Wilson Creek, and from there south along a trail that is now State Highway 145. From there, they would have passed Trout Lake and crossed over Lizard Head Pass to the Dolores River. Somewhere along the Dolores (which eventually leads to the town of Rico), they turned west and followed a trail to Hot Spring near the west fork of the Dolores. From that point, they most likely followed the west fork back to the main tributary of the Dolores before taking various trails west of the river, eventually ending up in Cortez.

Rambler implied that he may have actually participated in the robbery, or, at least, he waited with the first relay of horses at Keystone Hill. After descending the hill, the robbers were apparently confident that they had made a clean getaway. Although they were probably no more than four miles from the scene of the robbery by horseback, Rambler said they stopped long enough to divide up the money and have a quick lunch.[48]

While the robbers were eating, rancher Harry Adsit, owner of the Spectator Ranch for whom Bob and Matt had worked only weeks earlier, came riding up, and the boys invited him to join them for lunch, but he declined. In a slight variation, Adsit discussed the incident in more detail years later. He said that, on riding into Telluride that day, he passed the four men on the road coming from town and recognized Bob Parker and the other young man as the boys who had been at his ranch only a few weeks earlier. He said that he remembered wondering why they had not gone home to Utah as they had said they would. He learned only later that they had just robbed the San Miguel Valley Bank.[49]

Matt Warner described a similar incident without actually mentioning Adsit. According to him, he and his companions came out of a clearing to cross a road outside of Telluride when they came across two men. One of the men (apparently Adsit) knew him and Bob Parker and later identified them. Warner added, "Just that little accident made all the difference in the world to us the rest of our lives. It give 'em a clue so they could trace us for thousands of miles and for years. Right at that point is where we broke with our half-outlaw past, became real outlaws, burned our bridges behind us, and had no way to live except by robbing and stealing." After the encounter, according to Warner, McCarty remarked that he should have shot the two men.[50]

McCarty, in his account of the escape, doesn't mention encountering the men or Harry Adsit, but he recalled that, once they were five miles or so from town, one of the robbers' horses pulled up lame. McCarty said they waited near the road until a wagon came along. They stopped the cart and informed the driver that they were trading their lame horse for one of his. When the driver protested, McCarty said they gave him some money for his horse. Apparently, the money satisfied him, because by the time they had the animal unhitched and saddled, the man was smiling. He even tipped his hat and wished them good luck as they rode off.[51]

The robbers reached their second relay station at Hot Spring, well west of the Dolores River and the main road. It was a wise route to follow since authorities at Rico and Durango had been notified of the robbery and were organizing posses to head them off. The robbers had most likely left the main road at Cool Creek and reached the west fork of the Dolores by way of Morrison Creek, where they stopped to split up the loot.

After Hot Spring, according to Rambler, the four traveled on to West Fork, where they came upon two strangers with Winchesters, but they encountered no trouble from them. Around dark, the robbers stopped at their next-to-last relay point at Johnston's Horse Camp a few miles north of Haycamp Mesa. There they were served supper by the camp proprietor, Mrs. Olren. After leaving Johnston's, they backtracked along an old Indian trail that led to Italian Springs, where Rambler said they thought they had spotted three of their pursuers, but they eluded the men and rode on to the last relay stop, Mud Springs, arriving around ten o'clock. At that point, they had covered nearly eighty miles.

Rambler said that he left the group at Mud Springs and headed for Cortez, while Tom McCarty rode on to Mancos where he had "friends." Rambler probably meant Warner's friends rather than McCarty's. According to Warner, for some time before the robbery, he had maintained a horse camp near Mancos, which he had left in the hands of jockey Johnny Nicholson and two of Warner's wranglers, Neils Olson and George Brown. Warner was convinced that he'd been recognized along the trail and told his wranglers what had happened and that he was an outlaw on the run. Knowing that his property would be confiscated once he was named as a robbery suspect, he wrote out a bill of sale for his horses and equipment to the surprised wranglers, telling them that everything he had owned was now theirs. Here, Rambler's story may have deviated some from the truth, since it's more likely that Olson, Brown, and Nicholson were given the horses and equipment in payment for their help in carrying out the robbery, similar to the arrangement McCarty had made with Rambler.

As Warner told the story, he, McCarty, and Bob Parker made a fireless camp in the woods that night, hitting the trail again early the following morning after breaking camp minutes before a posse that had been trailing them for most of the night picked up their tracks.

The Telluride posse was led by San Miguel County sheriff James A. Beattie, who was later joined by Montezuma County sheriff J. C. Love. They most likely lead a sizable group because San Miguel County records show that nearly $900 was spent on the men and horses involved in the chase.

Tom McCarty also recalled that "quite a large posse was in hot pursuit,"[52] but he gave the impression that they lost their pursuers early on, possibly even during the second day's ride, after descending a steep mountain at a spot where such a descent was considered impossible.

Both Warner and McCarty told of throwing off their pursuers for a while, apparently during the second night, with a trick that later found its way into dozens of Hollywood's best Western yarns. As darkness was nearing, the outlaws found an abandoned Indian pony in a basin near the summit of one of the small mountain ranges they had to cross. They threw a lasso on the animal, tied branches and brush to its tail, and sent it back down the mountain toward the posse. As Warner described it, the frightened pony "shot back on the dead run in the direction he came from . . . [making] as much noise as our whole outfit would make bolting for safety."[53] McCarty added, "The noise caused by the breaking and snapping of dry timber . . . made it sound as though we had an army of men and were all making a charge at the posse."[54] The posse members, stunned and confused, thought the outlaws had turned to attack them, and the posse quickly mounted and rode off in the darkness.

Not long after at last realizing what had happened, the posse returned to Telluride to report that they'd lost the outlaws' trail. Warner wrote that he, Bob Parker, and Tom McCarty immediately beat out a getaway for Utah, while Rambler said that McCarty "and his little band"[55] remained in the high country near Mancos until the area had been thoroughly searched by the authorities with the help of Navajo trackers.

Back in Telluride, Sheriff Beattie and his men began scouring the area for witnesses, hoping to find someone to identify the robbers. Somebody (presumably Mrs. Hancock) remembered seeing Bob Parker hanging around town the month before the robbery, practicing fast getaways on his horse. Also, after Bert Madden's name came up as a suspect, authorities began watching the activities of his half brother, Bill. Sure enough, just short of a week following the robbery, authorities observed Madden leaving town with a loaded packhorse. One lawman named Wasson and perhaps others followed. Madden apparently turned south, probably taking the same road as the robbers, leading to the Dolores River. Wasson eventually saw him turning the packhorse over to another rider who had come from the opposite direction. Wasson moved in and arrested both men. Wasson searched Madden and found a letter from his half brother Bert. In it, Bert asked Bill to send supplies and gave instructions for how to reach him and the others.

Beattie immediately swore in another posse and struck out for the Mancos Mountains, but by the time they reached the location Bert had mentioned, the robbers were gone. The officers followed the outlaws' tracks for several days, eventually losing them to the wind and rain. Apparently the robbers knew they were being tracked, because just before the lawmen lost the trail, Beattie found a note from the robbers, warning them not to follow or somebody would get shot. At that point—for whatever reason—the posse gave up the ghost and returned home. There, they reported to the press that the robbers had once again eluded them when they "padded their horses' feet with gunny sacks and rode across slick rock."[56]

Other posses were still searching, though. On July 1, more than a week after the robbery, some twelve to fifteen lawmen were in pursuit, although their hopes for capturing the robbers were growing dim.[57] Bill Madden was eventually released by the San Miguel sheriff after finding no concrete evidence linking him to the robbery. Nor do records show that Madden's cohorts, Neils Olson, George Brown, and jockey Johnny Nicholson, were ever arrested for any part in the robbery. Regardless, the three failed to benefit from their "innocence." Over the next two years, local ranchers and others took justice upon themselves, gradually pilfering everything possible from the men because they "didn't feel bound to respect property that had come from a bank robber."[58]

The holdup men may have had other help, too. One intriguing tale claims that the outlaws were assisted by Telluride's own marshal, a man named Jim Clark. A shady character with a questionable past, Clark claimed to have been one of Quantrill's Raiders—a ruthless band of Confederate rebels who slaughtered nearly 200 civilians in Lawrence, Kansas, during the Civil War. Clark claimed to have received $2,200 of the stolen Telluride bank booty in return for being "conveniently out of town" on the morning of the robbery. The marshal supposedly admitted this years later to Colorado's legendary lawman, Gunnison County sheriff Doc Shores; Clark told Shores that the robbers left his share of the loot under a log along the trail they had taken during their escape.[59]

As an interesting sidebar, Marshal Clark—who was as corrupt a lawman as ever wore a badge west of the Mississippi—ended up with one of the horses used by the robbers in making their getaway. A large black gelding with a "CT" brand on its thigh was found at the top of Keystone Hill, apparently too winded for Rambler, Bert Madden, or anyone else to drive down the hill with the others. Clark took the horse home, named him Keystone, and kept him for several years until he disappeared one night, apparently stolen from Clark's corral right from under the marshal's nose.

Another of the robbers' horses was brought back by the posse. The dappled-brown colt that Harry Adsit had given Bob two weeks before the robbery was eventually taken by San Miguel County sheriff Jim Beattie, who claimed he was entitled to the horse because the county had never reimbursed him for money he had paid out of his own pocket to organize the manhunt. Adsit later said that, some ten days or so after the robbery, he received a letter from Bob Parker that went something like this: "Dear Harry: I understand the sheriff of San Miguel county is riding the dapple brown colt you gave me. I want you to tell Mr. Sheriff that this horse packed me one hundred and ten miles in ten hours across that broken country and declared a dividend of $22,580.00 and this will be your order for the horse. Please send him over to me at Moab, Utah, at the first opportunity."[60]

Adsit said that when he showed the sheriff the letter and pointed out that the animal carried the Adsit brand, the sheriff reminded him that Adsit had given the horse to Parker, so legally it was no longer his. Whether or not Adsit had received such a letter remains a mystery, but it's well known that the robbers, in their dramatic escape from Telluride, did pass through Moab.[61]

CHAPTER 8

And Baby Makes Three

[Butch] and the Sundance Kid—Harry Longabaugh—had a big haul
they took with them. The Sundance Kid brought along his lady friend,
Etta Place, a school teacher. Butch didn't want the woman to go along,
but Sundance insisted. They went to South America and, instead of
retiring, started all over again robbing trains and banks.
—LULA PARKER BETENSON, LOS ANGELES TIMES, APRIL 3, 1970

WHILE HARRY AND ETTA WERE RIDING HIGH—ESCAPING THE PINKER-
tons for New York City—the detectives weren't exactly resting on their
laurels. They knew that both Butch and Sundance had been reported
nearby, and they knew that both had been observed in the company of a
stunningly attractive beauty whom they quickly began to call Ethel for
lack of a better name.

On a visit to Fannie Porter's place in San Antonio, the Pinkertons
asked the notorious madam for an interview, giving her the cipher of
Hen in their files. Fannie told the undercover agents everything she could
recall about her outlaw clients—to a degree, of course—including her
recollections of Sundance. "Fanny Porter knows Harry Longbaugh [*sic*].
He used to have a gold tooth in front, left side, but he had it taken out
and white one placed in its stead." Fannie mentioned Sundance's tooth;
it was also mentioned in the wanted poster after Malta. "Teeth white and
clean with small dark spot on upper front tooth."[1]

Perhaps Fanny shared such intimate details with the Pinkertons because she'd learned from the boys themselves that they had long since departed for New York, from where they had likely sailed to South America, beyond the jurisdiction, one would suppose, of mere mortal Americans—or even the Pinkertons.

But the Pinkertons, as they would soon reveal, were anything but mere mortals, and their jurisdiction, while nowhere in particular, spread everywhere in general, and that was good enough to keep Butch, Sundance, and Etta in their sights.

Meanwhile, in South America, Sundance had told Etta of his intentions to settle down on a ranch and live a peaceful life with her; he was going to be a law-abiding rancher. Even though it was the outlaw Harry Longabaugh to whom Etta was first drawn, by the time she had traveled around the country and ended up with him in South America, she must have been ecstatic to hear the news. She was not getting any younger, after all, and it's likely she entertained, like most women of her day, the prospect of settling down, having children, and raising a family the best she knew how.

So, Sundance and Butch sought out the US vice consul, Dr. George Newbery, a Buenos Aires dentist who was an American immigrant from New York, for his advice on where and how to buy a ranch in Argentina. Newbery suggested the lush, grassy fields near Cholila, a sparsely settled area that the vice consul secretly hoped would one day grow into a colony of transplanted Americans. Sundance and Butch also learned that Cholila was near the border of Chile, nestled into the foothills of the Andes Mountains on the east bank of the Blanco River. Remote at best, it lay more than four hundred miles from the nearest railroad and had no telegraph—all fresh pollen to honeybees on the prowl for elusive peace and anonymity.

The three went to Cholila, looked around the area, and were pleased with what they found. They began building a small ranch. On June 11, 1901, Butch and Sundance purchased "16 colts from an estancia near Cholila with a $855 check drawn on the Banco de Londres y Rio de la Plata. In October 1901, they registered their brands in Rawson, the Chubut capital."[2]

On March 1, 1902, nearly a year after arriving in Argentina, Sundance and Butch applied to homestead four leagues of land in Cholila. A month later, on April 2, 1902, Butch finalized the application for "four square leagues of Government land within the Province of Chubut, district 16 of II Octuber, near Cholilo [*sic*]."[3]

On March 3, 1902, while Butch was filing the necessary paperwork in Buenos Aires, Sundance and Etta boarded the SS *Soldier Prince* for a trip back to the States. Arriving in New York on April 3, they registered at Mrs. Thompson's rooming house, 325 East Fourteenth Street. During their visit, according to the Pinkertons, they spent part of their time at Coney Island, a well-known beach resort and amusement park of the day, just outside New York City.

Afterward, they rode a hundred miles by train to visit Harry's family in Pennsylvania once again. He and Etta spent time with Harry's brother, Harvey, who was working at the beach resort town of Atlantic City, New Jersey, at the time. That June, they returned to New York and made another purchase at Tiffany's—this time a watch for which Harry paid $15.35. Once again, he complained to the family of an old gunshot injury for which he may have sought treatment in Chicago or, perhaps, on a return trip to Buffalo to coincide with the May 10, 1902, date on the report sent to the Pinkertons.

Regardless, Harry and Etta were in Chicago during the summer of 1902. On July 3, the Chicago–Rock Island Railroad Express No. 5 was held up by two men near Dupont, Illinois. The spoils tallied less than $500 plus some jewelry and a few other items. The safe wasn't characteristically blown, even though a bag of dynamite was later found nearby.

A hobo on the train claimed to have recognized a photograph of Sundance as one of the thieves, which brought the Pinkertons into the chase. But it's doubtful that Sundance could have—or *would* have—participated in the robbery and still have been in New York City in time to depart again for Argentina one week later.

On July 10, 1902, Mr. and Mrs. Harry Place sailed out of New York Harbor aboard the steamer *Honorius*. Since the ship was registered as a freighter not consigned to carry passengers, Harry had to hire on as purser, and Etta, a steward. They arrived back in Buenos Aires on August 9, 1902, and again checked into the Hotel Europa.

Sundance closed out his bank account in Buenos Aires on August 14, 1902, and a day later, he and Etta boarded the SS *Chubut*, a small steamer traveling along the Atlantic coast, before they set out on the remainder of their trip home on horseback. It was not a simple journey, but they were headed back to the ranch. That meant they were headed back to the safety, comfort, and security that only the ranch could afford them. An unsigned and undated memo in the Pinkerton files describes the couple's trip as taking a steamboat to Bahia Blanca and a smaller boat from Bahia Blanca to Rawson on the coast at the mouth of the "Chubute [*sic*] River." From there, they rode on horseback for another two weeks.

* * *

Once more settled into his home in Argentina with Etta and Butch, Sundance was amused to learn of an accusation against him for a July 3, 1901, train robbery in Wagner, Montana. The authorities in St. Louis, Missouri, were thrilled to report that they were holding the Sundance Kid in their local jail. On November 5, 1901, the St. Louis police had arrested Ben Kilpatrick for passing stolen banknotes, but he refused to identify himself or to answer any other questions. When searching his pockets, the authorities found a key to the Laclede Hotel, where Ben and his girlfriend Laura Bullion were staying. The following morning, the police arrested Laura, who was about to leave with a case filled with forged banknotes.

Both Ben and Laura refused to provide any information so as to avoid revealing their identities. When the St. Louis police contacted the Pinkerton Detective Agency and received wanted circulars from Wagner, they believed they had apprehended the Sundance Kid and Wild Bunch gang member Laura Bullion.

The police went through Laura's belongings. The *Daily Globe Democrat* reported, "In a notebook found among Miss Bullion's personal effects were written these lines: Harry Longbaugh [*sic*] very black hairs, steel gray eyes, very fair skin when not tanned by the sun."[4] They questioned

Laura about her companion, and she answered, "I have known the prisoner whom you call Longbaugh [*sic*] since the latter part of last April."[5]

According to authorities, Laura also reportedly claimed of Ben Kilpatrick that she had "found in his coat a pocket dictionary, on the jacket of which was written the name 'Harry Longuebaugh' [*sic*]." She asked him if that was another of his names and "he replied evasively."[6] The police were convinced beyond a doubt that they had captured the Sundance Kid.

Then, on November 15, 1901, Ben Kilpatrick was correctly identified; word spread quickly that Sundance was no longer in custody in St. Louis, Missouri. And the authorities there never did realize that he was already settled peacefully on a ranch in Argentina with his wife, Etta Place, and Butch Cassidy.

* * *

Meanwhile, back in South America, Sundance and Etta clearly made a new home for themselves. Their ranch consisted of a spacious four-room cabin as the main house, a stable, a chicken coop, a smaller bunkhouse for the local cowhands, and what Butch referred to as a "wearhouse." As the ranch business grew, they even built a small store for their neighbors and ranch hands. Although Sundance, Etta, and Butch probably lived together in the four-room cabin at first, there is some evidence that Butch also built a bachelor pad for himself.

Primo Caprara, an Italian immigrant who once passed through Cholila in 1904, later wrote about staying with the gang, referring to his hosts as peaceful ranchers.

> *The house was simply furnished and exhibited a certain painstaking tidiness, a geometric arrangement of things, pictures with cane frames, wallpaper made of clippings from North American magazines . . . many beautiful weapons and lassos braded [sic] from horse hair. The men were tall, slim, laconic and nervous, with intense gazes. The lady, who was reading, was well-dressed. I had a friendly dinner with them. Other neighbors recalled that she kept perfumed water in the house's wash basins, spoke some Spanish, and rode and shot like*

a man. Later, I learned that they were famous robbers of trains and banks in North America.[7]

Their neighbors, including a select few who knew of their past as out-laws, accepted them with open arms. "Their law-abiding activities, their proper manners, and their pleasant dispositions soon led them to be held in high regard by neighbors and authorities," wrote Marcelo Gavirati. After a local party on March 9, 1904, thrown for territorial governor Dr. Julio Lezana, one neighbor observed, "They were not good mixers, but whatever they did was correct . . . no one suspected they were criminals. The governor was entertained by three of the most respectable neighbors, Americans James Ryan and Mr. and Mrs. Harry Place. . . . Hospitality that the governor accepted, staying overnight at the cabin of the trio of American ranchers in Cholila."[8] Several sources mention that the new governor even enjoyed dancing with his hostess, Mrs. Ethel Place.[9]

No doubt, Sundance, Etta, and Butch had made a home together in Cholila. Shortly before Sundance and Etta returned to the ranch follow-ing their visit to the States, Butch wrote a letter dated August 10, 1902, to his friend Matilda Davis in Utah.

> *I visited the best Cities and best parts of the countrys [sic] of South A. till I got here, and this part of the country looked so good that I located, and I think for good, for I like the place better every day. I have 300 cattle, 1500 sheep, and 28 good Saddle horses, 2 men to do my work, also good 4 room house, wearhouse, stable, chicken house and some chickens.*[10]

Because he was, at last, a law-abiding citizen, settling down appar-ently for good, Sundance, too, began corresponding—with his sister Samanna—regularly. She kept the books and business ledgers for her husband and occasionally entered a personal note under the daily head-ings of the accounting book in a diary format. She wrote to her brother on July 22, 1902, and again on January 3, 1903, and he answered. What Samanna never knew was that their letters were often read by local postal clerks who had been hired as informants by the Pinkertons. The law, at last, had a solid clue as to where Butch and Sundance had gone.

In early March 1903, Pinkerton agent Frank Dimaio finished an assignment in Brazil and was sent by his employer to Argentina to locate the outlaws. Upon arriving in Buenos Aires, he interviewed Dr. George Newbery, who had met the outlaw trio when they landed in Argentina. Newbery recognized photos of Butch and Sundance as his neighbors some 130 miles south of his ranch. He told Dimaio that

> It would be impossible to apprehend these criminals at that time due to the fact that about May 1st the rainy season would set in and the country would become so flooded it would be impossible for the authorities to reach Cholila and bring about their arrest. That in order to reach Cholila it would be necessary to go to Puerto Madryn, 250 miles south of Buenos Aires, and then travel by horseback for about 15 days through the jungle. That it would be necessary to hire a peon familiar with the trail. Upon arrival in Cholila the commandant of the garrison at the 16 Octobre would have to be seen and the arrangements made for the arrest of these criminals.[11]

So, instead of traveling to Cholila, Dimaio contacted the local Buenos Aires authorities and warned them of the presence of American outlaws in their midst. Then he flooded the area with wanted posters written in Spanish and devised a code to be used in communicating with the Pinkertons.

Under the heading of "Castleman, New York," Newbery and local authorities were to wire the Pinkertons a shipment of fruit:

Longabaugh = lemons
Cassidy = citron
L & wife = apricots
Mrs. L = peaches
L wife & Cassidy = oranges
sailed on = pears.

These new cipher words replaced earlier ones the agency had used in the States, in which Sundance had been "sand" and Butch, "primer."[12]

Not realizing that Dimaio had located them, Sundance and Etta again returned stateside. A Pinkerton memo confirms that they were believed to have been in the area of Baggs, Wyoming, most likely in the spring of 1903.[13] More than likely, Harry shared the Robbers Roost hideout with Etta and possibly even took her to the Bassett Ranch to meet old friends.

The following year, the couple was back in Argentina. On February 29, 1904, Butch wrote a short letter in which he said Sundance planned on going to the lake on March 1 to buy bulls. The allusion was most likely to Lake Nahuel Huapi in Rio Negro, a few days' ride north of an *estancia*, or ranch, owned by a fellow Texan, Jared Jones. The trip took place around the same time as the party was thrown for Governor Lezana, at which Carlos Foresti, a professional photographer accompanying the governor's party, took several photographs of the ranch that Sundance mailed back home to Samanna. The *Tea Party* shows Sundance and Butch seated on chairs behind their ranch house, with Etta standing between them, holding a teakettle. The scene looks as tranquil as any other twentieth-century setting, right on down to Etta's apron and the two dogs sitting at their feet. The cocker spaniel was reportedly Etta's favorite and accompanied her everywhere.

A second photograph shows nine people standing in the front yard of the ranch along with an assemblage of horses and dogs. The family refers to these photos as the Cholila Post Card Scenes. There is a second copy of the scenes in a single photograph format owned by a descendant of Jared Jones, one of Sundance's Patagonian neighbors.[14] Remarkably, these photographs were somehow missed by the postal clerk in Mont Clare, Pennsylvania, and they remain in the family's collection today.

As the cold weather arrived in the Southern Hemisphere, Etta and Sundance again boarded a ship to head north for the warmer climes of the States. Emma received an unsigned postcard, presumably from Harry, from the 1904 St. Louis World's Fair and Exposition. A Pinkerton memo written on October 24, 1904, identified a couple around Fort Worth, Texas.

Our report here shows that Longbaugh [sic] and his wife Ethel Place are probably now in the United States. This information is partially confirmed through an informant who has been to our Denver office and reported conferences he has had with Longbaugh and his wife and Cassidy in the vicinity of Fort Worth. . . . We definitely recommend that your Protective Committee authorize us, first, to make an investigation at Fort Worth, Texas, San Antonio, Texas, and such other points.[15]

By the time the memo was written, Etta and Sundance were already back in Cholila.

On November 26, 1904, Samanna wrote her brother again. A month later, on December 30, Butch ordered supplies for the ranch from local merchant Richard Clarke. The order included six pairs of socks, one sweater, two pairs of slippers, and two handkerchiefs and totaled 18.40 pesos. All in all, their lives finally seemed to be normal.

But those lives were about to change.

Around 3 p.m. on Tuesday, February 14, 1905, two English-speaking men robbed the Rio Gallegos bank, making a clean getaway. They headed toward the towering Patagonian Andes to the north. Police later identified a "tall, slight man and the other a shorter man, fair complexion, and both clean shaven." They were known as "Henry Linden and Co."[16]

Although Butch and Sundance were soon implicated in the robbery, they were—for a change—innocent. An acquaintance, Robert Evans, most likely orchestrated the theft. At the time, Butch and Sundance were being interviewed for inclusion in a Cholila Agricultural Census Survey. They were still living the peaceful, law-abiding lives of respectable ranchers. One of the most critical aspects of the census was that it provided an unquestionable alibi to Sundance and Butch for the robbery. Although there's a remote possibility that they may have known about it, they weren't involved in it.

The theft, though, was pulled off in typical Wild Bunch fashion, and this brought attention to the outlaws' presence in Cholila. Things were beginning to unravel, and it would eventually put an end to the trio's idyllic life in Cholila for good.

The most accurate version of the robbery comes from Argentine historian Osvaldo Topcic, whose work was brought to light by Anne Meadows and Dan Buck. Topcic's account, appearing in the newspaper *El Antdrico* and in local police files, details two North Americans who called themselves Brady and Linden. After arriving in Rio Gallegos, they checked in to the Hotel Argentino. They claimed to be two Rio Negro livestock representatives looking for land. They opened an account at the Banco de Tarapaca and spent the next couple of days dining at the best restaurants and impressing the locals. They even made a point of buying a telescope and compass to use in scouting the countryside for just the right piece of property.[17]

On February 13, 1905, the two men returned to the Banco de Tarapaca and closed their account, their business in Rio Gallegos apparently concluded as they prepared to return to Rio Negro. But the next day, they came back to the bank, wielding long-barreled revolvers.

It was shortly before closing time when assistant manager Arturo Bishop and cashier Alexander Mackerrow began totaling the day's transactions. One of the gunmen forced the two employees to put all their loose cash into a large white canvas sack. The shorter of the two robbers, who called himself Brady, also picked up a small cash box containing some silver. Later estimates put the value of the purloined cash and silver at about $100,000 in today's currency. Once finished with their work, one of the robbers held Bishop and Mackerrow at gunpoint while the other went outside and tied the canvas sack to his horse. A few minutes later, they rode off toward the Gallegos River. Police and soldiers scoured the back trails for days but found only a pair of abandoned horses and an empty cash box.[18]

Despite the similarity between this holdup and the Wild Bunch bank robberies in the United States, there was no proof that Butch, Sundance, or Etta was involved, even though the descriptions given to the authorities were similar. The shorter bandit had green eyes, a sunburned complexion, and a closely cropped beard that was somewhere between chestnut and black, while his taller compatriot stood five feet ten inches tall and had a narrower face with a light complexion, green eyes, blond hair, a regular nose, and an upper lip that moved perceptibly when he spoke. There was only one disqualifying physical factor: The robbers were described as between twenty-five and thirty years of age. In 1905, both Butch and Harry were nearing forty.

Another reason Butch and Sundance couldn't have been involved in the holdup was the fact that, according to several neighbors' sworn testimonies, both Butch and Sundance were in Cholila at the time. Butch's name appears on a purchase order at a store in Sunica just outside Cholila around the time of the holdup, emphasizing the impossibility of his being in two different places at once. Also, a government agricultural survey taken in Cholila in February 1905 showed that both Butch and Sundance were present at their ranch 750 miles from Rio Gallegos at the time of the holdup.

Regardless, authorities insisted that the Americans be brought in for questioning in connection with the bank heist. A warrant was issued by the police chief in Buenos Aires: "As their specialty is armed robbery of banks, trains and public buildings in broad daylight, and they were in the country . . . it is presumed they are the perpetrators."[19]

Despite their innocence, the law drawing down on them left the three Americans apprehensive; they decided the better part of valor was to flee. On June 28, 1905, Sundance wrote to their neighbor, Dan Gibbon of Valparaiso, Chile, that they had just arrived home and that "our business went well and we received our money." Sundance then informed Gibbon that in two days he and Etta were leaving for San Francisco, adding, "I don't want to see Cholila ever again, but I will think of you and all of our friends often, and we want to assure you of our good wishes."[20]

Butch and Sundance had gotten word from local sheriff Edward Humphries that the law, thinking the two were guilty of the Rio Gallegos job, was closing in on them. Humphries most likely had been ordered by the authorities in Buenos Aires to investigate the duo's criminal activities. But Humphries was close friends with both men, and he allegedly had a massive crush on Etta, so he warned the three to start packing. Humphries was later relieved of his position, according to a fellow policeman, for "failing to carry out his orders and conducting himself in a manner unbecoming a police officer."[21]

So, the long arm of the law had finally reached Butch, Sundance, and Etta at their little piece of paradise in Cholila. True, it had sought them for the wrong reason, but poetic justice was nothing to laugh at as far as Butch and Sundance were concerned. Once they made the decision to pull up stakes, things unfolded quickly.

On April 19, 1905, Butch wrote a note to Richard Clarke asking that his previously ordered merchandise be delivered not to the ranch but, instead, to Dan Gibbon because Sundance was packing to leave Cholila.

Unaware of the rapidly deteriorating situation in Argentina, Samanna wrote her last letter to her brother on April 22, 1905. It's doubtful that he ever saw it.

On May 1, 1905, Butch wrote his nearest neighbor, John C. Perry, to say that the three of them were leaving Cholila later that day. Before moving to Argentina around 1901, Perry had been the first sheriff in Crockett County, Texas. He knew the outlaw past of both Sundance and Butch, but he accepted them as friends and good neighbors in Cholila. Perry's wife, Bertie, casually wrote in a letter to a friend in Texas that they had recently visited some Texans living nearby only to discover that they were outlaws whom her husband had known in the States.[22]

In his interviews with author James D. Horan, Percy Seibert—an American engineer employed by Concordia Tin Mines in Bolivia—mentioned a growing affection between Sundance and a neighbor's wife. Horan's notes read: "ranch, neighbor—deputy sheriff in west, wife, thought Sundance paying too much attention . . . neighbor had been Deputy Sheriff, knew of Butch, & didn't like wife falling for Sundance,"[23] although nothing existed to substantiate the rumor.

So, with visions of prison dancing in their heads, Butch, Sundance, and Etta packed up a few of their belongings and traveled to Lake Nahuel Huapi on May 9. They were accompanied by their employee and devoted friend Wenceslao Solis. From there, the three Americans sailed across the lake on the steamer *Condor* to Chile while Solis returned with their saddles to Cholila to begin carrying out his orders to dispose of the ranch holdings.

Solis eventually sold the ranch buildings and supplies to Thomas T. Austin, the manager of Cochamo Company, a Chilean land and cattle company, for 18,000 pesos. They left the bulk of their personal belongings, including a trunk filled with private letters, with Dan Gibbon, John Perry, Solis, and other close friends. Their livestock was also to be sold and the money held for them by Gibbon, their ranch foreman. Because the ranch was still considered to be homesteaded property belonging to the government, the land itself could not be sold.

On June 28, 1905, Sundance wrote to Gibbon from Valparaiso, Chile, saying that he and Etta had arrived safely and intended to leave for San Francisco on June 30.

> *Dear Friend:*
>
> *We are writing to you to let you know that our business went well and we received our money. We arrived here today, and the day after tomorrow my wife and I leave for San Francisco. I'm very sorry, Dan, that we could not bring the brand R with us, but I hope that you will be able to fetch enough to pay you for the inconveniences.*
>
> *We want you to take care of Davy and his wife and see that they don't suffer in any way. And be kind to the old Spaniel and give him pieces of meat once in a while and get rid of the black mutt.*
>
> *I don't want to see Cholila ever again, but I will think of you and of all our friends often, and we want to assure you of our good wishes.*
>
> *Attached you will find the song "Sam Bass," which I promised to write down for you. As I have no more news, I will end by begging that you remember us to all our friends, without forgetting Juan and Vency-low [sic], giving them our regards and good wishes, keeping a large portion for yourself and family.*
>
> *Remaining as always your true friend,*
>
> *H. A. Place*[24]

CHAPTER 9

On the Run Again

Three of the "Wild Bunch" escaped paying the immediate penalty of their crimes only by fleeing the country. "Butch" Cassidy, Harry Longbaugh, the "Sundance Kid," and Etta Place, who also poses as Longbaugh's wife, went to Argentina. All of them were experts with horse and rifle. Etta Place is a markswoman equalled by few men, and with what they had left of their share of the loot they bought a ranch in the interior. Here they were joined later by Harvey Logan.
—Tacoma Times, Tacoma, Washington, September 2, 1913

Sundance and Etta set off for the States once more, this time on June 30, 1905. Even though Valparaiso was a large seaport with a reasonably quick, direct route to San Francisco, one local police report had them traveling overland to Buenos Aires, according to a deposition taken in 1911 regarding the outlaws Williams Wilson and Robert Evans. The two had occasionally associated with Butch and Sundance, so the Cholila trio was sometimes mentioned in the deposition. The territory of Chubut police chief, Leandor Navarro, later wrote, "The fugitives went to Chile where they boarded a steamship and sailed to Valparaiso. . . . Place and his wife [traveled] as Matthews. . . . In Valparaiso, they boarded the trans-Andean train"[1] and traveled east toward Buenos Aires.

The last occasion upon which Etta's presence was mentioned was in Sundance's letter of June 29, 1905, which, according to Dan Gibbon in the 1911 deposition, stated that Etta wasn't with Butch and Sundance, saying that she had gone to San Francisco and remained there at least until 1906.[2] But on July 29, 1905, according to a shipping manifest discovered in New York, the SS *Seguranca* arrived in New York City carrying 105 passengers from Colon, Panama, which was a common transfer point for those who wanted to travel through New York rather than San Francisco. Although the Panama Canal hadn't yet been completed, passengers often took a railroad across the forty-mile isthmus between the Pacific and Atlantic Oceans. Navarro may have alluded to that overland journey when saying that the two traveled by train.

Aboard the ship entering New York Harbor, according to the manifest, was Mrs. E. Place, an American citizen who was born in 1879. She was apparently married since she gave her name as Mrs. Place; she marked "married" under the "marital status" column, and she claimed to be a wife under the "occupation" column. Although she gave only an initial for her first name, the rest of the information matches the description of Etta. It appears she hadn't gone to San Francisco at all but rather to New York.

The name appearing on the ship's manifest directly above Etta's was that of Mr. R. Scott, an American citizen; he was born in 1867; he was married, and his occupation was listed as that of a merchant. Although "R. Scott" would have been a first-time alias for Sundance, the other descriptions fit him perfectly. He, too, had apparently traveled to New York with his wife.

Possibly the two had changed their plans about sailing to San Francisco at the last minute to once again enjoy the sights and sounds of New York City. Or, because their trip had been a spur-of-the-moment venture, they may have discovered upon arrival in Colon that they would have to wait for months for a ship bound for San Francisco while they could board the *Seguranca* for New York immediately. And the *Seguranca*'s departure from Colon on July 22, 1905, would have coincided precisely if Sundance and Etta had left Valparaiso on June 30, 1905, as his letter stated.[3]

By the time December 1905 rolled around, Etta was back in South America with Sundance, where they joined Butch and an unknown accomplice in planning an assault on a bank in the city of Villa Mercedes.

On Tuesday afternoon, December 19, 1905, four robbers hit the Banco de la Nacion in Villa Mercedes de San Luis, Argentina; the armed *Banditos Yanqui* escaped with 12,000 pesos. Witnesses were quick to attribute the robbery to three men and a woman, and bank officers identified Butch, Sundance, and Etta from their photos on Pinkerton's wanted posters. On December 24, two Buenos Aires newspapers, *La Prensa* and *La Nacion*, each credited the robbery to the three Americans plus Kid Curry, a common alias of Harvey Logan. He'd been falsely accused of joining Butch and Sundance in South America, although he had already died in a shootout with Colorado police on June 9, 1904, some six months earlier. Researchers Dan Buck and Anne Meadows believe the fourth outlaw was, instead, a man named Robert Evans, an acquaintance of Sundance and Butch from Cholila.[4]

One local newspaper described the smallest of the outlaws as "beardless, had small feet and delicate features . . . it is supposed that the woman was in charge of cooking the meals . . . the woman is a fine rider."[5]

While two of the robbers held the bank employees and several customers at gunpoint, the other two emptied the safe. When the bank manager resisted, one of the men struck him with the butt of his revolver, opening up a small head wound. Within four minutes, the gang was gone, mounted up and racing out of town. A posse gathered quickly and raced off after them, possibly wounding one of the outlaws as they fled, but when the police drew too close, the bandits dismounted and fired back. A bullet struck the lead horse, dampening the posse's ardor for continuing the chase. The gang remounted and escaped. If Etta were the wounded robber, that would explain why she disappeared from the record one more time, raising the possibility that she'd had enough of outlawry and decided to return to the States.

A series of newspaper articles, such as this one from the *Ogden (Utah) Standard*, described the incident months later, mistakenly referring to the bank as a hotel:

"BUTCH" CASSIDY ALIVE. Hold-ups In Argentine Republic Are Attributed to Him By Eastern Paper.

"Butch" Cassidy is alive and at his old practices. The New York Herald of Sunday, Sept. 23, says "Butch," with three others of his kind, is holding up the Argentine republic. His present aides are Harry Longbaugh, alias "The Sun Dance Kid:" Mrs. Harry Longbaugh and Harvey Logan. Harvey Logan, Longbaugh and Cassidy have operated throughout the west. These men and Bill Caver [sic], now dead, and Ben Kilpatrick, now in the Ohio penitentiary serving a term of fifteen years were for years active in Wyoming, Utah, Colorado and Montana. They were so active in their operations that Utahns felt disappointed if their morning paper had no thrilling story of a fresh train holdup or exciting account of a duel between these desperadoes and town officers on the previous evening. Anything less than a $30,000 haul was thought worthy of little comment.

"Butch" Cassidy was born in southern Utah. He has relatives living in that region today. It is generally believed that he died near the Hole-in-the-Wall country a few years ago and is buried, there. The news furnished the New York Herald that he is alive and as active as ever will be news, indeed, throughout the west, and particularly in Utah. Those who remember Harvey Logan and others of Cassidy's "gang" will be also interested in learning that a few of them are still alive.

Under the heading, "Yankee Desperadoes Are Holding Up the Argentine Republic," the New York Herald says Cassidy, Longbaugh, Mrs. Longbaugh and Harvey Logan have been performing startling stunts in the hold-up line in that country. One exploit was a hotel hold-up turned last March in Villa Mercedes in the province of San Luis. While one of the horsemen watched outside three entered the hotel office and secured between $15,000 and $20,000. One man covered the clerk on duty with a revolver while the other two gathered the loose cash and valuables. Before they had completed this work the manager of the hotel entered the office and, for his intrusion, was shot through the head. The three men then mounted their horses and the quartette was out of sight before the little town had recovered sufficiently to start after them. Similar deeds have thrown the southern *republic into a fit of fear and made the mysterious quartette several thousand dollars richer.*

Color is added to this story by the announcement that one of the desperadoes is a woman, a pretty little woman, 20 years old, with, gracefully girlish figure, flashing eyes, regular features, brilliant white teeth and a mass of wavy heavy black hair. She is supposed to be Longbaugh's wife, but nothing is known of her pedigree or early life. It was she who held the horses in front of the Villa Mercedes hotel while her three companions performed the nasty work inside. She was dressed in men's clothes.

The authorities of the southern republic are greatly excited by the outrages being committed with persistent frequency by the quartette. In looking through old police documents they found a notification from the Pinkerton National Detective agency that a band of North American train and bank robbers had landed in Buenos Ayres in 1901 and had taken up a permanent residence in the remote interior. This gang comprised Cassidy, Longbaugh and the latter's wife. These were joined later by Harvey Logan. After touching at Buenos Ayres the original trio took a steamer for Bahia Blanca, and from this point proceeded to an inland point called Rawson. They then rode mules to an almost inaccessible table land in the province of Chibute. Here they are supposed to have made their home, raising cattle and farming. For reasons known to them alone they have again started their operations.[6]

The trio of robbers had stashed supplies en route from town, aiding their escape, and even though the posse supposedly wounded one of them, they never did catch them. Etta, who had always been a crack shot, reportedly handled herself utterly fearlessly, and *La Prensa* (which gave her the nickname of "Miss H. A. Place") said that she was "an interesting woman, very masculine, who wears male clothing with total correctness, and who is dedicated more to the occupations of men than to those of women . . . a fine rider, handles with precision all classes of firearms, and has an admirable male temperament."[7]

No one from the Cholila ranching community ever saw Etta Place afterward, and for good reason. She moved with Sundance from

Argentina to the Chilean port city of Antofagasta, settling there while Sundance experienced some unspecified "difficulty" with the Chilean authorities:

> *On January 26, 1906, a Pinkerton memo issued from the Philadel-phia office mentioned that Sundance was using the name Frank Boyd or H. A. Brown and he had been in trouble with the Chilean gov-ernment "a short time ago." The Pinkertons' source for the information was a letter Sundance had written to Samanna that was found by an informant in the Mont Clare, Pennsylvania, post office. No rea-son was given for the problem, and nothing has been found after an exhaustive search of Chilean records by present-day researchers. How-ever, the United States vice-consul, Frank Aller, assisted Mr. Boyd/ Brown in clearing up the problem at a cost of $1,500.[8]*

Aller worked at the time for the American Smelting and Refining Company in Antofagasta. He moonlighted as vice consul, a political go-between for Americans in foreign countries. He most likely never real-ized Sundance's true identity when he extended his services.

In the 1950s author James Horan interviewed the Concordia Mines' Percy Seibert in New York City about his friendship with Butch and Sundance. Although Horan's notes are abbreviated and at times chal-lenging to read, they may contain a possible explanation of the Chilean "problem" Sundance had experienced:

> *Sundance, going back, 1905, woman, . . . restaurant posters, depicting 75000, 10,000 joked with constable if found, split . . . got stouter . . . woman started to go out. number of deputies, to pick him up—as was custom, no single action .45—use black jack or billy, cock it faster ordinary man . . . Smith Wesson lawman . . . covered man, chief police shot, no intention, accident, showed cops gun, held week, had lawyer . . . sent message to Butch, who had 1,000 English, gave bill, northern Argentina—1906 . . . picked up Sundance to help him.[9]*

From the note's cryptic nature, it's difficult to know precisely what Horan meant to say, although it's likely that Sundance and a woman (Etta) were eating dinner in a restaurant before leaving the country when a constable noticed a wanted poster of Sundance. Sundance and Etta joked about a strong physical resemblance and turned to leave when more deputies entered. Sundance was concerned enough to draw his gun, even though the constables had only blackjacks or billy clubs with them. In the confusion that followed, Sundance's gun accidentally discharged, wounding the chief of police. Sundance was held in the local jail for a week while Aller rounded up $1,500, two-thirds of which came from Butch when he showed up to post Sundance's bail.

Following the Villa Mercedes holdup, Butch and Sundance parted ways, Butch taking a job with the Concordia Tin Mines while Sundance hired on breaking mules for Roy Letson, a contractor driving the animals from northern Argentina to a railroad encampment near La Paz, Bolivia. Although Letson found Sundance to be inordinately shy, he liked him.

Longabaugh kept very much to himself most of the time. I told him my destination was Bolivia and he said that he would be glad to go along. We were several weeks on that trip. . . . He was employed by our company to break the mules to harness and saddle and done a very good job . . . well dressed . . . did have a very fine Tiffany gold watch. . . . It was not long before he was on the go again.[10]

By the end of 1906, Butch and Sundance had reunited, this time at the mines southeast of the city of La Paz, Bolivia. These particular shafts were seated some 16,000 feet above sea level in the Santa Vela Cruz Mountains, part of the central Bolivian Andes. The two Americans had been hired as payroll guards by Clement Rolla Glass, the mine manager.

Glass's assistant, Percy Seibert, had met the two at a Christmas party at the Grand Hotel Guibert in La Paz. Seibert at the time knew nothing of their checkered past, although he soon began hearing rumors. His cryptic notes state, "Look here I hear you are Yankee American bandit rumor Butch—come in and talk—light electric light—treated decent we're hole in wall gang."[11]

During their employment, Butch and Sundance were known as Santiago Maxwell and Harry Brown. Despite their disparate backgrounds, the three soon became close friends, the two outlaws often dining with the Seibert family for Sunday dinner. As for Sundance's legendary accuracy with a pistol, Seibert recalled, "Sundance, 2 bottle of beer right—and left, hands, threw in air, draw single action revolver."[12]

Seibert also recalled that Butch sat facing the door so he could see anyone entering. Seibert even sketched his living quarters to show a man with his back to the rear wall. Their friendship was cemented when Butch ordered two local outlaws out of the mining camp. He wrote, "Nation came in Clifford—wanted pay roll robbery—wanted gringo camp, give bad name, wanted horseshoes made, out of money, gave $50—get out!"[13] The two local outlaws, Nation and Clifford, had planned on robbing Seibert's payroll because they were out of money. Butch wouldn't hear of it, so he gave them fifty dollars and sent them packing.

Either from boredom or empty pockets, the American bandits sporadically left the mines on short trips. When they returned, according to Seibert, they were always flush with cash, and rumors of another small robbery quickly surfaced. But the gringos' devotion to their boss and to Concordia was unquestioned. Except for those times when they *weren't*, the two were the perfect law-abiding citizens—to their own employers, at least.

But all good things eventually come to an end. With Butch and Sundance, it came shortly after Sundance began drinking heavily and boasting about the past. Butch no doubt talked to him about it, and no doubt it did little good, because not long after, the two left their positions at the Concordia. The tale that broke the donkey's back may have been the inside scoop on the Winnemucca bank robbery, the details of which ended up in the newspapers following Sundance's demise.

So, by November 12, 1907, the pair found themselves in Santa Cruz, Bolivia. Butch sent a letter to his friends and former employees at the Concordia, suggesting that he and Sundance were thinking of settling down again, making another attempt at going straight.

To The Boys At Concordia:

We arrived here about 3 weeks ago after a very pleasant journey and found just the place I have been looking for 20 years and [Sundance] likes it better than I do. He says he wont try to live any where else. . . The grass is good. . . . Land is cheap here and everything grows good that is planted. . . . It is pretty warm and some fever but the fever is caused by the food they eat. At least I am willing to chance it. . . . We expect to be back at Concordia in about 1 month. Good luck to all you fellows.

J. P. Maxwell[14]

Around this time, according to Frank Aller, who had provided help for Sundance's earlier problem in Chile, Sundance received his mail at the American Hotel in Oruro, Bolivia. Aller wrote in a letter that Sundance was known as "H. A. Brown or Frank Boyd. . . . I have a letter from him in which he stated that he would use the former name in Bolivia, in order to get 'honorable employment.'"[15]

As was the case back home, many unsolved robberies in South America were pinned on Butch and Sundance. This was no surprise since most of the official information given by the police and newspapers came from the Pinkertons through Frank Dimaio. Articles appearing in newspapers in both the United States and South America suggested at times that Sundance was the leader of the gang. The *New York Herald* and the *Denver Republican* each printed an article saying, "It is apparent that Longbaugh, the leader of what is left of one of the most noted bands of robbers in this country."[16] Another article claimed, "Harry Longbaugh became the accepted leader of the outlaws" and referred to the gang as the Sun-Dance Kids and the Sun Dance Gang.[17]

Then, in May 1908, two Americans stole the payroll from a railroad construction camp in Eucalyptus, Bolivia. The thieves took 15,000 bolivianos or about $15,000 and were assumed to be ex-employees of the railway. Three months later, on August 19, the station was robbed again by the same two bandits, according to authorities. This time, according to Seibert, the bandits were fingered as Butch and Sundance.

But the Americanos' involvement at Eucalyptus is doubtful. By August 1908, both outlaws were working at the headquarters of A. G. Francis near Esmoraca, Bolivia. Francis was a British engineer employed by the San Juan del Oro Dredging Company, supervising a gold dredge that was being moved on the river. Francis knew Sundance as Frank Smith and Butch as George Lowe, and he assigned them to bunk with his crew. What he didn't realize was that they were there, lying low, while they planned another bank job.[18]

While Sundance busied himself around camp during the day, Butch often snuck off to Tupiza, a mining town fifteen miles north of camp, where he spent several days at a time scouting out the local bank's layout. One day, when Butch rode into town, he was surprised to learn that a Bolivian cavalry unit had taken up residence in a hotel next to the bank. He and Sundance could do nothing more than wait. And watch. And wait some more.

Finally, by late October, the two realized the job was too risky and changed their plans. Butch had heard that an 80,000-peso payroll was being shipped by Aramayo Francke & Company, a mining enterprise with an office in Tupiza. Both outlaws left camp and registered at the Hotel Terminus, from which they kept an eye on the Aramayo company office for signs of the shipment.

Sure enough, on November 3, 1908, Carlos Pero, the company manager, left the Aramayo office with his son, Mariano, and an employee named Gil Gonzalez, trailing two pack mules headed for the mines at Quechisla. It was a rugged and hazardous three-day journey, and Butch and Sundance followed behind, their thoughts on the 80,000 pesos and, after one more robbery, another "go" at retirement from outlawry.

As Pero's group stopped to rest for the night at the village of Cotani, Butch and Sundance slipped quietly on ahead to Huaca Huañusca ("Dead Cow"). At the foot of a mountain named for the shape of its spiny ridge, Huaca Huañusca was a promising site for an ambush. About 9:30 the next morning, November 4, Pero and his payroll escort rounded the bend and found themselves face-to-face with Butch and Sundance brandishing new, small-caliber Mauser carbines. The two were also armed with Colt revolvers, Browning pistols, and enough rifle ammunition to last a week, according to Pero's later reports. He described the thieves as wearing dark red corduroy suits and bandannas pulled up over their faces, their hat brims turned down over their eyes. Pero's note read:

> We encountered two well-armed Yankees, who awaited us with the faces covered by bandannas and their rifles ready, and they made us dismount and open the baggage, from which they took only the cash shipment. They also took from us a dark brown mule, which is known to the stable hands in Tupiza, with a new hemp rope.
>
> The two Yankees are tall; one thin and the other—who carried a good pair of Hertz binoculars—heavyset.
>
> They clearly came from Tupiza, where they must have been waiting for my departure to make their strike, because from the beginning they did not ask me for anything other than the cash shipment.[19]

Pero added that Sundance kept silent watch from a distance while Butch rode up to Pero and, in English, demanded the 80,000-peso payroll. Pero replied that they were carrying only 15,000 pesos, amounting to a little less than $100,000 in today's currency. Obviously disappointed, Butch and Sundance tied the packet of money wrapped in a cloth to one of the mules and told Pero, his son, and Gonzalez to continue on their journey. When Pero crossed paths with a mule driver named Andrew Gutierrez a short while later, he jotted down a note reporting the robbery. Gutierrez took the note back to Aramayo headquarters while Pero continued on to the mine minus one payroll.

By that afternoon, nearly every town in the area had been alerted to be on the lookout for two Americano robbers. Sundance and Butch arrived in Tomahuaico, where A. G. Francis was camped. They woke him and told him they were looking for a place to bed down for the night. Butch was apparently sick and went to bed while Sundance fixed himself something to eat and regaled Francis with tales of their latest heist.[20]

The following morning, as they prepared breakfast, a mutual acquaintance rushed into camp to warn Francis, Sundance, and Butch that a military patrol from Tupiza was headed for Tomahuaico. At first, the outlaws seemed unconcerned, finishing breakfast before packing their horses. After that, they decided that Francis should accompany them as a "guide" to Uyuni in the north. Francis felt more like a hostage. "Needless to say, that was the last thing I wished to do, but argument was useless. Reflecting upon my position, I felt it to be a very unenviable one. . . . However, no other course being open to me, I decided to put as good a face on the matter as possible."[21]

The three men traveled as far as the Indian pueblo of Estarca, where they spent the night of November 5. In the morning, Butch and Sundance thanked Francis and said goodbye, much to their host's relief. They also said that he should tell anyone he met along the road that he had seen the two outlaws headed south to Argentina while the two actually continued north. Although Francis believed they were heading for Uyuni, they were probably hoping to get to Oruro, where Sundance had recently been living in the American Hotel.[22]

At about sundown the following evening, Butch and Sundance arrived in the small mining village of San Vicente, Bolivia. At 14,500 feet, the Cordillera Occidental Mountains were definitely no place to spend a night outdoors in the bitter cold and wind. Above tree line, the tundra was stark and without shelter, so they asked if they could spend the night at the home of Bonifacio Casasola, who referred them to Cleto Bellot, the town *corregidor*, a mayor or chief administrative officer. Bellot replied that there was no local inn but that the men should tell Casasola to put them up for the night. When the men said they also wanted some sardines and beer, Bellot sent Casasola to purchase their supper with several pesos that Sundance had given him.

Bellot then reported the pair of strangers to a military patrol that had arrived in town from Uyuni only a few hours earlier. The four-man patrol—Captain Justo P. Concha, Uyuni police inspector Timoteo Rios, soldier Victor Torres, and another soldier—was looking for the two Yankees who had stolen the Aramayo payroll and company mule.

With Concha inexplicably absent—most likely either napping or sleeping off drunkenness—Torres took the lead, and the men entered Casasola's patio. Butch saw them first and, wasting no time, shot from the doorway, hitting Torres in the neck. Although mortally wounded, Torres was able to return fire as he backed out of the patio. The others retreated, firing from a safe distance. Bellot later reported hearing "three screams of desperation . . . no more shots were heard, except that the inspector [Rios] fired one shot at about midnight."[23]

After the initial gunfight, according to author Donna Ernst, Concha appeared with the remainder of his patrol, and they waited outside the rest of the night. In the quiet that fell across the following morning's sunrise, Concha sent Casasola into his house, and he emerged excitedly to report two dead bodies. When Concha entered the casita, he had discovered the shorter outlaw (Butch) stretched out on the floor, shot in the arm and in the temple. The taller man (Sundance) was behind the door with his arms wrapped around a ceramic jar; he had several wounds in his arm and was shot in the forehead. "Wounded, not wishing to rot in a Bolivian jail, or simply inextricably trapped, Butch had shot Sundance and then himself."[24]

Although an inquest was held by the authorities in Tupiza, copies of that legal document have not been found. There are, however, other reports and depositions that verify both the shootout and the apparent suicide deaths of the two Yankee bandits in the small town of San Vicente. A copy of the summary memorandum, discovered later, was signed by all who gave testimony. In it, Cleto Bellot wrote,

This is to inform you that yesterday, at 3 P.M., a force from Uyuni commanded by Captain Justo P. Concha arrived in this vice canton with the aim of pursuing the robbers of the Aramayo, Francke and Company's cash shipment.

The presumed robbers arrived here at about 7 P.M. Having been advised [of this fact], those in charge of the pursuit, in the company of the undersigned, presented themselves at the lodging of the men in order to identify them. We were fired upon, which caused a battle to be joined between the pursued and the pursuers, resulting in three dead—one soldier from the Uyuni column, Victor Torres, and the two foreigners, the alleged robbers.[25]

Also, Remigio Sanchez, a miner from San Vicente, testified regarding the battle's outcome.

Two mounted gringos came from the east. . . . The police inspector, with two soldiers and the corregidor, immediately came to look and find out who the men were. . . . One of the gringos—the smaller one— appeared and fired one shot and then another from his revolver at the soldier. . . . He died in moments. . . . We remained all night until, at dawn, the captain ordered the owner of the house to go inside . . . . and found the smaller gringo stretched out on the floor, dead, with one bullet wound in the temple and another in the arm. The taller one . . . was dead, also, with a bullet wound in the forehead and several in the arm.

At about six in the morning, we were able to enter the room and found the two foreigners dead.[26]

A local magistrate, Aristides Daza, testified that he aided the authorities in a postmortem examination of the bodies. "I found a body in the threshold of Bonifacio Casasola's house with a revolver that appeared to have been fired . . . the other individual, who was on a bench, having used an earthen jug as a shield . . . finding him dead."[27]

Daza proceeded to help inventory the personal effects of the two deceased outlaws. Sundance had, among other items, a total of 93.50 bolivianos in his pocket; a dictionary; a new modified Winchester carbine; 125 Winchester cartridges; and an 18-carat gold watch without crystal—a symbol of more memorable times. In the luggage packs on the mules were a pair of binoculars, guns, more ammunition, and 14,400 bolivianos of Aramayo payroll money.[28]

The two deceased outlaws were buried in the San Vicente cemetery on November 7, 1908. "For Sundance and Butch," Ernst concluded, "the Outlaw Trail ended in San Vicente, Bolivia."[29]

CHAPTER 10

Someone Was Killed

As Etta Place, this master criminal was noted as a cow-woman in the North American Wild West of years ago. She married Harry Long-baugh, and when she discovered he was one of a band of holdup men and bandits, not only joined the gang, but became its leader. Dressed in man's clothing, Etta became "outside man" for the gang—the one who held the horses and remained on guard, who bore the brunt of attack by aroused citizens, and always was the last in the getaway.
—THE TIMES, SHREVEPORT, LOUISIANA, NOVEMBER 25, 1917

HARRY ALONZO LONGABAUGH WAS BORN IN THE SPRING OF 1867 AND, according to Donna Ernst, died on November 6, 1908, at forty-one years old. "His family did not acknowledge him for over sixty years; his sister Emma changed the spelling of the family name and disowned him when writing her will; and nearly three generations passed before his name was again mentioned by anyone in the family. He clearly broke the law, but others apparently remembered him in a better light."[1]

In 1913, A. G. Francis recalled Sundance's death:

I must confess that it was with a feeling very much akin to grief that I wended my way home. [Sundance] told me once that he had made several attempts to settle down to a law-abiding life, but these attempts had always been frustrated by emissaries of the police and detective agencies getting on his track, and thus forcing him to the road. He claimed that he had never hurt or killed a man except in self-defense, and had never stolen from the poor, but only from rich corporations well able to support his "requisitions."

I certainly knew him as a most amiable and cheerful companion, possessed of a very equable temper.

To conclude, I may mention that his favourite book was Rolf Boldrewood's "Robbery Under Arms," in which he greatly admired the character of "Old Man" Marston.[2]

On November 7, 1908, Francis met a local tribesman who confirmed that two Yankee outlaws had been killed in a shootout in San Vicente. Their descriptions matched those of Butch and Sundance, the men Francis had known as Smith and Lowe. He began asking questions and eventually learned more about their final hours, leading to his writing an article for *Wide World Magazine* titled "The End of an Outlaw." Unfortunately, Francis's use of several of his characters' false aliases muddied their true identities for years.

Dan Gibbon, John Perry, and others living near Cholila learned of their friends' deaths in Bolivia by 1911, while giving depositions about two local outlaws, Wilson and Evans. Fred Ings and Ebb Johnson, friends of Sundance from their days spent working their Canadian stomping grounds, also heard that Sundance and Butch had died; both of the friends wrote memoirs during the 1930s in which they mentioned Sundance's death in South America, lending credibility to the dictum that stories based on stories are still stories, whether real or not.

Other outlaw pals from the States also learned that Sundance and Butch were deceased. Two of them, William Simpson and Matt Warner, claimed that men had been sent down to South America to verify their deaths. Warner also mentioned their deaths in a 1937 letter to author Charles Kelly as well as in his own 1939 autobiography. "[Butch] went to South America . . . and partnered with Harry Longabaugh. The two of 'em ranched and robbed in Bolivia and Argentina and was finally killed in a fight with soldiers that had been chasing 'em." As for the outlaw duo's possible escape from harm's way and ultimate return to the States, Warner's opinion was, "It's all poppycock."[3] No doubt about it: Matt Warner was sure the two died that night.

When Butch and Sundance were buried in San Vicente, they were interred as *desconocidos*, or unknowns, a fact that created a debate among historians that continues to this day. It also posed a problem for the country of Chile. On July 31, 1909, Frank D. Aller, then vice consul from Antofagasta, wrote to the American minister at the American Legation in La Paz, Bolivia, attempting to verify the identities of the two outlaws who died in San Vicente on November 6, 1908. He wrote,

> *An American citizen named Frank Boyd is wanted in Antofagasta and letters addressed to him in Bolivia have failed to receive reply. . . . The last address of Frank Boyd or H. A. Brown was "American Hotel," Oruro. . . . I have been informed by Mr. Wm. Grey of Oruro, Mr. Thomas Mason of Uyuni and many others that Boyd and a companion named Maxwell or Brown were killed at San Vicente near Tupiza by natives and police and buried as "desconocidos." I have endeavored by correspondence to obtain confirmation and a certificate of death, but this has been impossible. . . . It is very important to locate Boyd alive, or failing this, to produce legal proof of his death. Everybody in Bolivia, except the authorities, seem convinced that the larger of the two men was Boyd and that possibly he had assumed the name of Brown.[4]*

The question of why Aller wanted to verify Sundance's death is still open to speculation. Most likely it was to satisfy the demands upon the Longabaugh estate. But whose demands? Certainly not his family's, who wrote him off as "lost" long before his death. Might the inquiries have been at the insistence of Etta Place? Could Etta have gone back to Chile, trying to file a legal claim against her husband's estate only to return empty-handed? If so, of what did the estate consist? Aller added that everyone believed Sundance was dead. Why was there no proof?

A confirmation of the *reason* for—if not the *source* of—Aller's request written to the American minister came from Alexander Benson of the American legation in La Paz, Bolivia, who wrote, "Legal proof of his

[Sundance's] death is wanted by a Judge of the Court of Chile, in order to settle his estate."[5]

The answer to these questions, according to Ernst, would be definitive after examining the proceeds Sundance left behind. Unfortunately, the evidence of a surviving estate has yet to be found.

Bolivian authorities eventually replied to Aller's request, saying, in rough translation, "I also submit to you the death certificates of the two said persons whose identifications are not known."[6] Obviously, this was not the answer Aller had hoped to receive—or needed. On January 21, 1911, Aller must have been overjoyed to receive a second letter from the Bolivian authorities, who were "pleased to enclose herewith a complete record of the case of Maxwell and Brown, drawn up by the authorities of the district where they were killed."[7] Although no copy of that complete record has been located, the letter states that Maxwell and Brown were killed, and those were known to be the names used in Bolivia by Butch and Sundance.

Game, set, match? Perhaps not.

In 1918, Emma Longabough, Sundance's sister, wrote a disclaimer in her will to avoid probate upon her death. In the will she stated, "Whether my said brother Harry be living or dead, is not to change or affect this will." The family never officially heard of his death, and many of them apparently believed the rumors of his demise, although Emma obviously had some doubts. Sundance's sister Samanna ended her diary with her last letter to her brother on April 22, 1905, after which she'd never heard from him again.

Finally, the general public learned of the deaths of Butch and Sundance in an article written by Arthur Chapman titled "Butch Cassidy," which appeared in the April 1930 issue of *The Elks Magazine*. Chapman's source for the piece was Percy Seibert of the Concordia Tin Mines. Seibert, a close friend of both Sundance and Butch, believed that they died in San Vicente that fateful night.

In recent years, researchers Dan Buck and Anne Meadows have discovered numerous documents and local histories in South America that verify both the San Vicente shootout and the deaths of Butch and Sundance. In addition to the mound of evidence Buck and Meadows claim, William H. Longabough (who was Sundance's nephew and author Donna Ernst's grandfather by marriage) took his grandfather's oft-reiterated words to heart: "Grand-pop once said, 'I had an uncle who died in South America; he robbed banks and trains for a living and died in South America.'"[8]

Chapter 11

What About Etta?

Now comes word that Etta Longbaugh is dead and that her band is broken up. Old police officials are skeptical. It would be just like her, they say, to send word to this country that she was dead, wait for the belief to become firmly entrenched, then quietly return. For, after all, the United States is Etta's native land, and perhaps the call to die in it is too strong to be resisted. She may be planning to come back and live quietly if she can avoid capture. Who can tell?
—Wichita Daily Eagle, Wichita, Kansas, January 1, 1918

Throughout the annals of history, neatly tied stories begin with a beginning and end with an end and have just the right amount of material in the middle to make them palatable—if, for no other reason, than to prove that something of historically valuable significance took place. And so it might have been with Etta.

Instead, her life's story was just the opposite. We don't know where she was born or where she lived until she moved as a young woman to Fort Worth to begin life anew. There, she met some bank robbers and train holdup men and had some frolicking good times both in the United States and in South America.

When she returned to San Francisco, her newly adopted home, where no one likely knew her and no one ever would, she allegedly left behind the one man she truly loved in Bolivia to die. And so, too, did

Etta Place die—perhaps of a broken heart; perhaps of a broken neck in a car accident; perhaps in a train wreck or of old age while traveling the world, trying to make sense of a life that bore little semblance to any other American woman's life before or since.

That would certainly be a fitting conclusion to the history of Etta place—any one of those scenarios—except for one thing: As with the beginning of her life, it has no end.

Or, at least, it has no *conclusive* end.

A person whose life has no accountable beginning, no accountable end, but an undeniably verifiable middle is an enigma. Such a person can't possibly have existed. And yet, she did.

So, the historical researcher, in unearthing the history of the mysterious life of Etta Place, is faced with digging deeper, attempting to uncover a hidden piece of information here, a miscellaneous and seemingly unimportant nugget there, to shed a modicum of light on the mystery. That we know little if anything of Etta's early life is not critical because she popped up mid-life and lived to her mid-twenties as richly, thoroughly, and openly as any person could, if not more so. That we know so little if anything of her later life is staggering because this woman whom we know existed simply disappeared into thin air. That is not an easy task for anyone to pull off, particularly not anyone so notorious for being the moll and member of one of the most infamous outlaw gangs in the history of the Old West. And beyond.

So, the question for the researcher remains: Where do we search next?

And the answer, in this case, is the same answer that any one of several Pinkerton agents hot on the trail of the Wild Bunch would have given—and that several did: In the last place the person was thought to have lived. In San Francisco.

In researching the Longabaugh family history, Donna Ernst came up with this usual conclusion regarding Etta: "Except for the six or seven years she spent with Sundance, very little is truly known about her."[1] She went on to recite her own contention: "Writer Horan's notes from his interviews with Percy Seibert read: 'Eltel [*sic*] Place, ailing chronic appen. Sundance took her to Denver, went to cathouse, woke up alone, drunk fired, wanted coffee, got out town.'"[2] Thus began Ernst's story that

Etta returned to the United States in 1906 because of a recurring battle with appendicitis. While it seems highly unlikely that someone with an attack of appendicitis would travel from South America to Denver for treatment—a long and arduous trip under normal conditions—this presents one of the earliest explanations for her departure.

Ernst was correct in assuming that no one suffering from *acute* appendicitis would make a month-long journey before seeking emergency aid, but someone suffering from *chronic*, or long-term and recurring, appendicitis might. And Etta, based on several comments from Butch and others, had suffered from the chronic disease for years.

But Ernst also points out that, assuming Etta didn't return for the appendectomy, she would have needed another reason for departing South America for the States. Ernst's conclusion was obvious: Etta returned because she'd had enough notoriety and was ready to escape to the vanishing pages of history. At that point, of course, facts about her life grow muddy.

When Butch and Sundance sold their holdings in Cholila in June 1905, Sundance wrote that he planned on taking Etta back to San Francisco. Whether or not she remained there as is commonly thought, offering one last, lingering goodbye to the man she loved, is open to conjecture and discounts the apparent trip to Denver for emergency medical treatment a year later. More likely, Etta first traveled to San Francisco in 1905 but then returned once more to South America alone on the SS *Seguranca*. She may also have visited San Francisco for a short time and returned with Sundance, where the two lived together in the port city of Antofagasta, Chile. The last official sighting of her was reportedly on a raft crossing the Salado River while escaping shortly after the December 19, 1905, bank robbery in Villa Mercedes, Argentina, which would have confirmed her return to South America after her June 1905 visit to the States.[3]

Although she never again surfaced to public view, a specific reference to her popped up in the 1911 deposition concerning outlaws Wilson and Evans provided by Daniel Gibbon, the ranch foreman at Cholila at the time. Gibbon swore under oath that Sundance told him Etta was living in San Francisco in 1906. If this is true, she may have been there when the great earthquake struck the vicinity in the early morning of April 18, 1906, recording 7.9 on the Richter scale and leveling more than 80 percent of the city, reducing it to rubble. If so, she may well have been among the three thousand people killed as a result of the disaster. Although the impact of the quake on San Francisco was the most pronounced, it also inflicted damage on several other cities, including nearby San Jose and Santa Rosa, the latter of which saw its entire downtown district devastated.

But if that were the final curtain call on the life and times of Etta Place, speculation regarding the unnamed woman inquiring into the settlement of Sundance's estate in 1909 would have eliminated her from contention. Yet, it could be that the local authorities—not Etta Place, the bereaved widow of Harry A. Place—initiated the inquiry into the standing of the estate.

However, yet another fly in the ointment exists in the speculation that Etta died unexpectedly during the earthquake of April 1906. According to Ernst,

> *A summary of the Argentine depositions taken in 1911 states that on their final trip out of the country Sundance and Ethel traveled under the name Mr. and Mrs. Matthews. Using this as a possible identity clue, together with the belief that she originally came from Texas, this author made a thorough search comparing Texas census records with California census records and San Francisco City directories.*
>
> *In 1907, there was a listing for an E. Matthews living at 1417 San Bruno Avenue in San Francisco; but there was no indication as to the sex or full name of "E" Matthews. No Ethel Matthews appeared in the 1910 California census records. Because of the method in which California keeps marriage records, with both date and names required, no search for a possible second-marriage record was possible.*
>
> *However, the search of Texas census and birth records did reveal a possibility. Ethel Angie Matthews was born October 3, 1877, to J. B. and S. E. Matthews in Morgan Mill, Erath County, Texas. After the 1880 census record, there is no further local record of her. She*

filed a delayed birth record with the Social Security Administration on August 16, 1944, and a family member verified her information. But there was no mention of a married name for Ethel Angie Matthews, and she again disappeared. Although much easier to research than the California records, no marriage record has yet been found in Texas for Ethel Angie Matthews. For that matter, no marriage record has yet been found in Texas for anyone named Harry Longabaugh, Harry Alonzo, Harry Place, or Ethel Place. [4]

Were Ethel Place, E. Matthews of San Francisco, and Ethel Angie Matthews of Morgan Mill, Texas, the same person? Ernst believes the possibility is likely.

Yet, other sources add still more complexity to the speculation, throwing cold water on the Ernst supposition. In a May 1995 article, author W. Paul Reeve suggests that a Brown's Park, Utah, woman named Ann Bassett may have actually been Etta Place, lending credence to the theory that Etta had been born not out east or in Texas but, instead, in the Beehive State, likely very near the Parker family home. Reeve points out that Bassett and Place shared the same physical description and many coincidental appearances: When Bassett left Utah, Place turned up in Texas. When Place left Texas, Bassett turned up elsewhere. "Moreover," according to Reeve, "both women were noted for their classic good looks, intelligence, expert horsemanship, prowess with guns, and reputations as 'loose' ladies. Adding to the likelihood that the two women were actually the same person is the fact that soon after each of Bassett's disappearances from Brown's Park, Place turned up with Cassidy and Sundance."[5]

Adding veracity to his claim, Reeve cited other sources:

Ann took to cattle rustling and sabotage to defend her family's holdings against the Two-Bar Ranch, a large cattle company vying for control of Brown's Park. Meanwhile, the Wild Bunch left Utah and congregated in Texas in the fall of 1900. A few months later Ann left Brown's Park and Etta Place turned up in Texas. A February 2, 1901, article in the Vernal Express noted that "Miss Annie Bassett left on this morning's stage for Texas." Again, using the alias Etta

Place, Bassett met Cassidy and Sundance, this time as a companion
of the latter, and the trio journeyed to New York and then sailed to
South America. Pinkerton records indicate that Place and Sundance
returned to the US in July 1902. Six months later Ann reappeared
in Vernal, and the newspaper reported that she had been "traveling"
for two years.[6]

History, however, doesn't smile too kindly upon Reeve's speculations. Too many documented elements of Bassett's life conflict with the acknowledged facts of Etta's life to dismiss. During two separate periods, when Etta was known to have been in South America with Butch and Sundance, Annie Bassett was either under arrest, on trial, in jail, or getting married in the States. "Difficult to do," says author Tony Hays, "if you're in South America."[7]

So, a young Utah-bred cowboy named Robert LeRoy Parker showed up at the Bassett Ranch looking for work one day, and Herb Bassett hired him as a hand. Before long, he looked at him as part of the family. According to author Richard Patterson,

Butch apparently had the run of the Bassett home. Herb was the local
postmaster, and when Butch was not needed in the barn or corral, he
spent much of his time reading the newspapers and magazines that
accumulated in Herb's office. Also, Butch took advantage of the Bassett
family's extensive library. On Sundays, Butch would sometimes join
in when neighbors gathered at the Bassett home for church services,
and he was always welcome at social gatherings hosted by the family.
Occasionally he attended local dances, probably escorting the Bassetts'
daughter Josie, then fifteen. Some say that Butch may have even
courted Josie briefly. In later years, when Josie was asked about this,
she would neither confirm nor deny it but would merely say that she
and Butch, whom she referred to as "a big dumb kid who liked to joke,"
were just "good friends."[8]

On the other hand, on at least one occasion she was heard to refer to Butch as her beau. "Josie's younger sister, Ann, then eleven, evidently adored Butch and would tag after him when he was working."[9]

In fact, the two sisters may have been more contentious over the "big dumb kid" than initially thought. When ranch hand Elzy Lay came to work at the Bassett Ranch, Josie took a liking to him. "In talking to Josie years later, Elzy's grandson had the impression that she may indeed have been in love with Elzy. But Josie was also taken with Butch, as was her sister, Ann. This conflict may have caused problems between the two women. According to a neighbor, a man named Meacham, one day he watched the sisters actually get into a 'knock-down-drag-out' fight over Butch."[10]

Later, when Butch and Elzy were being sought for suspicion of committing the Montpelier bank robbery, the outlaws decided to hide out in Brown's Park. But the park was familiar territory to Sheriff John Pope, who had prospected there and had even owned a ranch on Red Creek. Eventually, with enough manpower, Pope could have flushed them out. On the other hand, Pope was likely not all that serious about making the arrests. At least, that was the opinion of Ann Bassett, who, according to author Richard Patterson, "said later that Pope probably intentionally delayed rushing into the Overholt Saloon at Vernal so that Butch could escape."[11]

Ann's involvement with Butch and, for that matter, with Elzy Lay, long preceded Etta Place's introduction to the members of Butch Cassidy's inner circle, including Sundance, eliminating her from contention as being one and the same as the Bassett daughter.

* * *

Wherever Etta came from or whoever she was, the last recorded public sighting of her was when she crossed Argentina's Salado River on a raft. From that point forward, the path of speculation roams wider than her own travels. Some researchers allege she went back to Denver, not to have an appendectomy but rather a baby—or at least an abortion, perhaps as a result of her alleged affair with a Cholila neighbor, John Gardiner. In fact, she may have been living in Denver as late as 1924, sixteen years after the famous shootout in San Vicente. Others say she returned to the United States and had several children, including a daughter who carried on the family trade and became the leader of a minor gang of bank robbers active in the Midwest in the 1920s and early 1930s. In addition to moving to Tacoma with Sundance and begging for money from elderly relatives who didn't have any to spare, Etta allegedly spent six years fighting in the Mexican Revolution, with or without Sundance, depending on whether or not one believes he survived the gunfight in Bolivia.

Some accounts go wildly astray from the usual assumptions, one claiming that she returned to or remained in South America following the Bolivian shootout. One story says that, after marrying an "Irish adventurer who led Argentine troops to one of [the Wild Bunch's] strongholds and killed Longabaugh, her husband," Etta was slain in a Buenos Aires hotel by Mateo Gebhart. In another version, after Butch and Sundance died in the shootout with soldiers, Etta began keeping company with Elzy Lay in Buenos Aires, where they were married, moved to La Paz, and lived happily ever after. This is highly unlikely for several reasons, though, not the least of which is that Elzy Lay married a woman named Mary Calvert on March 27, 1909.

In another "Where in the World Is Etta Place?" scenario, Welsh novelist Richard Llewellyn (*How Green Was My Valley*), while living in Argentina in the late 1940s, was told that Etta had wed a Paraguayan government official. No one has found any evidence of the marriage, nor is there any proof that Etta married yet another Paraguayan, a boxing promoter named Tex Rickard who temporarily retired to the Chaco region in 1910. Rickard's wife, Edith Mae, accompanied him there and returned to the States with him five years later, so that rumor was squashed. Similarly puzzling, an outlaw named George Musgrave, who had been recruited to work at Rickard's ranch, remained in Paraguay and was married for a time to Janette Magor, who later ran an Arizona sanitarium with Elzy Lay's second wife, Mary Calvert, and briefly drew attention as a possible stand-in for Etta Place. But in the final analysis, she proved to be too young for the role.

While no book on Etta Place would be complete without at least some mention of the immensely popular 1960s film *Butch Cassidy and the*

Sundance Kid, featuring Paul Newman as Butch Cassidy, Robert Redford as Sundance, and Katherine Ross as Etta, the film was commendable if less than historically accurate. It's true that, in the loosely sculpted biopic based upon real life, the outlaw duo was forced by the law to leave the Wild West with Etta for South America. But in the last scene of the movie, the two bandits are shown surrounded by dozens of South American soldiers after a robbery gone bad. Facing capture and extradition to the United States, the two bad men charge out of their hiding place, guns blazing. The film stops there, giving the impression that the outlaws died in a blaze of glory—with their boots on, of course.

But, the scene didn't play out quite that way. Urban legends about the survival of the two outlaws persisted for long after the Bolivian shootout because so little information had trickled out of the small town where it had transpired. Most clues came from newspaper articles based on information that the Pinkerton Agency had placed with the papers to declare the men dead. As a result of renewed interest in the subject following the premiere of the film, several Wild West experts and historians, including Anne Meadows and Daniel Buck, traveled to Bolivia for a firsthand look. In the late 1980s, Buck and Meadows unearthed a letter written by the chief of the American embassy in Chile that gave the following account of the outlaws' alleged final years:

Following their close call in Argentina, Butch, Sundance and Etta Place headed for Chile. Most of the money that the three had had gone into the ranch in Cholila. Needing money to start over in Chile, the two American outlaws went back to their old ways. The first victims were two Argentinean banks that were robbed in 1905 of a combined total of 400,000 dollars. After the two robberies, Butch and Sundance lay low for a while. During the interim, the two banditos worked at the Concordia tin mine run by their old Cholila neighbor, Percy Seibert. On Tuesday, November 3, 1908, the paymaster for the Aramayo, Franke & Company silver mine left the mine's office in Tupiza, Bolivia for the corporate headquarters in Quechisla. The next day, the payroll caravan ran into two white-masked men armed with rifles and pistols. The two robbers demanded that the paymaster hand over the two mules carrying the payroll. After the bandits had left, the paymaster hurried off and warned police and the Bolivian army of the robbery. A posse composed of soldiers, police and armed citizens were organized to track the fugitives. On November 7, three days after the robbery of the payroll, a three-man Bolivian army patrol ran into the pistolaires in the village of San Vicente. The bandits opened fire, killing one of the Bolivians. A standoff ensued, followed by a long period of silence. Suddenly, two gunshots broke the quiet. The two remaining soldiers rushed the outlaws' hideout, only to find the two men dead from self-inflicted gunshot wounds. The soldiers recovered the 90,000-dollar payroll only to have it seized by a Bolivian judge investigating the incident. The money was never returned to the Aramayo, Franke, & Company silver mine. The bodies of the two men were buried in the cemetery in San Vicente side by side.[12]

While this account answers several questions (before the Bolivian documents were discovered, people had claimed that over one hundred Bolivians were killed by the outlaws in the final shootout), many others were raised. Chief among those was the question of whether or not the two bandits killed in San Vicente were actually Butch and Sundance. The two descriptions that were given by witnesses of the Argentinean bank robberies matched descriptions of the two Western icons, but when Aramayo's paymaster initially notified the police, he said the two robbers were a gringo and a fat Chilean fugitive by the name of Madariaga.[13] Only later did he amend his claim to say they were both gringos. Why did the man change his story?

The answer may be simple. The United States was pressuring South American governments to locate outlaws such as Butch and Sundance. Perhaps the Bolivians forced the paymaster to change his story so that the government could claim it had killed some prominent American bandits. If so, as Leonard John Lanier wondered, why didn't they attempt to collect the $15,000 reward placed by the US government and railroads for the capture of the two outlaws? And why did the two men, who were supposedly Butch and Sundance, shoot themselves? Both had been in tighter scrapes in the past than simply being surrounded by a three-man Bolivian posse![14]

So, the question arises: Were Butch and Sundance actually gunned down on that day in Bolivia? Were they actually buried in that grave? Are there any doubts? Of course. Yet, according to Lanier:

> *A hundred years have passed since the disappearance and supposed deaths of Butch and Sundance, and no one is any closer to solving the mystery. One explanation is not going to solve the problem, but the research uncovered so far has led the author to believe that the two men died in Bolivia. Most people agree that the two men fled to South America and did engage in criminal activities there, such as the bank robberies in Argentina. The descriptions given by the paymaster in Bolivia match known descriptions of the real Butch and Sundance. In all likelihood, though, no smoking gun will ever be found that says that the two men did indeed die in Bolivia. Butch and Sundance probably would have liked it that way.[15]*

Of course, no matter what happened to Butch and Sundance in Bolivia that event-filled day, we still have no indication of what happened to Etta after she returned to the States, presumably for an appendectomy. But Percy Seibert, who knew the three Americans better than anyone else in South America, believed he knew when he published his conversations with the trio years later. Often houseguests and Sunday dinner companions at the Seibert home, the three eventually warmed up to Seibert and his wife, opening up about their pasts and speculating about their futures. Butch in particular shed some illuminating light on Etta following her last appearance in the Southern Hemisphere. Says Seibert,

> *We talked generally of the West and ranching, and gradually as he [Butch] came to trust us; he told us about his life as an outlaw—never naming names of men who had ridden with him—and his technique, so to speak.*
>
> *"I came down to South America with the idea of settling down," he said. "In the States there was nothing but jail, the noose, or being*

shot by a posse. I thought maybe I could change things but I guess things at this late date can't be changed."

One day when the Kid didn't come along with him for dinner, [Butch] told us about Etta Place. Privately he described her to me as "the best housekeeper in South America but she has the heart of a whore."

One day, he said, Etta had severe stomach pains. They got worse and finally the Kid took her to the nearest doctor, who diagnosed her condition as acute appendicitis. He wanted to put her in the local hospital but Etta refused. Frankly, I didn't blame her. Medical conditions were crude and unsanitary, and unless you were treated by Doctor Lovelace and his staff, who were attached to the Railway Commission in the interior, you were at the mercy of a native doctor who did everything from treating mules to pulling teeth.

Etta begged the Kid to take her back to the States; finally Cassidy and the Kid agreed that had to be done. The Sundance Kid and Etta went back to Denver, where Etta entered the hospital. The next day the operation was to be performed. That night the Kid went on a high lonesome and came back to his boardinghouse roaring drunk. He woke up with a terrible hangover and shouted for someone to bring him a cup of coffee. Of course, no one did. Then he grabbed one of his guns, which hung in a holster at the side of the bed, and fired a few rounds into the ceiling.

The Kid had forgotten he wasn't in a cow camp twenty-five years before. Denver was no longer a frontier town. The outraged landlord shouted that he was going to call the police. The Kid suddenly realized he would make a fine catch, so he threw on his clothes and ran out to hire a carriage to take him to the railroad station, where he finally got connections back to New York and a steamer to South America, where he rejoined Cassidy.

When I asked Cassidy if they had ever heard of Etta again he just shook his head.

This story is mostly corroborated by author James D. Horan in notes taken during his interviews with Seibert. In typical Horan self-styled shorthand, the notations read: "Eltel [*sic*] Place, ailing chronic appen. Sundance took her to Denver, went to cathouse, woke up alone, drunk, fired, wanted coffee, got out town."[16]

So the tale of Etta Place could end right then and there. Those were the last of the facts commonly acknowledged about her. But that is not all there was to know about her existence—far from it. She was not only a flesh-and-blood woman whose mysteriously shrouded disappearance into thin air occurred practically overnight. Logic tells us that she did *not* disappear from life any more than Sundance went up in a puff of smoke when he left his Denver boardinghouse room headed for South America that fateful morning. We know nothing of Sundance's travels following this incident; yet when he arrived safely in South America, we are comfortable enough with the facts to state emphatically, "He got there safely."

While we may not be so emphatic about Etta's whereabouts following her apparent admission to and discharge from the Denver hospital, we can rely upon the "facts" deduced by logic to reduce the mystery of her disappearance from public scrutiny to one of a handful of options, among which are these:

- Etta was admitted and scheduled for the operation, very possibly in St. Joseph Hospital, but died in the process. Acute appendicitis was nothing to be taken lightly in those days, as is the case today. If her appendix had burst during or before the operation, she might well have not survived. Unfortunately, this scenario has one gaping hole in it: No medical records exist stating that anyone named Ethel Place, under whose name she would almost certainly have been admitted, died as a result of appendicitis while a patient in the hospital. Even more unfortunately, no records of her hospitalization exist at all, at least none that Denver's St. Joseph Hospital has been able to provide.[17]

- Etta's operation was a success, and after checking out of the hospital, she found a position as a schoolteacher in Denver under the name of Ethel Place or another pseudonym, after which she may have married and settled down to a pedestrian lifestyle more in keeping with her upbringing.

- Following her successful operation, Etta remained in Denver only long enough to recuperate fully before traveling on to San Francisco or, perhaps, Texas where she carried on with her life as she knew it before Sundance exploded into her world.

Of course, other hypotheses exist. At one time or another, "researchers" have claimed she was a madam in San Francisco, a madam in Fort Worth, the wife of a boxing promoter, a soldier in the service of Pancho Villa in Mexico, a victim of the great San Francisco earthquake of 1906, the owner of a sanitarium, the head of an outlaw gang in Argentina, a robber of banks during the Roaring Twenties, the mother of a daughter who became a bank robber, the mother of a son who inspired the character of James Bond, the wife of a wealthy Argentinian landowner, and the victim of a shootout in South America. Along the way, she was alleged to have died in 1918, 1922, 1924, 1935, 1959, 1962, and sometime in the 1970s.

Most likely, Etta's real-life existence wound down slowly, painlessly, as it does for most of us. The chronology of the last known years of Ethel "Etta" Place includes the December 19, 1905, bank robbery in Villa Mercedes, a sighting of Etta on a raft in South America following the holdup (probably in early 1906), and a medical junket to Denver with Sundance later in 1906. She could have remained in Denver following a successful appendectomy (no medical records were ever found indicating that she died around that time) and Harry's unexpected exodus from the States. If so, she most likely would have run out her life as a schoolteacher or a newly remarried housewife—ironically enough, most likely to someone with money who would have allowed her anonymity and insulation from notoriety.

If the Denver theory of Etta's final disposition is correct, then Etta Place truly entered the world with a whisper, not a bang, and departed it in precisely the same way. But, oh, what a fireworks display of a life she lived in between!

Of course, others say Ms. Place may well have traveled to Texas to reunite with old friends and live out her remaining days there with them, but doing so seems unlikely since it would have opened up painful memories she would most likely have wanted to forget. Similarly, there was no longer any reason for her to return to San Francisco, since by then more than two-thirds of the city, along with any fond memories she might have once held for the City by the Bay, lay smoldering in the ashes following the great quake of 1906. If Butch and Sundance were dead, and Etta felt the horrendous pain of losing the two men who were the most significant part of her life for nearly a decade, then she was decimated.

Or was she?

ANOTHER POSSIBILITY

According to Percy Seibert, not long after the employees at the Concordia mine learned of the outlaw past of Butch and Sundance, the two men settled their accounts at the company stores and told Seibert they'd be leaving their positions at the mine. Seibert believed this was because Butch didn't want to shed a poor light on the company by letting the world know it had hired acknowledged criminals. But this would probably ascribe more honor to the duo than they deserved. More likely, Butch would simply have decided it was time to move on.

After Concordia, Butch and Sundance probably went to work for a transportation company in southern Bolivia operated by a Scot named James "Santiago" Hutcheon. The company hauled passengers and freight in mule-drawn coaches and wagons. Hutcheon may have known them as Maxwell and Brown, but it's possible that, by then, they introduced themselves to others as the Lowe brothers.[18]

Percy Seibert later heard that the two outlaws went across the border to Peru, where they held up a stagecoach they thought was carrying remittance money belonging to the Santo Domingo Mine. But Seibert believed the Santo Domingo officials, wary of robbers on the lonely mountain trails, had sent a dummy wagon ahead of the money coach, and the boys rode off empty-handed. Their next holdup, said Seibert, was a train robbery back in Bolivia, near the town of Eucalyptus in Oruro Department, about fifty miles southwest of Concordia.[19] Seibert did not give the date of this holdup, but the newspapers of the day reported two robberies near Eucalyptus in 1908. In May, a railroad paymaster was robbed of what in today's currency would be approximately $90,000. The suspects were thought to be two American gringos who had worked for the railroad that ran between Eucalyptus and La Paz.[20]

Seibert said that, following the Eucalyptus robbery in 1908, the boys returned to Peru and hid out on the eastern slope of the Andes Mountains at Sacambaya, an abandoned Jesuit mission near the headwaters of the Amazon. Local authorities knew of their presence but weren't anxious to run the risk of trying to flush them out. That August, with Etta still spirited away somewhere in the States, bandits robbed the paymaster of a construction company of an undetermined payroll while traveling on the same railroad. Whether or not Butch and Sundance were responsible is unclear, although officials at the time believed the robbery was committed by the same men who struck at Eucalyptus.[21]

Then, on November 4, 1908, researchers believe Butch and Sundance may have held up an official of the Aramayo-based Francke y Compania mining company and taken the firm's payroll. The official, Carlos Pero, was traveling by mule on an isolated trail south of Quechisla, Bolivia, with his son, Mariano, and a servant, Gil Gonzalez. At a place called Huaca Huañusca, they were surprised by two well-armed "Yankees" whose faces were covered with bandannas.[22] According to Pero, one of the bandits was "thin and of normal stature," and the other was "heavyset and taller," a description that seems to be just the opposite of Butch and Sundance, but in the heat of the moment, mistakes in judgment happen. Pero went on to say that both men wore "new, dark-red, thin-wale corduroy suits with narrow, soft-brimmed hats." When the bandits ordered Pero's group to dismount, they did so in English and "in a very pleasant manner." However, he noticed that the bandits' rifles "were cocked and ready to fire," adding that they also each carried a Colt revolver and possibly a small Browning revolver on their cartridge belts, which were filled with rifle ammunition.[23]

The bandits knew that Pero was carrying the company payroll. They also knew which package among several contained the money. According to Pero, there were two "very similar" packages in his saddlebag, and they immediately picked the correct one without bothering to check the other. They did, however, apparently overestimate the size of the payroll, asking if Pero was not carrying 80,000 bolivianos when the actual amount was 15,000.[24]

Before they left, they ordered Pero's servant to turn over his mule to them but left the other two mules where they were. According to Pero, "they undoubtedly planned their retreat carefully; otherwise, they would not have left us with our animals or they would have killed us in order to avoid accusations or to gain time."[25]

Three days later, on November 7, Malcom Roberts, the manager of Aramayo Francke & Company, received a message from Captain Justo P. Concha of the Bolivian army that the bandits who had stolen the Aramayo payroll had been confronted by an armed patrol in San Vicente, a small village some thirty miles southwest of the site of the robbery. According to the report, both robbers had been killed, and the payroll had been recovered.[26]

There are several versions of this shootout. Seibert, in support of the robbers being Butch and Sundance, said that, after the payroll holdup, the thieves rode to the village of Tupiza, which is southeast of the holdup site. There they learned that word of the robbery had preceded them and that the authorities were looking for two North Americans. Worried, they made a hasty departure, intending to go north to Uyuni and possibly from there leave Bolivia for sanctuary in the Peruvian Andes at Sacambaya.[27]

At San Vicente, on the way to Uyuni, the two made a fatal mistake. Rather than camp somewhere along the trail, the bandits, in an act uncharacteristic of Butch, rode into the village and rented a room in a small house. Apparently somebody became suspicious of the pair of well-armed "foreigners" and sent word to a Bolivian army patrol stopping off in Uyuni. The captain of the detail, Justo P. Concha, accompanied by two soldiers and local sheriff Timoteo Rios, set out for San Vicente to check on the situation. According to an article appearing later in *La Mañana* in the nearby town of Sucre, the four-man posse confronted the two foreigners in their casa. Shots were fired, and one of the soldiers was killed. Concha ordered the two men to surrender; the men responded with more shots, and a gun battle erupted that lasted for half an hour. In the end, both foreigners lay dead. On searching the bodies, Captain Concha found the stolen Aramayo payroll plus a map of Bolivia on which the outlaws had marked the route they were taking. It included the towns of La Paz, Santa Cruz, Cochabamba, and Potosi. From San Vicente, they had intended to go to Santa Catalina and then to La Quiaca.[28]

According to Meadows and Buck, the *La Mañana* article was mostly accurate, except that Captain Concha wasn't likely to have been among the first group to engage the bandits. A search by the authors eventually turned up a file containing a Bolivian magistrate's investigation of the shootout. Included was a statement by the local *corregidor*, or mayor, who testified that he had encountered the two bandits earlier in the evening while they were looking for a place to spend the night. The corregidor, Cleto Bellot, said that he saw the strangers at the door of local Bonifacio Casasola, where they asked about a place to stay the night. Since there were no hotels or inns in San Vicente, Bellot advised Casasola to rent them a room. Bellot said that the two men unsaddled and fed their mules before asking Bellot if they could get some beer and sardines. Bellot sent Casasola to buy them with money provided by "the taller one."

Bellot said that when he left, he went directly to the "lodging of the commission" (most likely the town council) to tell them about the foreigners. The "commissioners," with loaded rifles, took two Bolivian soldiers and returned with Bellot to the house. According to Bellot, one of the soldiers, Victor Torres, went ahead, and "from the door he was shot once with a revolver, wounding him, to which he responded with a rifle shot." Bellot apparently decided that this sort of affair was not for him and quickly departed. On his way home, he ran into Captain Concha, who asked him to try to round up help from the villagers.[29]

While rounding up volunteers, Bellot said he heard "three screams of desperation" but couldn't tell where they came from. He related that a single shot was fired by the "inspector" around midnight, with no response from the casa. By six the following morning, the men approached the room and found the two Yankees dead: "One was in the doorway and the other behind the door on a bench."[30]

According to Victor Hampton, a mining engineer who worked in San Vicente during the 1920s, the two bandits were buried in an Indian graveyard near where they were killed. Hampton claimed he got this information from Malcom Roberts, the Aramayo company manager.

When Butch's friends back in the States heard rumors that he and Sundance were dead, they didn't believe it. This wasn't the first report of their demise, and they'd always turned up alive in the past. What *was* troubling, though, was that Butch had apparently written to some of his friends that things were getting a little hot down in South America, so he might be returning soon to the States. In time, the letters stopped coming, and letters to him to his various addresses were returned unclaimed.

While Butch's letters may have stopped flowing, the stories in the newspapers recounting their South American escapades didn't. In February 1910, numerous papers carried an eastern dispatch about the State Department in Washington receiving word from Argentina that Robert Parker and Harry Longabaugh, believed to have been joined by Harvey Logan, had formed a bandit gang so powerful that the government was forced to pay them tribute just to keep them at bay. That same month, Pinkerton hearts must have leaped for joy when news came to the Denver office that a train robbery arrest in St. Louis resulted in the incarceration of one "Jim Lowe," aka Butch Cassidy. Not long after, though, the excitement turned cold when officers discovered that the suspect in custody was a small-time outlaw from Kansas City.

Despite conflicting reports, at least one person, Butch's old outlaw pal Matt Warner, believed that Butch was dead. In 1937 or 1938, he wrote that Butch and Sundance were killed in a fight with soldiers who had been chasing them. Whether or not he based his knowledge on Arthur Chapman's account in *The Elks Magazine*, published in April 1930, isn't clear. Warner's version varied somewhat from Chapman's account but reached the same conclusion. He disagreed, though, with the final analysis of *how* the boys met their end. In Warner's opinion, Butch wouldn't have shot himself. Warner believed that he would have kept all his shots down to the very last one for the men who were trying to kill them.

Will Simpson, the prosecuting attorney who had Butch sent to prison in 1894, also believed that Butch met his end at San Vicente. In 1939, Simpson, then in private practice in Jackson, Wyoming, said that he knew two men who went to South America to verify the story and that he had talked to one of them "no more than three months ago," which would have been around February 1939.[31]

Over the years, naysayers who believe Butch and Sundance weren't the two banditos killed in San Vicente that night point out that Bolivian officials never identified the two men who were killed. While local authorities apparently believed that the men were the same ones who stole the Aramayo payroll, the men's names, if they were known at the time, were not released to the public. Judicial records obtained by Buck and Meadows contained a statement from a man named Remigio Sanchez who claimed to have been an eyewitness to the San Vicente shootout. He recounted that when the soldiers entered the hut, they found "the smaller gringo stretched out on the floor, dead, with one bullet wound in the temple and another in the arm. The taller one was hugging a large ceramic jug that was in the room. He was dead, also, with a wound in the forehead and several in the arm." Both of the dead men, according to Sanchez, were "unshaven blonds, with somewhat turned-up noses, the small one a bit ugly and the large one good-looking."[32]

A Bolivian official, Aristides Daza, testified that he had also entered the hut where the battle occurred and found a body in the threshold of the door "with a revolver that appeared to have been fired. Presently, I focused in on the other individual, who was on a bench, having used an earthen jug as a shield, finding him dead. . . . I proceeded to remove the bodies, beginning with the first one, who was in the doorway. In his pockets were money, personal effects, and some pounds, as described in the inventory."[33]

The list of the dead men's personal effects included several notable items. On the body of the smaller victim (Butch) were the usual personal items (money, comb, pocket mirror, etc.) as well as seven calling cards inscribed with the name Enrique B. Hutcheon. He also had an ammo belt with 121 unspent Winchester cartridges. On the body of the other man (Sundance) were similar personal items, plus 149 Mauser and Winchester cartridges and an English dictionary (apparently not a Spanish-English dictionary, but an English-only dictionary). Also in the pair's saddlebags were 14,400 bolivianos.[34]

The cards with the name of Enrique B. Hutcheon were a mystery. If Hutcheon and Butch were the same, why would he need seven cards to prove it? Did Butch intend to establish a new alias to avoid potential skepticism? Or was the bullet-riddled body actually that of a man named Hutcheon?

Butch and Sundance apparently once worked for a man named James Santiago Hutcheon after leaving the Concordia mines. Was Enrique a relative who was one of the Aramayo bandits killed in the shootout? Buck believes that local authorities would have revealed this fact if they thought it were true. The conclusion makes sense except that the authorities never released the names of *anyone* believed to have been killed in that battle, so why would Hucheon have been handled any differently?

The possibility that the dead man could have been Enrique Hutcheon coincides with a local legend saying that one of the two bodies buried in the San Vicente cemetery after the shootout was that of a Chilean. Also, several reports of the South American robberies attributed to Butch and Sundance (including the holdup of the Aramayo payroll) mentioned that one of the robbers appeared to be Chilean rather than North American. Buck attributes such stories to careless local reporting. But what if it were *more* than that?

Also, according to Buck, "Carlos Pero, the man they held up, says the bandits were Yankees and spoke English."[35] But this is not entirely true. Pero said in his deposition following the robbery that *one* of the men, the shorter of the two, had spoken to him in English; the other remained silent, standing several feet away with his gun drawn, watching. Not that it mattered conclusively. Chileans have been known to be bilingual; nothing says one of the Aramayo holdup men couldn't have been Chilean and still spoken English.

To Dan Buck and Anne Meadows, who were consumed by the riddle of the fate of Butch and Sundance, the only logical solution was to attempt to have the bodies in the San Vicente cemetery exhumed to prove their identities once and for all. While asking around for the names of reliable forensic experts, a stroke of good fortune brought an undisputed expert to *them*. He was Clyde Snow, a forensic anthropologist from Oklahoma, who had an impressive record of working on high-profile cases, including the identification of Nazi war criminal Josef Mengele in Brazil. His stumbling across Buck and Meadows was apparently pure chance. While on a project in Argentina, Snow had become curious about what really happened to Butch Cassidy and the Sundance Kid. When he heard about the exhumation, he decided to check it out.[36]

With Snow's reputation and Buck and Meadows's enthusiasm, they had little difficulty finding a sponsor for a proposed expedition: The project was made to order for a PBS documentary. Boston public television channel WGBH and the producers of the TV program *Nova* quickly signed on.[37]

With the help of local officials, Buck and Meadows located what they believed to be the graves of the outlaws, obtained permission from the appropriate Bolivian officials to exhume the bodies, and began excavating under Snow's supervision.[38]

After several false starts, the team eventually removed one skeleton from the grave plus a skull fragment from a second corpse.[39] According to Snow's estimate, the skeletal remains fit those of Butch and Sundance. Snow obtained permission to take some of the bones back to his laboratory in Oklahoma for a more detailed forensic analysis. There, he conducted x-ray studies of the skeletal remains to confirm the presence of metal fragments embedded in the bones; they revealed an old wound, perhaps from a gunshot to the lower left leg, in one of the skeletons. This sparked interest because Sundance was once treated for an alleged gunshot wound to the leg.

The next obvious step was DNA analysis. But, after an arduous series of tests on Sundance, no match was found, thus excluding the possibility that one of the skeletons belonged to Sundance.

The DNA from the remains was also compared with Butch's family samples, with the same results: no matches.[40] Worse, the partial skull from the second corpse was found to be that of a Native American and not Caucasoid.[41]

The conclusion: The exhumation team had most likely excavated the wrong site, which may have explained why the name of German miner Gustav Zimmer appeared on the headstone that once marked the grave, even though it had been removed sometime between 1972 and the researchers' first visit to the cemetery.

So, while the search for the true identity of the victims at San Vicente was not at all conclusive, Buck and Meadows still believe that the evidence uncovered strongly points to Butch and Sundance being the bandits who died in San Vicente that night.[42] Others disagree. And that disagreement brings us closer than ever to the answer to "Whatever happened to Baby Etta?"

BACK FROM THE GRAVE

When Butch's family heard the news that Butch and Sundance had been shot to death in Bolivia, they initially doubted the stories. Then, according to Butch's sister Lula Parker Betenson, they began to fear the reports might be true. The family was devastated to learn that, if the story was true, the fatal shootout with Butch and Sundance may have added murder to their list of crimes.[43]

Then, one day—Lula did not give the year—a childhood friend of Butch's, a Utah neighbor named Jim Gass from Circleville, came home from a trip to California with startling news. He had just seen Butch getting on a train in Los Angeles. He said he was sure it was Butch—they had even waved at one another—but then the train pulled out, and the man was gone. According to Lula, it was the first time she'd heard that her brother was alive and well and somewhere in the States.[44]

After years of agonizing, Lula said the Parker family's prayers were answered in 1925. By then, the family had moved from the ranch into town, but they still owned the homestead in Circle Valley. It was a fall day, she said, and her brother Mark was working out at the ranch mending fences. As Mark told the story later, a new black Ford touring car pulled up to the house, and a man got out and started across the field toward the spot where Mark was working. From a distance, he thought it was his cousin, Fred Levi, but as the man got closer, he recognized that "characteristic Parker grin." It was Robert LeRoy.

After several minutes of back-slapping and hugging, the two brothers climbed into Bob's car and drove into town to the old brick house where their eighty-one-year-old father, Max, was living with several of his bachelor sons. Lula, married and with her own family, lived only a short distance away, so Mark called her to come over to fix supper for the boys. When she arrived, she at first failed to recognize her brother, whom she hadn't seen in decades. She recalled her reaction when she realized who he was: "My knees felt like rubber, and my insides turned upside down."[45]

But why had Butch waited so long to get in touch with his family, she asked? The answer was simple: He wanted to reach out but was too ashamed of having brought so much sorrow upon the family name.

Lula recalled that Butch said he and Sundance had planned to return from South America together, but Sundance had developed a leg problem (he thought it was the result of a scorpion bite) and was laid up for several weeks. When the time came to go, Sundance was still too weak to travel, so he remained behind.[46]

When asked about the shootout in San Vicente, Butch said that he had read about it after he'd returned to the States, but that's all he knew. He said he'd heard that Percy Seibert had identified him and Sundance as the victims, apparently thinking he would do them a favor by allowing them to bury their past and taking the heat of the law off their backs.[47]

According to an interview that Lula granted years later, Butch added, "Would I be dumb enough after all those years to steal a white, clearly branded mule and ride him into an area where the police and Bolivian Army were in evidence?"[48] Researcher Dan Buck is reasonably sure that Lula's conversation with Butch never took place, and he bases his conclusion on two points. First, according to the report of the Aramayo payroll robbery, the mule in question was not white. Second, the area (the village of San Vicente) where the shootout occurred was not infested with Bolivian soldiers when Butch and Sundance were said to have ridden in.[49]

But Buck's contention is flawed on both counts. If Butch hadn't been part of the Aramayo payroll robbery, he *couldn't* have known the color of the mule and, thus, could easily have assumed it was white. Similarly, if Butch hadn't been in the village of San Vicente on that fateful day, he couldn't possibly have known it *wasn't* saturated with Bolivian soldiers. Both points support Lula Betenson's contention regarding Butch's statement to her.

Lula also relayed that Butch told her he'd spent a good bit of time in Mexico after leaving South America. While in Mexico City, he said he ran into Etta Place, who told him that she and Sundance were living right there in the city. He said she invited him over, and he visited with them for several days before getting restless and deciding to move along. He said he hadn't seen them since. After leaving Mexico, Butch traveled throughout Europe, particularly Italy, which he enjoyed, before returning to North America to visit Alaska. That, he said, was too cold for his old bones. He did find the northwestern United States more to his liking—so much so that he'd made the area his new home.[50]

According to Lula, Butch and the family visited together long into the night, recalling childhood events and all the good times they'd once shared. Butch stayed with his father for several days before he rode up into the hills with Mark to visit some brothers who had a cabin there. In total, Butch's visit lasted more than a week. Before he left, he asked everyone not to mention his presence there for obvious reasons, and they all agreed. For the rest of Butch's life, Lula said, they lived up to their word and kept his existence a secret.[51]

When news leaked in the early 1970s that Lula was writing a book about her brother, it created a stir among the handful of Wild Bunch historians thumbing the pages of history at the time. At first, Lula was receptive to their letters, but then she began complaining about being misquoted, and she stopped talking, telling those who wanted to know more about Butch that they would just have to wait for the book. Before she quit responding to their questions, some of what people said about her brother may have been the result of sloppy reporting—or worse. One tabloid account had Butch revealing to her that the victims of the shootout at San Vicente were just a couple of "greenhorns," that on the night of the confrontation, Sundance was off somewhere tending to business matters, and Butch was several miles away in an Indian hut recovering from a scorpion bite.[52]

While the book was still in its early stages in the late 1960s, the film *Butch Cassidy and the Sundance Kid* was released. Lula completed her work and turned it over to the publisher, which changed its mind about publishing it because Lula refused to reveal the date and place of Butch's death. Eventually she found another publisher—Brigham Young University Press—and the book was released in 1975 to immediate accolades.

Naturally, Lula had her detractors. Foremost was Wild Bunch researcher Jim Dullenty, who at the time was working on his own book on Butch. Dullenty cast doubt on the veracity of Lula's story about Butch's return to the States, and he found similar doubts among members of Lula's own family. Dullenty had interviewed Max and Elinor Parker, son and daughter-in-law of Dan Parker, Butch's brother. According to Dullenty, the couple said that Butch came back all right, though not in 1925 as Lula had said, but five years later.[53]

Larry Pointer also interviewed Max and Elinor. Pointer says they told him that Butch visited them in Milford, Utah, in 1930, while they were taking care of Butch's brother Dan, who was then in his early sixties and in poor health. The Parkers said that Butch came to the house with two other men and talked to Dan for several hours. Elinor Parker said that she remembered the day clearly because Butch sat and rocked her young son, Max Jr. The Parkers said that, following the visit, Dan regularly received letters from Butch, some of which contained money. Dan always destroyed the letters, but the Parkers said that he revealed to Elinor that Butch was living in Spokane under the name William Phillips. According to Pointer, when Lula began releasing information in 1970 about Butch's return, Elinor Parker wrote to her about the 1930 visit and told her what Dan Parker had said about Butch using the alias of William Phillips. Elinor said that Lula wrote back, asking her not to share that information with anyone else for fear that he would be discovered and arrested.[54]

According to Bill Betenson, Lula's grandson, some members of the Parker family did not want Lula to write the book at all because of the agreement made between Butch's father and the family that they would never reveal the true details of Butch's return. But Bill Betenson clearly challenges Jim Dullenty's view that Lula's statements deserve scrutiny. "Lula did not lie," Betenson says flatly.[55] He insists that Butch's visit to Circleville in 1925 was confirmed by Lula's son Mark.[56]

Lula Parker Betenson and her brothers were not the only people who claimed to have seen Butch after his alleged death in South America.

Josie Bassett, who considered Butch her "Brown's Park Beau," said she visited with him several times in the late 1920s and early 1930s. The first time was in Nevada in 1928, and the second time was in Baggs, Wyoming, in 1930. According to Josie, Elzy Lay accompanied Butch to where she was staying in Baggs. "We had a good visit, talking over old times." Josie saw Butch two more times, once in Rawlins and again in Rock Springs, Wyoming. Harv Murdock, Elzy Lay's grandson, said that Josie's recollection of the date of the meeting in Baggs with Butch and Elzy was probably correct because Elzy visited Harv's mother at the Murdock ranch near Baggs at about the same time.[57]

Still not satisfied with the accuracy of Josie's recollections of meeting Butch, Murdock decided to test her memory during a visit to her home in her later years. He said he challenged her with, "You know very well Butch was killed in South America," to which Josie replied, "I know Butch Cassidy a hell of a lot better than I know you. He was here in Baggs in about 1930." Murdock said he tested her three more times, and she succeeded in repeating the story verbatim each time.[58]

A Rock Springs resident also reported seeing Butch, although at an earlier date. John Taylor, a local auto dealer and garage man, told Brown's Park historian John Rolfe Burroughs that one day in 1922 Butch drove into Taylor's shop in a Model T to get some work done on the car. "He was pulling a two-wheel trailer loaded with camping gear," Taylor said, and he "asked me a lot of questions about old-timers around Rock Springs. He didn't tell me who he was, but I recognized him."[59]

Two years later, Larry Pointer said that Tom Welch, a Wyoming pioneer who claimed to have known Butch in the old days, told him that Butch stopped by to visit him in Green River, Wyoming. Welch, too, said that Butch was driving a Model T and was towing a two-wheel trailer filled with camping gear.[60]

Another old-timer from Butch's Wild Bunch days, Tom Vernon, the unofficial "mayor" of Baggs, told of a reunion with his old pard "sometime in the twenties." Vernon said that Butch stayed with him in Baggs for two days. There was no mistake that it was Butch, Vernon said, recalling the days when Butch and his gang had the run of the town. "I played at the dances he and the other members of the Wild Bunch threw in Baggs."[61]

In the summer of 1925, Boyd Charter, then a boy of seventeen, said that a man whom his father knew from the old days spent part of the summer camped in a grove of trees near the Charter ranch in Jackson, Wyoming. Boyd said that Butch didn't talk much, but he did invite Boyd to hunt sage chickens with him. Later, after the man had left, Boyd overheard his father tell Will Simpson, the prosecuting attorney who had sent Butch to prison in 1894, that it was Butch who had camped on his ranch.

Another eyewitness who claimed to have seen Butch and recognized him from bygone days was Edith MacKnight Jensen, daughter-in-law of Josie Bassett. Edith was seventeen when her family moved to Brown's Park. Her father, Stephen Embrey, homesteaded in Moffat County, Colorado, on the lower end of Pot Creek. In 1928, following her marriage to Chick MacKnight (Josie's son), Jensen said she and Chick went on a trip to Nevada with her aunt, Ann Bassett Willis, and Ann's husband, Frank Willis, to check out a mining claim in which Ann held an interest. Jensen always felt the real reason, though, was to see Butch, who had been staying in a cabin in Pahrump Valley about fifty miles west of Las Vegas. Edith said she knew for sure it was Butch. "If you ever got a close look at [him], you'd never forget those eyes."[62]

Crawford MacKnight, Ann Bassett's nephew, tells of an earlier trip Ann took to the Nevada mining camp and her first reunion with Butch. MacKnight said that a man known around the area as Doc Masson came into camp one day and kept "looking Ann over." Later, when the man got Ann alone, he asked about certain events that occurred at Brown's Park when Ann was young. He would not come right out and tell her who he was, but he did say that she knew him. Finally, he said, "When we were young I knew you well. I had many a meal at the Bassett cabin." Then she recognized him. It was Butch, wearing a black goatee. Afterward, when he wasn't looking, Ann snapped several photographs of him and later shared them with her nephew. They compared the newer photos with earlier shots of Butch that Maude Davis had kept. According to MacKnight, the man's goatee was definitely distracting, changing the entire look of the subject. But, he added, if you held your hand over the lower part of the man's face in the picture, you could clearly see who it was.

It was Butch.

CHAPTER 12

The Mystery Solved

THERE COMES A TIME IN EVERY BIOGRAPHER'S LIFE WHEN HE'S READY to set his pencil down, take a deep breath, and bask in the knowledge that he's done all he can do—captured the essence and the elegance of his subject, and removed all doubts surrounding that subject's persona. There also comes a time when he realizes he simply can't do that. And that time is now.

To say that the riddle of Etta Place is solved is tempting. But wrong. We don't know where she came from—not for sure. And we don't know where she ended up—not for sure. But we do know where she went, what she did while she was there, and what likely happened to her and the two most important men ever to grace her life when at last she was finished with it. And we know just a little more of her life now than we did before.

What we know with relative certainty comes from eyewitness accounts and printed resources. In his book *The Outlaw Trail*, published less than a decade after the release of the film *Butch Cassidy and the Sundance Kid*, author Robert Redford says he had a conversation about Sundance's mysterious girlfriend with Western writer Edward Abbey and historian Kerry Boren. Boren claimed to have met a son-in-law of Etta Place, who gave him the following information about her:

- She was born around 1874, the daughter of the Honorable George Capel and the granddaughter of Arthur Algernon Capel, sixth Earl of Essex.

- Her father was killed before 1892 near Tombstone, Arizona, after which Etta was virtually raised by the very outlaws with whom her father had associated; they even paid to provide her with an education.

- She was living in the bordello district of San Antonio, Texas, when Butch Cassidy and his friends, including the Sundance Kid, brought her to Utah, where she stayed with a Mormon family for a year.

- She attended a teacher's college in the East and taught school for about one year in Telluride, Colorado, before joining Butch at Robbers Roost in 1895.

- She traveled with Butch and Sundance to New York and then on to Bolivia.

- She was accompanied by Sundance to Denver before returning to South America in 1909.

Boren couldn't relay more than that except to say that he believed Etta lived a long life and had at least one daughter who died in 1971. He doesn't say why the son-in-law's timeline is suspect. For example, if Etta had been born "around 1874," she would have been twenty-five or twenty-six years old when she met Sundance at Fannie Porter's house. It is highly unlikely for her to have been that age and still working at a Western whorehouse where young girls were chewed up and spit out nearly as fast as they were found.

As for her father, the "Honorable George Capel," being an associate of outlaws in Arizona—this, too, makes little sense absent a mechanism for the man suddenly moving to the Southwest and going rogue.

Similarly, there's no specific reference to Etta having lived with any Mormon families in Utah and no conclusive evidence that she attended a teacher's college in the East—or anywhere else for that matter—which certainly would have been a long way to travel for a single year; and afterward, there's no evidence that she ever taught school in Telluride, Colorado, although she may have done so briefly in Denver. No records exist because teachers at the time were unlicensed by the state.

But let's not forget that neatness counts, just as it did on our fifth-grade exams in school. At first glance, the list from Etta's son-in-law appears to be nicely organized and, thus, authoritative. Unfortunately, neatness doesn't count in researching biographical subjects, and as for substance, the collaborative book effort between historian Boren and Etta Place's son-in-law was apparently never consummated. One can only speculate as to why.

So, by far the most robust evidence we have of Etta's post-Argentinian life and activities comes from firsthand accounts given by Butch and Sundance themselves and passed along from Butch through Lula Parker Betenson, his sister.

Could Betenson have manufactured details to shore up a potential role in the upcoming film starring Paul Newman and Robert Redford? According to the timeline, yes. Is it likely? No. She had been talking with family members about her brother's visit for years before the announcement of the film, and those family members have all substantiated the substance, if not the verbatim recitation, of her stories.

Which brings up a question: Might Betenson, despite the best of intentions, simply be mistaken—the recipient of false information from an age-soiled mind? The answer: Yes. Is it likely? No. This thumbnail sketch of the woman appeared in a newspaper clipping in 1962, describing her and her accomplishments:

A dainty lady with a twinkle in her brown eyes is Piute County's new representative to the Utah Legislature. And behind that twinkle is a store of knowledge and zest for public life sparked by the girlhood experience of Mrs. Lula. Betenson as a member of Walter's Stock Co., one of those traveling theatrical groups of the dear-old days when entertainment was personal, not electronic.

Mrs. Betenson's appointment by Gov. George D. Clyde was to fill the vacancy created when Thomas D. A. Smith resigned to accept a federal appointment as postmaster of Circleville.

She's no newcomer to politics. She has served as Piute County Democratic chair-woman for 28 years and for several Legislature sessions served as a messenger. In those roles she acquired a thorough working knowledge of the legislative process in action. A mother of five and a great-grandmother as well, she maintains an active interest in current events. For fun, she also has participated in many local entertainments and was a stalwart in the old Circleville Glee Club.

As a legislator, she is particularly interested in:

- *Defining the State Board of Examiners' role in Utah government.*
- *Better schools through the State Equalization Fund.*
- *Decentralization of government to enable as much local control as possible.*
- *Better roads through Increased B and C Road Fund allocations.*
- *Projects to consume the idle time of youth, through employment and education.*
- *Boosting the economy of Utah's rural counties.*[1]

Obviously, Lula Parker Betenson had an active body and a sharp mind despite her advancing years. She is not a person who would likely forget or even "misremember" anything that had happened to her in her earlier years.

Although the 1969 film adaptation of the two outlaws' notorious heists and final days on earth met with wide critical and box-office acclaim, it wasn't universally heralded as a harbinger of truth or a bellwether of historical accuracy. For instance, numerous historians faulted the final shootout as overly dramatic, as more than two hundred Bolivian soldiers converged upon a Hollywood stage set to simulate the duo's final moments when their bullet-riddled bodies were sent off to an early grave.

Still, most historians have accepted the pair's participation in the 1909 Aramayo payroll robbery and their ultimate fate. And it's basically true. Or, at least, the facts surrounding the heist are true. The only problem is that the two robbers who pulled it off weren't Butch and Sundance.

As early as 1963, Lula Betenson was telling the *real* story of the effect that the last two major outlaws in the American West had on the nation.

The biggest shock from her, of course, was that Butch lived to be sixty-nine and died of natural causes in this country and that, years earlier, he had met Sundance and Etta in Mexico City, where he spent several days with them before returning to the States. The false narrative that Butch and Sundance had pulled the Aramayo job and paid the ultimate price was mostly a result of the Pinkertons and the Bolivian government, both anxious to put an exclamation point, albeit for different reasons, on the end of the outlawed Wild Bunch.

Said Betenson: "Everyone in the family and a few others have always known my brother was not shot down and left for dead in South America. He visited me years after his reputed death. We heard from him from time to time through the years until he died."[2]

As if begging for confirmation, newspapers in Wyoming, Utah, and Colorado carried stories of reported "Butch sightings" throughout the twenties and thirties, always naming Butch but never offering conclusive proof of his existence. Butch's sister was the last surviving child of thirteen in a tightly knit pioneering Mormon family. She didn't need the newspaper stories to confirm what she knew.

"We never talked about my brother outside the family," she said. "We were ashamed and embarrassed about the things he did. But within the family, seems like it's all we ever talked about. He broke my folks' hearts. I can still hear my mother praying every night of her life that Butch would come home and lead a good life again."[3]

Betenson decided to take her story public in 1961, "while there was still someone alive that could tell it."[4] She set about doing just that while writing a book that eventually was published and met with critical and popular success. The reason for the book: While some of the tales about Butch, Sundance, and Etta were true, many more weren't. She felt her brother's life was colorful enough without dressing it up with fantasy.

So, on the one hand, with a staggering amount of firsthand information from original sources, we have Butch, Sundance, and Etta nowhere near the Aramayo payroll robbery and subsequent deadly shootout in San Vicente. On the other hand, we have the dedicated and well-meaning explorations of several researchers who, with no firsthand information from original sources, no positive results from DNA tests conducted on remains, and no other correlating identification of skeletal exhumations, produced only conflicting information about the remains of the exhumed.

We also have written proof in the form of several letters saying that Butch and Sundance were preparing to leave South America, where the pressure for their capture was growing daily. We have substantial evidence that the trio had more than enough money salted away from their work, both unlawful and otherwise (primarily their ranching, which was an extremely lucrative business in those days), to last them the rest of their lives. Would it make sense for the bandit duo to pull one last hit before departing South America for safer climes?

Finally, we have dozens of people with no incentive to lie or even to fantasize, saying that the San Vicente massacre of the two never happened, that Butch had been spotted dozens of times over the years following South America, and that his own family members met with him and enjoyed his company on several occasions.

All of this weighs heavily on one side of the scale—the one, unfortunately, that has not received much serious attention over the years.

But for Etta Place, that scale has expanded our knowledge of her life to include more information about where she was—and with whom—before she did, indeed, finally succumb to the pages of history.

Did Etta and Sundance live out their final days in Mexico City, destined to die peacefully under false identities? Did Sundance die a natural death, after which Etta decided to return to Denver for one reason or another? Did she succumb to disease or even old age and pass on in the Mile High City?

These theories are just that—*theories*. They may all be wrong. Or perhaps all are wrong except for one. Whatever ultimately happened to a woman named Etta Place, she led one hell of a life, and she packed more into a few short years than most women—or *anyone*—could hope to see in a lifetime.

Is she dead? Most assuredly. How do we know? Science tells us so. Yet a part of her lives on in history as well as in our own minds. Death is undoubtedly a finality of life, an outcome as unavoidable as getting wet when caught in a thunderstorm. But without a fingerprint to read beneath the ocular magnifying glass of a microscope, without a confirmed newspaper article or a verified magazine account, without an official government document, her death remains as nebulous and fleeting as her birth.

And just as alluring.

Notes

CHAPTER 1: THE EARLY YEARS

1. Daniel Buck and Anne Meadows, "Wild Bunch Dream Girl," *True West Magazine*, May 1, 2002. Accessed July 9, 2019. truewestmagazine.com/wild-bunch-dream-girl/.
2. Ibid.
3. Ibid.
4. Ibid.
5. Ibid.
6. Tony Hays, "The Mysterious Disappearance of Etta Place," Criminal Element, August 14, 2011. Accessed July 18, 2019. www.criminalelement.com/the-mysterious-disappearance-of-etta-place/.
7. Maggie Van Ostrand, "Fannie Porter of San Antonio," Texas Escapes. Accessed July 19, 2019. www.texasescapes.com/MaggieVanOstrand/Fannie-Porter-of-San-Antonio.htm.
8. Hays, "The Mysterious Disappearance of Etta Place."
9. Ibid.
10. Buck and Meadows, "Wild Bunch Dream Girl."
11. Ibid.
12. Ibid.
13. Ibid.
14. Ibid.
15. Ibid.
16. Mitchell Smyth, "Some Doubt It, but Town Finds Butch Cassidy Crime Pays," *Chicago Tribune*, October 12, 1986. Accessed July 16, 2019. www.chicagotribune.com/news/ct-xpm-1986-10-12-8603170251-story.html.
17. Ibid.
18. Ibid.
19. Ibid.
20. Buck and Meadows, "Wild Bunch Dream Girl."
21. David James Horan, *Desperate Men: The James Gang and the Wild Bunch* (Lincoln: University of Nebraska Press, 1997), 287.

22. Richard F. Selcer, "Porter, Fannie," *Handbook of Texas*. Accessed July 19, 2019. www.tshaonline.org/handbook/online/articles/fpo51.

23. Ciaran Conliffe, "Ethel 'Etta' Place, Western Woman of Mystery," HeadStuff, September 16, 2017. Accessed July 15, 2019. www.headstuff.org/culture/history /ethel-etta-place-western-woman-of-mystery/.

24. Buck and Meadows, "Wild Bunch Dream Girl."

25. Ibid.

CHAPTER 2: TEARING UP THE WEST

1. *New York Tribune*, June 26, 1889, Wed., 1.

2. *Austin American-Statesman*, Austin, Texas, September 8, 1893, Fri., 1.

3. *The Salt Lake Herald*, Salt Lake City, Utah, April 25, 1897, Sun., 6.

4. *The Inter Ocean*, Chicago, Illinois, March 17, 1898, Sun., 33.

5. *El Paso Times*, El Paso, Texas, July 2, 1898, Sat., 1.

6. *Las Vegas Daily Optic*, Las Vegas, New Mexico, July 17, 1899, Mon., 1.

7. *Natrona County Tribune*, Casper, Wyoming, June 8, 1899, Thu., 1.

8. Robert Redford, *The Outlaw Trail* (New York: Grossett & Dunlap, 1976), 61.

9. Ibid.

10. Chas. A. Siringo, *A Cowboy Detective* (Chicago: W. B. Conkey Company, 1912), 310–12.

11. Ibid., 311.

12. Ibid., 312.

13. Richard Patterson, *Butch Cassidy: A Biography* (Lincoln: University of Nebraska Press, 1998), 153.

14. Ibid., 154.

15. Ibid., n. 183.

16. Ibid., 159.

17. Charles Kelly, *The Outlaw Trail: A History of Butch Cassidy and His Wild Bunch* (New York: Devin-Adair Company, 1959), 271.

18. Ibid., 172.

19. Patterson, *Butch Cassidy*, 190.

20. Ibid., 163.

21. *Grand Junction News*, Grand Junction, Colorado, June 11, 1904, 5.

CHAPTER 3: THE PINKERTONS MEET ETHEL PLACE

1. James D. Horan and Howard Swiggett, *The Pinkerton Story* (New York: G. P. Putnam's Sons, 1951), 130.

2. Ibid., 151–52.

3. Ibid., 152.

4. Ibid.

5. Morris Friedman, *The Pinkerton Labor Spy* (New York: Wilshire Book Company, 1907), 14.

6. Humanities, National Endowment for the Arts, "*The Wheeling Daily Intelligencer* (Wheeling, W. Va.) 1865–1903, July 07, 1892, Image 1," ISSN 2333-8547. Retrieved July 23, 2019.

7. Peter Carlson, *Roughneck: The Life and Times of Big Bill Haywood* (New York: W. W. Norton, 1983), 140.

8. James D. Horan, *Desperate Men: The James Gang and the Wild Bunch* (Lincoln: University of Nebraska Press, 1997), 283.

9. Ibid.

10. Fannie Porter's brothel is often misplaced in Fort Worth, when in reality it was in San Antonio. A woman named Mary Porter ran a bordello in Fort Worth.

11. Horan, *Desperate Men*, 283.

12. Ibid.

13. Ibid., 284.

14. Ibid., 284–85.

15. James D. Horan, *The Pinkertons: The Detective Agency That Made History* (New York: Crown Publishers, 1967), 389.

16. Ibid., 388.

17. Ibid., 391.

Chapter 4: The Death of Butch Cassidy

1. *Denver News*, March 6, 1898.

2. John Rolfe Burroughs, *Where the Old West Stayed Young* (New York: William Morrow & Company, 1962), 112–13.

3. James D. Horan, *Desperate Men: The James Gang and the Wild Bunch* (Lincoln: University of Nebraska Press, 1997), 234–35.

4. Richard Patterson, *Butch Cassidy: A Biography* (Lincoln: University of Nebraska Press, 1998), 135.

5. Ibid.

6. Charles Kelly, *The Outlaw Trail: A History of Butch Cassidy and His Wild Bunch* (New York: Devin-Adair Company, 1959), 213–15.

7. *Eastern Utah Advocate*, May 19, 1898.

8. Ibid.

9. Ibid.

10. Patterson, *Butch Cassidy*, 139.

11. Kelly, *The Outlaw Trail*, 179.

12. Patterson, *Butch Cassidy*, 140.

Chapter 5: New York, New York

1. *Salt Lake Herald*, September 17, 1900.

2. Charles Angelo Siringo, *Riata and Spurs* (Boston: Houghton Mifflin, 1927), 229.

3. Ibid., 238.

4. Letter from Charles A. Siringo to editor, *Frontier Times*, November 1928.

5. Lula Parker Betenson and Dora Flack, *Butch Cassidy, My Brother* (New York: Penguin Books, 1976), 157.

6. Richard M. Patterson, *Butch Cassidy: A Biography* (Lincoln: University of Nebraska Press, 1998), 175.

7. Ibid.

8. Ibid.

9. Ibid.

10. Ibid., 176.

11. Ibid.

12. Ibid., 177.

13. Ibid.

14. Arthur Chapman, "Butch Cassidy," *The Elks Magazine* (April 1930).

15. Patterson, *Butch Cassidy*, 178.

16. Ibid.

17. Jan MacKell, *Red Light Women of the Rocky Mountains* (Albuquerque: University of New Mexico Press, 2009), 327–28.

18. Ibid., 328.

19. Ibid.

20. Patterson, *Butch Cassidy*, 179.

21. MacKell, *Red Light Women*, 327.

22. Patterson, *Butch Cassidy*, 180.

23. MacKell, *Red Light Women*, 327.

24. Kerry Ross Boren, "Grandpa Knew Butch Cassidy," *Frontier Times*, February–March 1966.

25. Butch Cassidy to Mathilda Davis, August 10, 1902, reprinted in Dullenty, *Cassidy Collection*,

26. Chapman, "Butch Cassidy," 61.

27. Cy Warman, "Soldiers of the Rail," *Munsey's*, July 1900, 461.

28. Richard M. Patterson, *The Train Robbery Era: An Encyclopedic History* (Boulder, CO: Pruitt Publishing Company, 1991), 122–25.

29. Cassidy to Davis, in Dullenty, *Cassidy Collection*.

30. Ibid.

31. Betenson and Flack, *Butch Cassidy, My Brother*, 161.

32. Charles Kelly, *The Outlaw Trail: A History of Butch Cassidy and His Wild Bunch* (New York: The Devin-Adair Company, 1959), 285.

33. Mary Allison, ed., *Dubois Area History* (Dallas, TX: Curtis Media Corp., 1991), F7.

34. Donna Ernst, *The Sundance Kid: The Life of Harry Alonzo Longabaugh* (Norman: University of Oklahoma Press, 2009), 130.

35. Ernst, *The Sundance Kid*, 96.

36. Ibid., 131–32.

37. Ibid., 132.

38. Ibid.

39. Ibid.

40. Ibid.

41. *Pinkertons*, Sundance Kid file, Pinkerton Detective Agency Archives, Library of Congress, Washington, D.C.

42. *New York Times*, February 14, 1901.

43. Anne Meadows, *Digging Up Butch and Sundance* (New York: St. Martin's Press, 1994), 45.

44. Ibid., 37.

CHAPTER 6: HARRY ALONZO LONGABAUGH

1. Donna Ernst, *The Sundance Kid: The Life of Harry Alonzo Longabaugh* (Norman: University of Oklahoma Press, 2009), xv.

2. Ibid.

3. Ibid., xvii.

4. Ibid., xviii.

5. Ibid., xix.

6. Ibid.

7. Ibid., xix–xx.

8. *Proceedings of the Annual Conventions of the International Association of Chiefs of Police 1906–1912*, Vol. 2 (Grand Rapids, MI: Etheridge Printing Company, 1906), 63–65.

9. 1870 and 1880 US Federal Census Records, Pennsylvania.

10. US Government Pension records and army discharge papers.

11. Samuel Whitaker Pennypacker, *Annals of Phoenixville* (Philadelphia: Bavis & Pennypacker, 1872), 164–69.

12. Whaling ship records; Pinkerton Report dated April 23, 1902.

13. Pinkerton Detective Agency Archives, Library of Congress, Washington, DC.

14. Ibid., memo dated November 17, 1921, signed by Wm. A. Pinkerton.

15. Ibid., binder 6, p. 7.

16. Family records; Donna B. Ernst correspondence and interviews with family members.

17. Local head-tax records; Phoenixville City Directory.

18. Jim Gatchell, "Hole in the Wall Gang," *Annals of Wyoming*, 1958.

19. Diana Allen Kouris, *The Romantic and Notorious History of Brown's Park* (Ann Arbor, MI: Wolverine Gallery, 1988), 78.

20. *Craig (Colorado) Courier*, January 16, 1897.

21. Ernst, *The Sundance Kid*, 23.

22. Matt Warner, *The Last of the Bandit Riders* (New York: Bonanza Books, 1940), 143.

23. J. D. B. Grieg letter to the Pinkerton Detective Agency, Library of Congress, Washington, DC.

24. Letter from Sam W. Mather of Eldorado, Texas, to *Frontier Times*, Bonham, Texas, dated August 27, 1928 (published in October 1928).

25. *Daily Yellowstone Journal*, Helena, Montana, letter to the editor, June 9, 1867.

26. *Sundance (Wyoming) Gazette*, March 18, 1887.

27. Ibid., April 8, 1887.

28. *Daily Yellowstone Journal*, April 12, 1887.

29. James D. Horan in notes taken during interview with Percy Seibert, stating, "Sundance—slim wrists—slipped cuffs," in Robert G. McCubbin Collection, National Cowboy & Western Heritage Museum, Oklahoma City, Oklahoma.
30. *Miles City (Montana) Daily Gazette,* June 8, 1887.
31. *Daily Yellowstone Journal,* June 9, 1887.
32. Ibid., June 7, 1887.
33. Ibid., letter to the editor, June 9, 1887.
34. *Daily Yellowstone Journal,* June 21, 1887.
35. Crook County (Wyoming) Court Records, 1887.
36. Indictments in the records of Clerk of the Court Office, Crook County Courthouse, Sundance, Wyoming, 1887.
37. Court records provided at Crook County Courthouse, Sundance, Wyoming. Because the transcript of his appearance is missing, this was quoted by H. R. Bernd and placed in the court files, 1887.
38. *Sundance Gazette,* May 4, 1888.
39. Records of Charities and Reform, Minutes of the Penitentiary Commission, as found in Garman, "Harry Longabaugh," 5.
40. Moonlight, Governor Thomas. *Two Letters of Pardon for Harry Longabaugh.* 4 February 1989. Wyoming State Archives.
41. *Sundance Gazette,* February 8, 1889.
42. Arrest warrant, Sheriff's Records, Crook County, Wyoming, May 24, 1889.
43. *Rocky Mountain News,* Denver, Colorado, June 27, 1889.

CHAPTER 7: ROBERT LEROY PARKER

1. *Los Angeles Times,* April 3, 1970.
2. Lula Parker Betenson and Doris Flack, *Butch Cassidy, My Brother* (New York: Penguin, 1976), 47.
3. Pearl Baker, *The Wild Bunch at Robbers Roost* (Kearney: Bison Books, University of Nebraska Press, 1989), 172.
4. Betenson and Flack, *Butch Cassidy,* 31.
5. Morris Stegner, *Mormon Country* (Kearney: Bison Books, University of Nebraska Press, 2003), 38.
6. Larry Pointer, *In Search of Cassidy* (Norman: University of Oklahoma Press, 2013), 43.
7. Ibid.
8. Betenson and Flack, *Butch Cassidy,* 33–34.
9. *Dolores (Colorado) Star,* February 11, 1938.
10. Betenson and Flack, *Butch Cassidy,* 45.
11. Ibid.
12. Baker, *The Wild Bunch,* 14, 18–19.
13. Ibid., 27.
14. Matt Warner, *The Last of the Bandit Riders* (New York: Bonanza Books, 1940), 107.
15. Charles Kelly, *The Outlaw Trail: A History of Butch Cassidy and His Wild Bunch* (New York: Devin-Adair Company, 1959), 12–13.

16. Kerry Ross Boren, "Grandpa Knew Butch Cassidy," *Frontier Times*—Companion to *True West and Old West* 40, no. 2 (March 1966): 44.

17. Betenson and Flack, *Butch Cassidy*, 39, 50.

18. Ibid., 48–49.

19. Richard Poll, Thomas G. Alexander, et al, *Utah: A People's History* (Salt Lake City: Brigham Young University Press, 1978), 283–84.

20. Warner, *Bandit Riders*, 106.

21. David Lavender and George H. H. Huey, *The Telluride Story* (Ridgeway, CO: Wayfinder Press, 2007), 22.

22. Pointer, *In Search of Cassidy*, 48.

23. Betenson and Flack, *Butch Cassidy*, 55.

24. *Los Angeles Times*, April 3, 1970.

25. Warner, *Bandit Riders*, 111.

26. Baker, *The Wild Bunch*, 184.

27. *Dolores Star*, February 11, 1938.

28. Warner, *Bandit Riders*, 117.

29. Tom McCarty, *Tom McCarty's Own Story* (Hamilton, MT: Rocky Mountain House Press, 1986), 28.

30. Ibid., 34.

31. McCarty, *McCarty's Own Story*, 50.

32. Warner, *Bandit Riders*, 118–19.

33. Baker, *Wild Bunch*, 58.

34. Kelly, *The Outlaw Trail*, 30.

35. Richard M. Patterson, *Butch Cassidy: A Biography* (Lincoln: University of Nebraska Press, 1998), 22.

36. Don D. Walker, "The Carlisles: Cattle Barons of the Upper Basin," 275, *Utah Historical Quarterly* (Summer 1964) citing the diary of Henry L. A. Culmer, Utah State Historical Society, Salt Lake City.

37. Warner, *Bandit Riders*, 120–21.

38. *Pueblo Daily Chieftain*, Pueblo, Colorado, June 27, 1889.

39. Kelly, *The Outlaw Trail*, 30.

40. *Pueblo Daily Chieftain*, Pueblo, Colorado, June 26, 1889.

41. Warner, *Bandit Riders*, 121–22.

42. Ibid., 122.

43. McCarty, *McCarty's Own Story*, 28.

44. Warner, *Bandit Riders*, 122.

45. *Dolores (Colorado) Star*, February 11, 1938.

46. *Rocky Mountain News*, Denver, Colorado, June 27, 1889.

47. Ibid.

48. Patterson, *Butch Cassidy*, 27.

49. *Dolores (Colorado) Star*, February 11, 1938.

50. Warner, *Bandit Riders*, 123.

51. McCarty, *McCarty's Own Story*, 28.

52. Patterson, *Butch Cassidy*, 29.

53. Warner, *Bandit Riders*, 127–28.
54. McCarty, *McCarty's Own Story*, 28.
55. Patterson, *Butch Cassidy*, 30.
56. Kelly, *The Outlaw Trail*, 31.
57. *Rocky Mountain News*, Denver, Colorado, July 1, 1889.
58. Warner, *Bandit Riders*, 125.
59. Pointer, *In Search of Cassidy*, 62.
60. *Dolores (Colorado) Star*, February 11, 1938.
61. Warner, *Bandit Riders*, 129.

CHAPTER 8: AND BABY MAKES THREE

1. Donna Ernst, *The Sundance Kid* (Norman: University of Oklahoma Press, 2009), 128.
2. *Pinkertons*, Butch Cassidy file.
3. Ibid.
4. *St. Louis Globe Democrat*, St. Louis, Missouri, November 6, 1901.
5. Ibid.
6. *San Angelo Standard-Times*, San Angelo, Texas, November 8, 1901.
7. Anne Meadows, *Digging Up Butch and Sundance* (New York: St. Martin's Press, 1994), 5.
8. Ernst, *Sundance Kid*, 144.
9. Ernst, *Sundance Kid*, 146–47.
10. Meadows, *Digging Up Butch*, xi–xii.
11. *Pinkertons*, Dimaio report, Pinkerton Detective Agency Archives, Library of Congress, Washington, D.C.
12. Ibid.
13. *Pinkertons*, memo dated March 21, 1909, Pinkerton Detective Agency Archives, Library of Congress, Washington, D.C.
14. Meadows, *Digging Up Butch*, 57–59.
15. *Pinkertons*, Robert A. Pinkerton memo to American Bankers Association, dated October 24, 1904, Pinkerton Detective Agency Archives, Library of Congress, Washington, D.C.
16. Meadows, *Digging Up Butch*, 67–69.
17. Ibid., 67.
18. Ibid., 67–68.
19. Dan Buck, "Butch's Place at Cholila," *Lugares Magazine*, no. 10, 1992, 36–37.
20. Ernst, *Sundance*, 206.
21. Ibid., 206–7.
22. Anne Meadows, *Digging Up Butch and Sundance* (New York: St. Martin's Press, 1994), 10.
23. Horan's notes.
24. Dan Buck and Anne Meadows, "Leaving Cholila," *True West* (January 1996): 21–27.

CHAPTER 9: ON THE RUN AGAIN

1. Dan Buck and Anne Meadows, "Leaving Cholila," *True West* (January 1996): 21–27.

2. Daniel Gibbon, testimony, Cholila, Argentina, 1911.

3. Donna Ernst, *Sundance* (Norman: University of Oklahoma Press, 2009), 154–55.

4. Daniel Buck and Anne Meadows, "Neighbors on the Hot Seat: Revelations from the Long Lost Argentine Police File," *WOLA Journal* 5, no. 2 (Spring/Summer 1996): 6.

5. *La Prensa*, Buenos Aires, Argentina, January 26 and 27, 1906 (as translated by Dan Buck).

6. *Ogden Standard*, Ogden, Utah, September 27, 1906.

7. Ciaran Conliffe, "Ethel 'Etta' Place, Western Woman of Mystery," HeadStuff, September 16, 2017. www.headstuff.org/culture/history/ethel-etta-place-western -woman-of-mystery/.

8. Ernst, *Sundance*, 155.

9. Horan's notes.

10. Letter from Roy Letson in Charles Kelly's papers.

11. Horan's notes.

12. Ibid.

13. Ibid.

14. Letter dated November 12, 1907, sent by Butch to the "Boys at Concordia" from Santa Cruz, in Percy Seibert's scrapbook, Robert G. McCubbin Collection, National Cowboy & Western Heritage Museum, Oklahoma City, Oklahoma.

15. Anne Meadows, *Digging Up Butch and Sundance* (New York: St. Martin's Press, 1994), 127–28.

16. *New York Herald* and *Denver Republican*, September 23, 1906.

17. *Baltimore News*, Baltimore, Maryland, September 10, 1911.

18. A. G. Francis, "The End of an Outlaw," *Wide World Magazine*, May 1913, 46–53.

19. Meadows, *Digging Up Butch*, 229.

20. Ernst, *Sundance*, 165.

21. Francis, "The End of an Outlaw," 36–43.

22. Ernst, *Sundance*, 166–67.

23. Meadows, *Digging Up Butch*, 267.

24. Ernst, *Sundance*, 167–68.

25. Meadows, *Digging Up Butch*, 261–62.

26. Ibid., 262–68.

27. Ibid.

28. Ibid., 269–71.

29. Ernst, *Sundance*, 169.

CHAPTER 10: SOMEONE WAS KILLED

1. Donna Ernst, *The Sundance Kid* (Norman: University of Oklahoma Press, 2009), 170.

2. A. G. Francis, "The End of an Outlaw," *Wide World Magazine*, May 1913, 36–43.

3. Matt Warner, *The Last of the Bandit Riders* (New York: Bonanza Books, 1940), 322.

4. Aller correspondence in Bolivian Foreign Office files for 1910, National Archives Records, Washington, DC.

5. Ibid., 127.

6. Ibid.

7. Ibid.

8. Ernst, *Sundance*, 174.

CHAPTER 11: WHAT ABOUT ETTA?

1. Donna Ernst, *The Sundance Kid* (Norman: University of Oklahoma Press, 2009), 175.

2. Ibid.

3. Anne Meadows, *Digging Up Butch and Sundance* (New York: St. Martin's Press, 1994), 83.

4. Ernst, *Sundance*, 176.

5. W. Paul Reeve, "Just Who Was the Outlaw Queen Etta Place?" *History Blazer* (May 1995).

6. Ibid.

7. Tony Hays, "The Mysterious Disappearance of Etta Place," Criminal Element, August 14, 2011. Accessed September 16, 2019. www.criminalelement.com /the-mysterious-disappearance-of-etta-place/.

8. Grace McClure, *The Bassett Women* (Athens: Ohio University Press, 1985), 57.

9. Lula Parker Bentenson and Dora Flack, *Butch Cassidy, My Brother* (New York: Penguin Books, 1976), 68.

10. Ibid.

11. Doris Karren Burton, "Sheriff John Theodore Pope," *The Outlaw Trail Journal* 1, no. 1 (Summer 1991): 9.

12. Anne Meadows and Daniel Buck, "Running Down a Legend." *Americas* 42, no. 6 (1990–1991): 25–27.

13. Ibid., 25.

14. The Free Library, "Running Down a Legend." Accessed September 14, 2019. www.thefreelibrary.com/Running down a legend.-a010412357.

15. Lanier, "Legend."

16. Horan's notes.

17. Author's note: A request to St. Joseph Hospital for medical confirmation or denial was not received.

18. Arthur Chapman, "Butch Cassidy," *The Elks Magazine* (April 1930).

19. Meadows, *Digging Up Butch*, 101.

20. Chapman, "Butch Cassidy."

21. Ibid.

22. Chapman, "Butch Cassidy."

23. Meadows, *Digging Up Butch*, 231.

24. Ibid.

25. Ibid.

26. Ibid., 234.

27. Chapman, "Butch Cassidy."

28. Meadows, *Digging Up Butch*, 136.

29. Ibid., 267.

30. Ibid.

31. Meadows, *Digging Up Butch*, 265.

32. Ibid.

33. Ibid., 217.

34. Ibid.

35. Dan Buck, personal communication with Richard M. Patterson, August 30, 1997.

36. Meadows, *Digging Up Butch*, 207.

37. Richard M. Patterson, *Butch Cassidy: A Biography* (Lincoln: University of Nebraska Press, 1998), 224.

38. Ibid.

39. Ibid., 225.

40. Ibid.

41. Ibid.

42. Ibid.

43. Lula Parker Betenson and Doris Flack, *Butch Cassidy, My Brother* (New York: Penguin, 1976), 172.

44. Ibid., 177.

45. Ibid.

46. Ibid., 177–81.

47. Ibid., 181–83.

48. Ed Kirby, *The Saga of Butch and the Wild Bunch* (New York: Filter Press, 1977), 88.

49. Dan Buck, personal communication with Richard M. Patterson, August 30, 1997.

50. Betenson and Flack, *Butch Cassidy*, 186–87, 192–93.

51. Ibid., 192–93.

52. *National Enquirer*, June 10, 1943.

53. Dullenty, Cassidy Collection, 52.

54. Larry Pointer, *In Search of Cassidy* (Norman: University of Oklahoma Press, 2013), 19, citing interviews with Elinor Parker by Jim Dullenty on June 30 and July 12, 1975, as well as his own interview with Max Parker on September 12,1975, plus correspondence from Elinor to Dullenty dated July 20 and August 1975. See also Dullenty's "Interview with Max Parker, Kent, Washington, January 2, 1975," in Dullenty, Cassidy Collection, 77–82.

55. Bill Betenson, symposium panel member, "What Ever Happened to Butch and Sundance," Craig, Colorado, July 20,1996.

56. Bill Betenson, "Lula Parker Betenson," 9. According to Bill Betenson, Mark Betenson's statement that he saw Butch in Circleville in 1925 has in turn been confirmed by Mark's widow, Vivian Betenson, and by Mark's brother, Scott Betenson (Bill's grandfather).

57. Dick DeJournette and Daun DeJournette, *One Hundred Years of Brown's Park and Diamond Mountain* (Vernal, UT: DeJournette Enterprises, 1996), 223–24. According to

Daun DeJournette, this information came directly from Josie during an interview in the late 1950s.

58. Betenson and Flack, *Butch Cassidy*, 249, citing Flack's interview with Harv Murdock in Salt Lake City, April 1972.

59. John Rolfe Burroughs, *Where the Old West Stayed Young* (New York: William Morrow & Company, 1962), 135.

60. Pointer, *In Search of Cassidy*, 241, citing an interview with George Reynolds in Riverton, Wyoming, on May 7, 1974. The connection between Welch and Reynolds was not given.

61. Burroughs, *Where the Old West Stayed Young*, 135, citing a personal interview with Vernon.

62. Pointer, *In Search of Cassidy*, 240.

CHAPTER 12: THE MYSTERY SOLVED

1. *Salt Lake Tribune*, Salt Lake City, Utah, April 22, 1962.

2. *Los Angeles Times*, Los Angeles, California, April 3, 1970.

3. Ibid.

4. Ibid.

Index

About the Author

Born and raised in Chicago, **D. J. Herda** worked for years at *The Chicago Tribune*, as well as at numerous other Chicago-area newspapers and magazines, before becoming an internationally syndicated columnist. Herda's interest in Western Americana goes back to his childhood. He has published on the subjects of Calamity Jane, Doc Holliday, Frank and Jesse James, Billy the Kid, Butch Cassidy and the Wild Bunch, Wyatt Earp, and other Western legends. He has written "Forts of the American West" and other articles for *American West, Arizona Highways*, and other magazines. D. J. Herda has lived in the Rocky Mountains of the southwestern United States for nearly three decades.